MGB 1969-77 Autobook

By Kenneth Ball

Associate Member, Guild of Motoring Writers
and the Autobooks Team of Technical Writers

MG MGB Mk 2 1969-71
MG MGB GT Mk 2 1969-71
MG MGB Mk 3 1971-77
MG MGB GT Mk 3 1971-77

Autobooks

Autobooks Ltd. Golden Lane Brighton BN1 2QJ England

The AUTOBOOK series of Workshop Manuals is the largest in the world and covers the majority of British and Continental motor cars, as well as the majority of Japanese and Australian models.

Whilst every care has been taken to ensure correctness of information it is obviously not possible to guarantee complete freedom from errors or omissions or to accept liability arising from such errors or omissions.

**This book is to be returned on or before
the last date stamped below.**

RENEWALS   *Please quote:* date of return, your ticket number
and computer label number for each item.

CONTENTS

ISBN 0 85147 723 2

First Edition   1970
Second Edition, fully revised   1971
Reprinted   1971
Third Edition, fully revised   1972
Fourth Edition, fully revised   1972
Fifth Edition, fully revised   1973
Reprinted   1973
Sixth Edition, fully revised   1974
Seventh Edition, fully revised   1975
Eighth Edition, fully revised   1976
Ninth Edition, fully revised   1977

935

Illustrations reproduced by kind permission of the
manufacturers © British Leyland UK Limited.

Printed in Brighton England for Autobooks Ltd by G. Beard and Son Ltd
Bound in Hove England for Autobooks Ltd by Jilks Ltd

E

ACKNOWLEDGEMENT

My thanks are due to British Leyland Motor Corporation Limited for their unstinted co-operation and also for supplying data and illustrations.

Considerable assistance has also been given by owners, who have discussed their cars in detail, and I would like to express my gratitude for this invaluable advice and help.

Kenneth Ball
Associate Member, Guild of Motoring Writers

Ditchling Sussex England.

INTRODUCTION

This do-it-yourself Workshop Manual has been specially written for the owner who wishes to maintain his vehicle in first class condition and to carry out the bulk of his own servicing and repairs. Considerable savings on garage charges can be made, and one can drive in safety and confidence knowing the work has been done properly.

Comprehensive step-by-step instructions and illustrations are given on most dismantling, overhauling and assembling operations. Certain assemblies require the use of expensive special tools, the purchase of which would be unjustified. In these cases information is included but the reader is recommended to hand the unit to the agent for attention.

Throughout the Manual hints and tips are included which will be found invaluable, and there is an easy to follow fault diagnosis at the end of each chapter.

Whilst every care has been taken to ensure correctness of information it is obviously not possible to guarantee complete freedom from errors or omissions or to accept liability arising from such errors or omissions.

Instructions may refer to the righthand or lefthand sides of the vehicle or the components. These are the same as the righthand or lefthand of an observer standing behind the vehicle and looking forward.

CHAPTER 1

THE ENGINE

1:1 Description

The engine is a conventional four-cylinder, water-cooled model, using overhead valves operated by rocker gear and pushrods from a camshaft mounted in the block. On the original engines the crankshaft ran in three bearings but the models covered by this manual have five main bearings for the crankshaft. The cubic capacity remains unchanged at 1798cc (109.8 cu in).

The cylinder head components are shown in **FIG 1 : 2**, the crankshaft and camshaft components in **FIG 1 : 5**, and the block details are shown in **FIG 1 : 9**. Details of the bore and stroke are given in Technical Data at the end of this manual, together with an extensive coverage of further technical information.

The camshaft runs in three bi-metal, renewable bearings, and is driven by a duplex chain from a sprocket on the front of the crankshaft. The camshaft lobes move tappets which slide in accurately machined bores in the block. The pushrods seat into the tappets at one end and the rockers at the other end so that the motion is transmitted to the valves in the cylinder head. The camshaft also has a gear which drives the shaft for the distributor and oil pump. End float of the camshaft is controlled by

the retainer plate, and the tension of the timing chain is automatically set by a hydraulic chain tensioner.

The crankshaft main bearings and big-end bearings are renewable copper/lead, steel-backed shells. At the front end the crankshaft carries the sprocket for the camshaft and, outside the timing cover, a pulley for driving the alternator and water pump. Oil is prevented from leaking out along the crankshaft by an oil seal in the timing cover and another oil seal at the rear of the crankshaft. Crankshaft end float is controlled by renewable semicircular thrust washers on either side of the centre main bearing.

Oil for lubrication and cooling is contained in the pressed-steel sump. The oil pump is mounted on the lefthand side of the crankcase and draws oil from the sump through a gauze strainer. The pressurized oil then passes by internal passage and external pipe to the filter head on the righthand side of the engine. The oil passes through the fullflow filter and into the main gallery running along the side of the engine. A pressure relief valve vents off surplus oil back to the sump to limit the maximum oil pressure. From the gallery the oil passes by internal passages to the main bearings. Some oil is then led through internally drilled passages in the crankshaft to

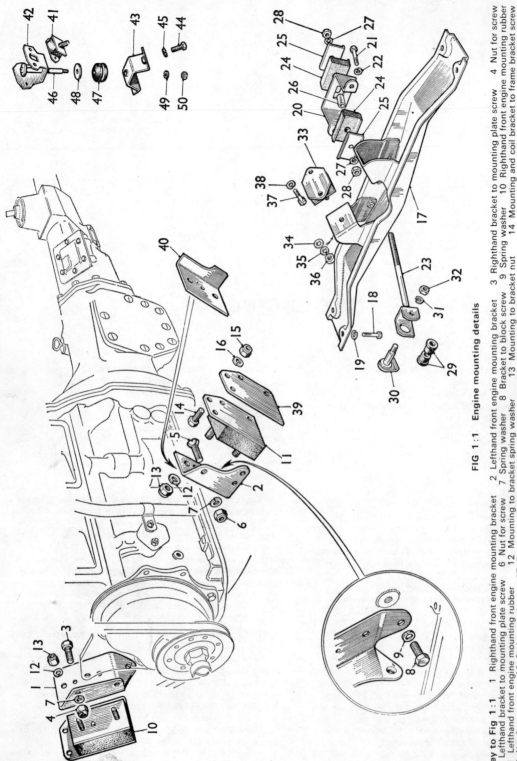

FIG 1 : 1   Engine mounting details

Key to Fig 1 : 1   1 Righthand front engine mounting bracket   2 Lefthand front engine mounting bracket   3 Righthand bracket to mounting plate screw   4 Nut for screw
5 Lefthand bracket to mounting plate screw   6 Nut for screw   7 Spring washer   8 Bracket to block screw   9 Spring washer   10 Righthand front engine mounting rubber
11 Lefthand front engine mounting rubber   12 Mounting to bracket spring washer   13 Mounting to bracket nut   14 Mounting and coil bracket to frame bracket screw   20 Engine stay rod bracket
15 Nut for screw   16 Spring washer   17 Rear mounting crossmember   18 Crossmember to frame screw   19 Spring washer   27 Stay rod spring washer
21 Bracket screw   22 Spring washer   23 Engine stay rod   24 Stay rod buffer   25 Buffer plate   26 Distance tube for stay rod   33 Rear engine mounting
28 Stay rod nut   29 Gearbox rear extension shouldered bush   30 Stay rod pin   31 Stay rod pin spring washer   32 Stay rod pin nut   37 Rear mounting to gearbox screw
34 Rear mounting to crossmember plain washer   35 Rear mounting to crossmember spring washer   36 Rear mounting to crossmember nut   42 Upper rear engine mounting bracket (GT)
38 Spring washer   39 Lefthand rubber packing plate   40 Engine mounting control bracket   41 Rear engine mounting (GT)   46 Rear engine mounting pin (GT)
43 Lower rear engine mounting bracket (GT)   44 Bracket to crossmember screw (GT)   45 Spring washer (GT)   47 Pin bush (GT)
48 Plain washer for pin (GT)   49 Spring washer for pin (GT)   50 Nut for pin (GT)

10

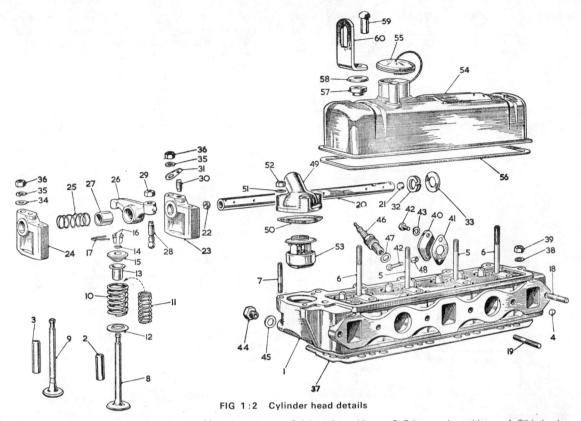

FIG 1 : 2   Cylinder head details

Key to Fig 1 : 2   1 Cylinder head assembly with guides   2 Inlet valve guide   3 Exhaust valve guide   4 Oil hole plug
5 Short stud for rocker bracket   6 Long stud for rocker bracket   7 Water outlet elbow to head stud   8 Inlet valve   9 Exhaust valve
10 Outer valve spring   11 Inner valve spring (Pre 18v)   12 Valve spring collar   13 Valve spring shroud (no longer fitted)
14 Valve packing ring   15 Valve spring cup   16 Valve cotter (halves)   17 Valve cotter circlip   18 Exhaust manifold to head stud
19 Inlet and exhaust manifold to head stud   20 Plugged valve rocker shaft   21 Valve rocker plain plug
22 Valve rocker screwed plug   23 Rocker shaft tapped bracket   24 Rocker shaft plain bracket   25 Rocker spacing spring
26 Bushed valve rocker   27 Valve rocker bush   28 Tappet adjusting screw   29 Tappet adjusting screw nut
30 Rocker shaft locating screw   31 Locating screw lockplate   32 Double-coil rocker shaft washer   33 Rocker shaft washer
34 Plain washer for rocker shaft stud   35 Spring washer for rocker shaft stud   36 Rocker bracket stud nut
37 Cylinder head joint washer   38 Cylinder head nut washer   39 Cylinder head stud nut   40 Heater outlet elbow blanking plate
41 Joint washer blanking plate   42 Plate to cylinder head screw   43 Spring washer screw   44 Thermal transmitter boss plug
45 Plug washer   46 Sparking plug   47 Steel plug gasket   48 Long screw distance piece   49 Water outlet elbow
50 Elbow joint washer   51 Plain washer for stud in cylinder head   52 Stud nut   53 Thermostat   54 Valve rocker cover
55 Oil filler cap and cable   56 Valve rocker cover joint washer   57 Rubber cover bush   58 Cup washer   59 Rocker cover
cap nut   60 Engine sling bracket

lubricate the big-end bearings. Some of this oil then passes into the drilled passage in the connecting rod and is jetted from the connecting rod to lubricate the cylinder walls and pistons. The main bearings also pass oil to the camshaft bearings. Oil from the rear camshaft bearing is passed up through the rear rocker pedestal and into the hollow rocker shaft to lubricate the rocker gear. This oil then finds its way back to the sump via the pushrod holes. Oil is metered from the front camshaft bearing to operate the automatic tensioner as well as to lubricate the chain and timing sprockets.

1 : 2 Removing the engine and gearbox

The engine mounting points are shown in **FIG 1 : 1**. The engine may be removed separately, though this is not advisable as there is danger of damaging the clutch if the engine only is taken out. It is safer and just as easy to remove the engine complete with gearbox.

The only operation for which it is essential to remove the engine from the car is when the crankshaft is to be taken out of the engine or the main bearings are to be renewed. Apart from this, other operations can be carried out in situ, though if a great deal of work is to be carried out it will probably be more convenient to have the engine out and on the bench.

1 Drain the oil from the engine and gearbox and the coolant from the cooling system. Disconnect both batteries. Remove the bonnet (see **Chapter 13**). Remove the radiator (see **Chapter 4, Section 4 : 3**), complete with oil cooler and oil pipes.

2 Disconnect the electrical leads to alternator, starter motor, distributor and temperature transmitter.

3 Disconnect the water hoses to the heater and the control cable from the water valve.

4 Disconnect the fuel pipe and carburetter controls from the carburetters and remove the air cleaners.

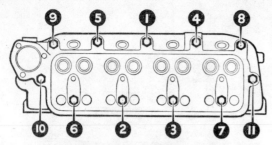

FIG 1:3 Cylinder head nut sequence

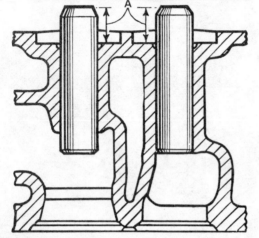

FIG 1:4 Protrusion of the valve guides above the cylinder head top face

5 Synchromesh gearbox only. Remove the gearlever surround and remove the gearlever by raising the rubber boot and taking out the lever retaining bolts. Disconnect the electrical leads from the reverse light switch and, if fitted, the inhibitor switch (overdrive units only). Remove the bolts securing the clutch slave cylinder to the gearbox casing, remove the clevis pin securing the pushrod to the clutch operating lever and move the clutch slave cylinder out of the way, still attached to its hose.

6 Automatic transmission only. Disconnect the downshift cable from the carburetters. **Disconnect the** manual control lever from the gearbox shaft. Disconnect the electrical leads from the reverse light and inhibitor switches.

7 On all models, disconnect the speedometer drive cable from the gearbox. Disconnect the propeller shaft from the differential pinion and the gearbox, remove the propeller shaft as instructed in **Chapter 8, Section 8:1**. Disconnect the exhaust pipe from the exhaust manifold and free the clip that secures it to the gearbox.

8 Support the engine with a sling and crane and support the gearbox, preferably with a trolley jack. Remove the nuts and bolts securing the engine front mountings to the frame. Remove the bolts supporting the crossmember to the frame and the two bolts securing the bottom tie bracket to the crossmember. Lower the gearbox until it rests on the chassis fixed crossmember.

Remove the stay rod on earlier engines from the gearbox. On later engines where fitted remove the engine restraint from the gearbox. Remove the crossmember.

9 Check that all connections are undone. On emission controlled engines there will be vapour pipes which need to be disconnected.

10 Move the engine and gearbox assembly forwards until the gearbox is clear of the crossmember, then tilt it downwards and lift the assembly out of the car.

Remove the gearbox from the engine after undoing the ring of securing nuts and bolts. Do not allow the weight of the gearbox to rest on the input shaft in the clutch otherwise the clutch may be damaged.

Refit the engine in the reverse order of removal. After all connections have been remade, refill the gearbox and engine to the correct levels, and refill the cooling system with coolant. Check all adjustments and controls before starting the engine.

1:3 The cylinder head

The cylinder head details are shown in **FIG 1:2**. The cylinder head can be removed with the engine fitted or removed from the car. If the valve rocker gear only is to be removed then the cooling system must be drained and all the nuts securing the cylinder head removed, as if only the nuts securing the rocker gear are removed then undue strain will be placed on the cylinder head, possibly causing it to distort.

Removal:

1 Drain the cooling system, keeping the liquid in a clean container for re-use if it contains antifreeze. Remove the carburetters (see **Chapter 2**). Disconnect the exhaust pipe from the exhaust manifold and disconnect the vacuum pipe from the inlet manifold. Remove the six nuts securing the manifolds to the cylinder head, noting that the four centre nuts have large washers which secure both manifolds.

2 Slacken all the securing nuts, evenly and part of a turn at a time, in the order shown in **FIG 1:3**. If this precaution is not observed the cylinder head may be distorted and the gasket will be unable to form an effective seal. When all eleven nuts are loose, remove them and lift off the rocker gear assembly. Withdraw the eight pushrods and store them in the order of removal so that they will be replaced in their original positions.

3 Disconnect the top radiator hose, the heater hoses and water valve control cable. Disconnect the electrical lead from the temperature transmitter. Disconnect any breather or vapour hoses that are connected or in the way. Unclip any hoses or pipes attached to the cylinder head. Disconnect the HT leads from the sparking plugs.

4 Break the cylinder head joint and lift the head squarely off the studs. The joint may be broken either by carefully levering the head at one end or turning the engine over with the sparking plugs in position.

The cylinder head is refitted in the reverse order of removal but noting the following points:

1 Make sure that the mating faces of the cylinder head, cylinder block and manifolds are perfectly clean and free from any small particles.

2 Use new gaskets for the cylinder head and manifolds.

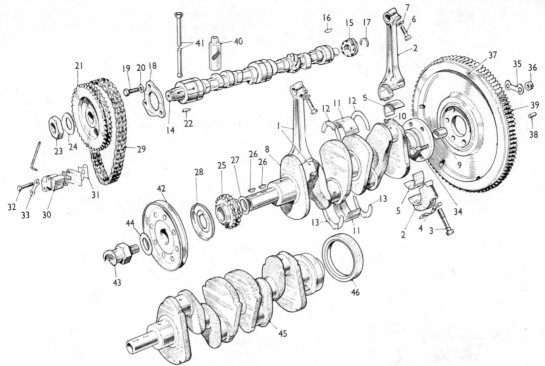

FIG 1:5 Crankshaft, camshaft and timing gear details

Key to Fig 1:5   1 Nos. 1 and 3 cylinders connecting rod and cap   2 Nos. 2 and 4 cylinders connecting rod and cap
3 Cap screw   4 Screw lockwasher   5 Standard connecting rod bearing   6 Connecting rod clamping screw (deleted)
7 Screw spring washer (deleted)   8 Crankshaft (superseded by 45)   9 First motion shaft bush   10 Plug
11 Standard main bearing   12 Upper thrust washer   13 Lower thrust washer   14 Camshaft   15 Tachometer driving gear
16 Tachometer gear key   17 Tachometer gear spring ring   18 Camshaft locating plate   19 Locating plate to crankcase screw
20 Screw lockwasher   21 Camshaft gear   22 Camshaft gear key   23 Camshaft gear nut   24 Locknut washer
25 Crankshaft gear   26 Crankshaft gear and pulley key   27 Crankshaft gear packing washer   28 Crankshaft front oil thrower
29 Timing chain   30 Chain tensioner   31 Tensioner joint washer   32 Tension to crankcase screw   33 Screw lockwasher
34 Flywheel to crankshaft bolt   35 Bolt lockwasher   36 Bolt nut   37 Flywheel   38 Clutch to flywheel dowel
39 Starting ring gear   40 Tappet   41 Pushrod   42 Crankshaft pulley   43 Starting nut   44 Starting nut lockwasher
45 Crankshaft   46 Oil seal

The cylinder head gasket is marked both TOP and FRONT to ensure that it will be correctly fitted. No jointing compound should be needed on any of the gaskets but a light smear of grease on both sides of the cylinder head gasket will assist in sealing.

3 Refit the cylinder head, replace the eight pushrods and fit back into place the rocker assembly. Do not forget to replace the locking plate 31 which secures the rocker shaft locating screw. Evenly and progressively tighten all eleven cylinder head nuts, in the order shown in **FIG 1:3**, to a torque load of 45 to 50 lb ft (6.2 to 6.9 kgm) and the four remaining rocker pedestal securing nuts to a load of 25 lb ft (3.4 kgm). During this operation take care to see that the pushrods are correctly seated and not jamming out of place. Set the rocker clearances.

4 Recheck the torque loading of the cylinder head nuts and the rocker clearances after 500 miles.

1:4 Servicing the cylinder head

Remove the cylinder head from the engine as described in the previous section.

Rocker assembly:

To dismantle the assembly, remove the locating screw 30 then the splitpins which hold the washers 32 and 33 to the rocker shaft 20. The pedestals, springs and rockers can then be slid off from the shaft. Store the parts in the correct order so that they can be replaced in their original positions. For cleaning out the shaft, unscrew the end plugs 22.

Light wear on the ends of the rockers 26 can be dressed out with a smooth carborundum stone but deep pitting necessitates renewing the rockers. The bushes 27 are renewable but as welding and very accurate reaming are required it is best to leave this operation to a service station.

Before reassembly, thoroughly clean all the parts in clean fuel or any suitable solvent. Reassemble in the reverse order of dismantling using clean engine oil on all the bearing surfaces.

When refitting the rocker assembly fit a .005 inch (.13 mm) shim where not already fitted, under the two centre brackets.

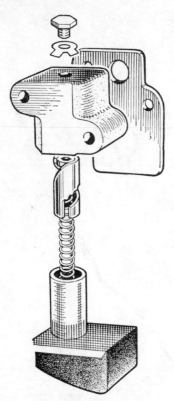

FIG 1:6 The automatic timing chain tensioner details

Removing carbon:

It is advisable to take off all the carbon and deposits before removing the valves, otherwise the valve seats may be damaged. Either scrape the deposits out of the combustion chamber or use rotary wire brushes with an electric drill. Emerycloth, preferably part worn, and paraffin may be used to clean the remaining deposits. The ports may be cleaned out in the same way but take great care not to damage the valve guides or valve stems. If any abrasive is used on the cylinder head it must be cleaned off completely before refitting the cylinder head. Remove deposits from under the valve heads by spinning them in the chuck of an electric drill and lightly pressing on emerycloth but do not score or damage the accurately machined valve stems and avoid polishing the valve seat.

No abrasives should be used on the pistons as it cannot be fully cleaned off and may work its way down the cylinder bores. Use a sharp stick of solder or hardwood to remove the deposits. Before removing the carbon smear grease lightly around the tops of the four bores and plug all waterways and oil passages with good-sized pieces of non-fluffy cloth. Turn the engine over until one pair of pistons is nearly at TDC. Preferably spring an old piston ring into the bore above the piston, but in any case avoid removing the carbon from around the periphery of the piston as this acts as an oil seal as well as protecting the top ring from direct heat. When all four pistons have been cleaned then the dirt should be blown away and the engine turned over so that the pistons scrape the particles

in the bore and the grease to the top of the bore where it can all be removed. Take out the pieces of cloth, making sure that none are left or have worked their way into the block.

Valves:

Use a valve spring compressor under the head of the valve and press down the cup 15. Extract the circlip 17 and remove the valve cotters 16. Carefully release the tool to allow the valve springs to expand and then remove the tool. Remove the valve springs 10 and 11, cup 15 and collar 12. The valve itself can then be slid out through the combustion chamber.

Replace the valves in the reverse order of removal, ensuring that the valves are replaced in their original positions. The old sealing rings 14 must be discarded and new ones fitted in their place. Soak the new seals in clean engine oil and press them into place when the cup 15 is held down by the valve spring compressor. The collets and spring clips can then be refitted.

Clean the valves and check that the stems are straight, using a steel straightedge. If the valve seats or the seats in the head are deeply pitted, then they should be recut using garage equipment. Do not attempt to remove deep pitting using grinding paste otherwise excess metal will also be removed from the mating seat. Renew the valves if the stems show signs of wear or 'picking up' or the seats are pitted beyond redemption. Seat inserts can be fitted to the cylinder head if the original seats cannot be rectified or are oversize.

To grind-in valves, put a light spring between the valve and cylinder head (this is not necessary but will assist in lifting the valve from the seat for inspection), and use medium-grade paste unless the seats are in good condition, in which case fine-grade paste may be used from the start. Use a suction-cup tool and grind with a semi-rotary movement, letting the valve rise off the seat occasionally by the pressure of the light spring. Use paste sparingly and change to fine-grade paste when the pits have been ground out. When both seats have a matt grey finish clean away all traces of grinding paste.

Valve springs:

Measure the free lengths of all the valve springs and renew any that are shorter than the dimensions given in Technical Data. The best test is to use a spring balance and steel rule to check that the springs supply the correct load at their fitted lengths. Renew the set if they are weak.

Valve guides:

Worn valve guides 2 and 3 or defective seals 14 will cause high oil consumption so renew the guides if they are worn. For both removing and refitting valve guides a hardened steel punch is required. The punch should be at least 4 inches (10 cm) long and turned from $\frac{9}{16}$ inch (14 mm) rod. At one end should be turned a spigot of $\frac{5}{16}$ inch (7.9 mm) diameter and 1 inch (2.5 cm) length. Use the punch to drive the old guide down and out into the combustion chamber. Insert the new valve guides, from the top of the cylinder head, with the smallest chamfer leading and drive them down towards the combustion chamber until the protrusion A, shown in **FIG 1:4**, is $\frac{5}{8}$ inch (15.875 mm) for the longer exhaust valve guides and

$\frac{3}{4}$ inch (19 mm) for the shorter inlet valve guides. Have the cylinder head seats reground after fitting new valve guides to ensure concentricity.

Distortion:

Both the face of the block and the mating face on the cylinder head should be checked for distortion. A long steel straightedge will give a reasonable guide but for best results the studs should be removed from the block (either using a stud extractor or by unscrewing them using two locked nuts) and the surface checked using engineers' blue on either a surface table or large piece of plate glass. High spots may be removed by the careful use of a scraper but the only cure for distortion is to have the surface ground flat by a firm of specialists.

The need for cleanliness and removing all traces of grinding paste or abrasive from the cylinder head before reassembly cannot be overstressed.

1:5 Overhauling the valve timing gear

The details of the camshaft and its driving gear, with double roller chain, are shown in **FIG 1:5** and the details of the hydraulic chain tensioner in use with this type of chain, are shown in **FIG 1:6**. Later engines are fitted with a single roller chain and a modified tensioner.

1 Drain the cooling system, remove the radiator and fan belt (see **Chapter 4**). Remove the cooling fan and pulley as necessary on later engines.
2 Remove the bolts on engines with a double roller chain securing the steering rack unit and ease the rack assembly forwards sufficiently to allow the crankshaft pulley to be withdrawn (see **Chapter 10**).
3 Free the lockwasher 44 and unscrew the nut 43. This nut will be very tight and it is best to use special tool 18G.98A which is a spanner with a reinforced handle for hitting on with a hammer. If all else fails, lock a solid spanner onto the nut, holding the other end firmly against a strong point on the chassis, and push the car slowly forwards in a forward gear.
4 Withdraw the pulley 42. Undo the securing bolts and remove the timing case cover. Discard the old gasket. Withdraw the oil thrower 28. Free the lockwasher 24 and remove the nut 23. Remove the bottom plug on the tensioner, if fitted, insert a $\frac{1}{8}$ inch (3.18 mm) Allen key into the cylinder and turn the key clockwise until the slipper head is fully retracted and locked behind the limit plug. **Never turn the key anticlockwise.** Free the tabs on the lockwasher 33 and remove the two bolts 32 to free the tensioner 30, its backplate and gasket 31. Where no plug is fitted to the tensioner retain the slipper head which is under spring pressure while removal takes place and allow the spring tension to relax when free and withdraw the slipper head, spring and inner cylinder from the body.
5 Use levers to move both the timing sprockets 21 and 25 together with the timing chain 29 so that the sprockets come off equally from the crankshaft and camshaft without stressing the timing chain. Take care to collect all the shims 27 when the crankshaft sprocket comes free.

Wash all the parts in clean fuel and remove any sludge from inside the timing cover. Renew both sprockets and timing chain as a set if the timing chain is worn or the

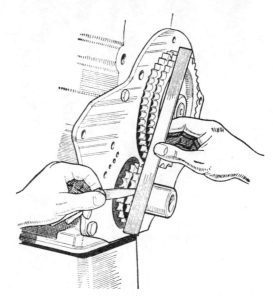

FIG 1:7 Determining the thickness of shims behind the crankshaft timing sprocket

teeth on the sprockets are worn to hooks. A new timing chain on old sprockets will soon become worn itself.

If a new crankshaft or sprockets have been fitted then the sprocket alignment should be checked as shown in **FIG 1:7**. Fit shims 27 until the gap between the straight-edge and the crankshaft sprocket is zero.

Turn the crankshaft until its key is vertically upwards and set the camshaft so that its keyway is approximately at 1 o'clock when viewed from the front. Encircle the sprockets with the timing chain so that their dimples are aligned as shown in **FIG 1:8**. Ease the sprockets into place, without turning the crankshaft, but aligning the camshaft so that its sprocket slides on and the alignment is still preserved.

Secure the sprocket in place with a new lockwasher 24 and the nut 23. Refit the tensioner and set it as described later. If the oil seal in the timing cover is defective or damaged drive out the old one and drive in a new seal so that its lips face inwards. Grease the seal and carefully twist the boss on the pulley through the seal. If the boss is scored or damaged then the pulley must be renewed. Fit the oil thrower 28, with the side marked F away from the engine, onto the crankshaft. Place a new gasket into position and refit the timing cover and pulley back into place, turning the cover about the pulley to align the cover with the securing holes. Replace the remainder of the parts in the reverse order of removal.

Chain tensioner:

Refer to **FIG 1:6**. To adjust or slacken the earlier tensioner, remove the bolt and lockwasher. Insert a $\frac{1}{8}$ inch (3.18 mm) Allen key through the bolt hole and turn the key clockwise until the slipper pad is fully retracted. **Never turn the key anticlockwise.** To dismantle the unit, carry on turning the key clockwise while holding the plunger and slipper securely, until the plunger comes free.

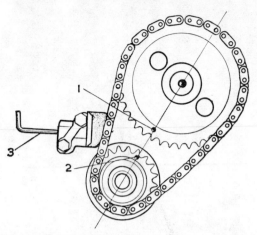

FIG 1 : 8 Dimples on timing sprockets correctly aligned at TDC on No. 1 (front) cylinder

Key to Fig 1 :8   1 and 2 Timing dimples
3 Allen key for adjusting tensioner

Wash the parts in clean fuel and then measure the bore in the body. If the ovality exceeds .003 inch (.076 mm) on the diameters near the mouth the unit must be renewed completely, otherwise renewing the slipper pad will recondition the unit.

When reassembling the unit, fit the spring between the plunger and the slipper cylinder. Compress the two together until the plunger enters the cylinder and then use the Allen key to turn the plunger cylinder clockwise until the spring is held compressed. Remove the Allen key and slide the cylinder into the bore of the body. Refit the tensioner to the engine in this state, using a new lockwasher 33. Check that the assembly moves freely in the body and does not catch against the engine plate, then use the Allen key to turn the cylinder clockwise until the spring pressure moves the slipper head against the timing chain. Replace the small plug bolt and its locking washer.

On tensioners without a plug, refit the inner cylinder and spring into the bore of the slipper head so that the serrated helical slot engages with the peg in the bore. Turn the inner cylinder clockwise against spring tension until the lower serration in the slot engages with the peg and locks.

Refit the slipper assembly to the body and insert a .06 inch (1.6 mm) spacer between the head and body to prevent disengagement.

After assembly to the engine remove the spacer, press the slipper head into the body and release it to disengage the inner cylinder.

1 :6 The tappets

Removal:

1 Remove the carburetters and manifolds. Remove the rocker assembly, noting that the cooling system must be drained and all the nuts securing the cylinder head slackened. Withdraw the pushrods keeping them in the correct order for refitting.
2 Disconnect the HT leads from the sparking plugs. Disconnect any breather pipes that are in the way.

Remove the tappet covers from the lefthand side of the block (see **FIG 1 : 9** for the block details) and lift out the eight tappets, carefully storing them in the order of removal.

Examine the tappets and renew any that are chipped or worn. New tappets should be fitted by selection so that they just slide down the bores in the block under their own weight when lubricated.

Refit the tappets in the reverse order of removal, remembering to adjust the rocker clearances and fill the cooling system before starting the engine.

1 :7 The sump

Drain the oil from the sump, preferably when it is hot after a run. Drain the cooling system and disconnect the radiator hoses. Support the engine with a sling and crane, or block and tackle, and remove the nuts and bolts holding the front engine mounting to the frame. Raise the engine until the sump securing bolts are all accessible. Remove all the bolts and take off the sump.

The oil strainer may be removed from the oil pump by taking out the two securing bolts. Dismantle the strainer for cleaning by taking out the centre nut and bolt and the two delivery pipe flange bolts. Note that there is a distance tube and a locating tongue on the side of the cover, both of which must be correctly replaced on reassembly.

Clean the parts using a suitable solvent such as fuel or paraffin (kerosene) and an old paint brush. Avoid the use of rags unless they are non-fluffy and not liable to leave fluff or threads in the parts.

Refit the strainer and sump in the reverse order of removal. It is most advisable to fit new sump gaskets rather than rely on the old ones. Hold the gaskets in place with a thin smear of grease while refitting the sump.

1 :8 The oil pump

Remove the sump and oil strainer as described in the previous section. The pump is secured to the engine by three studs and nuts. The pump may be dismantled by removing the two screws securing the cover and easing the cover off the two dowels securing it.

Reassemble and refit the pump in the reverse order of dismantling but using a new gasket between the pump and engine.

Before final reassembly, wash the pump parts in clean fuel and fit both rotors into the pump casing. Lay a steel straightedge across the bottom of the case and check that the rotor end floats do not exceed .005 inch (.127 mm). If the end float is exceeded then the dowels should be removed and the joint face of the pump lapped down using fine grinding paste on a piece of plate glass.

Check that the clearance between the outer rotor and casing does not exceed .010 inch (.254 mm) and that the clearance between the rotors, as shown in **FIG 1 :10** does not exceed .006 inch (.152 mm). If these clearances are exceeded either renew the rotors or the complete pump. Clean the parts very thoroughly if any abrasive has been used and then fully reassemble them using plenty of clean engine oil as lubricant.

1 :9 The camshaft

Removal:

1 Disconnect the HT leads from the sparking plugs and the ignition coil. Disconnect the vacuum pipe from the

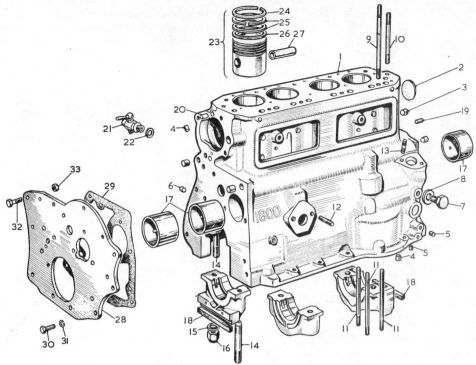

FIG 1:9 Cylinder block details

Key to Fig 1:9 1 Cylinder block assembly 2 Large Welch plug 3 Crankcase oil gallery plug 4 Crankcase oil hole taper plug 5 Oil relief valve vent hole plug 6 Chain tensioner oil feed plug 7 Screwed oil hole plug 8 Screwed plug washer 9 Long cylinder head stud 10 Short cylinder head stud 11 Short oil pump stud 12 Crankcase vent pipe clip stud 13 Tachometer spindle housing stud 14 Main bearing cap stud 15 Plain washer for main bearing stud 16 Main bearing stud nut 17 Camshaft bearing liner 18 Front and rear main bearing cap joint 19 Gearbox mounting plate dowel 20 Water pump dowel 21 Cylinder block drain tap 22 Drain tap washer 23 Standard high compression piston assembly 24 Top compression ring 25 Second and third compression rings 26 Scraper ring 27 Gudgeon pin 28 Engine mounting plate 29 Mounting plate joint washer 30 Mounting plate to crankcase screw 31 Screw spring washer 32 Righthand top engine mounting bracket to front plate bolt 33 Bolt nut

carburetter. Remove the two setscrews securing the ignition distributor clamp plate to the housing on the engine. Do not slacken the pinch bolt that secures the clamp plate to the distributor otherwise the ignition timing will be lost. Withdraw the distributor from the engine. Turn the engine so that all pistons are halfway up the bores. Screw a $\frac{5}{16}$ inch UNF bolt which is about $3\frac{1}{2}$ inches long into the threaded end of the drive spindle and withdraw this from the car, using the bolt to pull on.

2 Remove the tappets (see **Section 1:6**). Remove the sump and oil pump (see **Sections 1:7** and **1:8**). Remove the timing cover, timing chain and sprockets (see **Section 1:5**).

3 Refer to **FIG 1:5**. Remove the screws 19, washers 20 and the retaining plate 18. The camshaft 14 can now be withdrawn from the engine block.

Camshaft bearings:

If the bearings are worn they should be renewed. It is possible to drive out the old bearings and drive in new ones using a drift, though special tools are obtainable for this task. However when the new bearings have been fitted then they must be line-reamed to an accurate finish,

using special cutters and a bar for mounting the cutters on. For these reasons it is best to leave the work to a suitably equipped service station.

Examining the camshaft:

Check the cams and the journals for wear, also check the cams for chipping on the edges. Light wear on the cams may be ground off by a specialist firm but deep wear necessitates renewing the camshaft.

Refit the retaining plate 18, sprocket 21 and nut 23 to the camshaft. Use feeler gauges to measure the gap between the retaining plate and the camshaft, which should be .003 to .007 inch (.076 to .178 mm). If the gap is excessive then the retaining plate 18 must be renewed.

Refitting:

Thoroughly clean all the parts and refit them in the reverse order of removal, using engine oil liberally on all bearing surfaces.

Refitting distributor drive shaft:

Screw the $\frac{5}{16}$ UNF bolt into the threaded end of the drive shaft. Turn the engine so that all the pistons are

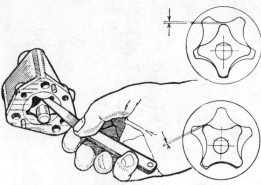

FIG 1:10 Measuring the clearance between the oil pump rotors

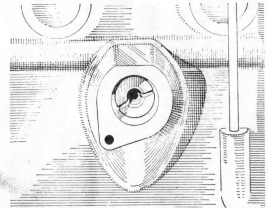

FIG 1:11 Correct position of the distributor drive spindle with No. 1 piston at TDC on the compression stroke

halfway up their bores, either 90 deg. before or after TDC. Refit the drive shaft, leaving the bolt in place. Turn the engine until No. 1 (front) piston is exactly at TDC on the compression stroke. If the timing cover is off this is indicated by the dimples on the timing sprockets being exactly aligned. If the timing cover is still fitted then TDC is indicated by the longest pointer on the timing cover being aligned with the groove in the periphery of the pulley, and the compression stroke will either have to be found by rotating the engine with a thumb blocking the sparking plug hole (pressure will rise as the piston reaches TDC) or by noting when the valves on No. 4 (rear) cylinder are at the point of rock.

Withdraw the drive shaft partially to clear it from the camshaft gear. Turn the drive shaft until the slot is below the horizontal, parallel to it, and the larger offset is uppermost. Press the drive shaft back into mesh, allowing it to rotate anticlockwise as it engages. The final position should then be as shown in **FIG 1:11**.

Refit the housing using the special bolt, and then refit the distributor. If the ignition timing has been lost then refer to **Chapter 3** for resetting the ignition timing.

1:10 Clutch and flywheel

This section will only deal with removing the clutch and further details on the clutch will be found in **Chapter 5**. Before gaining access to the clutch and flywheel, the engine and gearbox assembly must first be removed from the car and then the gearbox separated from the engine, although as mentioned in **Section 1:2** it may be possible to remove the engine only and leave the gearbox in the car. This latter procedure is not recommended.

Remove the clutch from the flywheel by progressively and evenly removing the six bolts and spring washers securing it and then easing the clutch off the three dowels.

Unlock and remove the six nuts 36 and three lockwashers 35 (see **FIG 1:9**) and then carefully withdraw the flywheel from the crankshaft. Tapping around the periphery of the flywheel with a rubber or copper-faced mallet will help to free it but take care to support the flywheel in case it suddenly comes free.

The parts are replaced in the reverse order of removal, tightening the flywheel nuts to a torque load of 40 lb ft (5.5 kgm) and the clutch bolts to a load of 25 to 30 lb ft (3.4 to 4.1 kgm). When tightening the clutch bolts the clutch driven plate must be aligned using a mandrel through its hub and the crankshaft spigot pulley. If this precaution is not observed then the gearbox input shaft cannot be slid back into place.

Flywheel ring gear:

If the teeth are worn or damaged then the ring gear will have to be renewed. Split the old ring to remove it, taking care not to damage or mark the flywheel. The ring can either be split using a hammer and cold chisel, or a weak point can be started by drilling holes along the root of a tooth.

When the old ring has been removed scrub the periphery of the flywheel with a wire brush to remove any dirt or rust and carefully file off any burrs. Lay the flywheel on a flat surface. Heat the new ring evenly to a temperature of 300 to 400°C (572 to 752°F), preferably in a thermostatically controlled furnace. The correct temperature will be indicated by light-blue surface colour. Do not overheat the ring otherwise the temper will be destroyed. If blowlamps and asbestos sheet are used, avoid localized overheating otherwise the ring will distort. Place the hot ring onto the flywheel, lead of the ring teeth facing the flywheel register, and tap it into place using a soft drift. Allow the ring to cool and contract fully into place before moving the flywheel.

1:11 Pistons and connecting rods

To change the big-ends, only the sump need be removed (see **Section 1:7**) but to remove the pistons and connecting rods the cylinder head must also be removed (see **Section 1:3**).

Big-ends:

With the sump removed, check that the connecting rods and bearing caps are marked at 4 (see **FIG 1:12**) to show both position and order. They should be stamped with numerals. Lightly pop mark them if they are not already marked.

Remove the nuts 5 from each bearing in turn. Pull off the caps and push the connecting rods up the bore of the cylinders to free them from the crankpins. Slide out the bearing shells from the caps and connecting rods, and store the shells so that they are identified with their bearing caps, unless new shells are to be fitted. New shells must be fitted if the old ones are worn, scored, pitted or show any defects.

Thoroughly clean the bearing caps and the recesses in the connecting rods for the bearing shells and also clean the crankpins. Examine the crankpins and measure them using a micrometer gauge. If they are scored, worn oval or tapered then the crankshaft must be removed and the crankpins ground down to the next suitable undersize.

Refit the big-ends in the reverse order of removal, but noting the following points:

1 Never file the bearing caps or connecting rods in an attempt to take up wear on the crankpin.
2 Refit the bearing caps in their original positions. Both these and the connecting rods have recesses for the tags on the bearing shells to seat into and prevent the shells from rotating, so make sure that the shells are properly seated.
3 The shell bearings are fitted so that the tags are both on the same jointing face between the connecting rod and the bearing cap but at opposite corners.
4 New shell bearings are fitted as received and only require removal of any protective (wash in clean fuel) and lubricating with clean engine oil when they are fitted. The bearings do not require scraping or boring as they are machined to provide the correct clearances.
5 Tighten the connecting rod nuts to a torque load of 33 lb ft (4.5 kgm).

Pistons:

Disconnect the big-ends as just described. With the cylinder head removed, push the connecting rods up the bores so that the pistons come out of the block and remove the assembly from the engine.

The pistons are marked on the crown to ensure that they are correctly refitted.

Press fit gudgeon pins are fitted and therefore it will be necessary to use Service Tool 18G.1150 and adaptor 18G.1150D if it is intended to separate the gudgeon pin from the piston.

Piston rings:

It is best to use a ring expander to remove and refit piston rings, though they can still be taken off and replaced without one if care is taken. Remove and replace rings from the top of the piston, never down the skirt.

Remove each ring in turn by raising one end of its groove and slipping a shim, such as an old .020 inch feeler gauge under it. Pass the shim around the piston at the same time gently pressing the ring onto the piston land above the groove. Three equi-spaced shims can then be used to slide the ring up and off the piston.

Clean carbon and dirt from the piston grooves using an old piece of broken ring, but taking care not to remove metal from the piston otherwise oil consumption will be raised and the gas seal lost. Make sure that any oil return holes in the bottom oil control ring groove are clear.

Check that the ring to groove clearance is correct, as shown in FIG 1:13. For the top rings the clearance should be .0015 to .0035 inch (.038 to .088 mm). If this

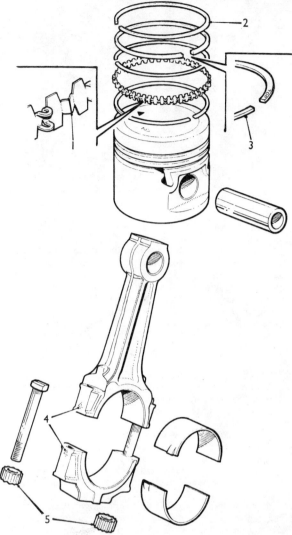

FIG 1:12 Piston and connecting rod details

Key to Fig 1:12   1 Expander rail   2 Top compression ring   3 Second compression ring   4 Identification marks   5 Multi-sided nut

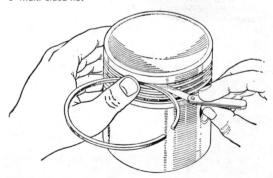

FIG 1:13 Checking the piston ring to groove clearance

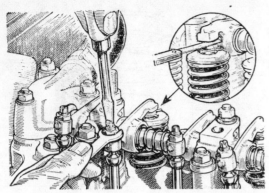
FIG 1:14   Adjusting the valve rocker clearances

clearance is exceeded with new rings then the pistons are worn and must be renewed.

If new rings are being fitted check that the gaps between the ends are correct when fitted. Spring each ring into the bore and use the inverted piston to press it squarely down until it is about one inch from the top of the bore. Measure the gap with feeler gauges and carefully file the ends of the ring to increase the gap. The correct gap for compression rings is 0.12 to .022 inch (.304 to .600 mm). For oil control rings the gap is .015 to .045 inch (.38 to 1.14 mm).

Cylinder bores:

With the pistons removed the bores should be examined, though the wear on the bores can still be checked when the pistons are fitted, provided the piston is moved to the BDC position.

The maximum wear will occur near the top of the bore and across the thrust axis (at right angles to the line of the engine block). Ideally a Mercer gauge should be used to measure the wear, but a reasonable judgement can be made by estimating the depth of the ridge at the top of the bore.

If the wear is excessive then the block will have to be rebored to the next oversize and oversize pistons fitted. Some firms will bring equipment to the car and perform the job in situ but most firms will require that the engine be brought to them for machining. Though it is convenient to have the block machined in the car this method presents greater problems in removing all the swarf.

If the bore wear is not excessive but compression is still lacking and oil consumption rising, new piston rings can be fitted. Before fitting new rings the wear ridge at the top of the bore should be removed, using garage equipment, and the bore lightly scuffed to break the glaze. The old rings will have worn together with the ridge and new unworn rings will probably hit this ridge at each TDC causing early failure of the new rings.

Connecting rods:

The renewal of the big-end bearings has already been dealt with.

The connecting rods should also be checked for twist and bend, using V-blocks, mandrels and a DTI (Dial Test Indicator).

Reassembling the parts:

1 Refit the piston rings in the reverse order of removal, bottom oil control ring first. The second compression ring is thinner and must be fitted to the second groove with the marking 'TOP' to the crown of the piston.
2 Refit the top compression ring.
3 Turn the rings so that their gaps are evenly spaced at 90 degrees and no gaps are in line with the gudgeon pin. Use a special ring clamp to compress the rings into their grooves after lubricating them with clean engine oil. In emergency a large hose clip can be used instead of the correct clamp though more care will have to be taken.
4 Lower the connecting rod down the correct bore, so that the FRONT, or arrowhead, on the piston faces forwards, and engage the skirt of the piston in the bore. Gently press the piston down so that the rings enter in turn and the clamp slides off them as they enter. Take great care not to force the piston as if a ring is slightly proud it can easily be snapped.
5 Reconnect the big-ends as described earlier.

1:12 The crankshaft and main bearings

To remove these, the engine must be out of the car and the gearbox removed (see **Section 1:2**). The crankshaft details are shown in **FIG 1:5** and the main bearing caps are shown in **FIG 1:9**.

Remove the clutch and flywheel (see **Section 1:10**), remove the timing chain and sprockets (see **Section 1:5**). Invert the engine and remove the sump (see **Section 1:7**) and the oil pump (see **Section 1:8**). Remove the engine backplate. Disconnect all four big-ends (see previous section).

Evenly slacken the securing nuts 16 and then remove them all. Note that only three bearings are shown in **FIG 1:9** whereas a five bearing crankshaft (item 45 in **FIG 1:5**) is actually fitted. Check that all the bearing caps are marked both for position and order before removing them and store them in the correct order for replacement. The front main bearing cap may be difficult to withdraw and special tool 18G.42 with adaptor 18G.42.B should be used to withdraw it. If the tool is not available take great care not to damage the mating faces or distort the cap.

Lift out the crankshaft, noting that thrust washers are fitted on either side of the centre main bearing. Slid out the bearing shells from the crankcase and bearing caps, keeping them in order.

Examination:

Clean the journals and measure them using a micrometer gauge. If the journals are scored, worn oval or worn tapered then the crankshaft must be reground to the next available undersize and new undersize shell bearings fitted. Never file the bearing caps in an attempt to take up wear on the crankshaft as if the crankshaft is later reconditioned the bearings will no longer be truly circular and the clearances will be incorrect. If for any reason the bearing caps have been filed then the bearings must be line-bored by a specialist firm.

If a bearing has run, or the crankshaft has been reground the oilways must be cleaned out though this should be done in any case. Use paraffin (kerosene) under pressure and then blow through the oil ways using compressed air either from an airline or a tyre pump.

If any of the bearing shells show signs of wear, pitting or scoring the complete set should be renewed. New bearings require no machining or scraping as they are manufactured to very close tolerances.

Replacing the parts:

Reassemble the parts in the reverse order of dismantling but note the following points:

1 The bearing shells are fitted with tags which fit into recesses in the crankcase and bearing caps. These tags fit on the same joint face but on opposite corners of the face.

2 The thrust washers on either side of the centre main bearing are fitted so that the whitemetal face is against the crankshaft. When the centre main bearing has been refitted the end float of the crankshaft should be checked. Use either feeler gauges or a DTI and firmly lever the crankshaft from one end to the other. The correct end float should be .002 to .003 inch (.051 to .076 mm). +.003 inch (.076 mm) oversize thrust washers are available if the crankshaft has worn so that the end float is excessive.

3 When refitting the front and rear bearing caps use a thin smear of jointing compound on the mating surfaces so as to ensure an oiltight seal.

4 Use clean engine oil to lubricate the bearings and the oil seals. Renew the front and rear oil seals if they are defective or damaged. Tighten all the securing nuts and bolts progressively and evenly until they reach the full torque load of 70 lb ft (9.7 kgm).

5 Refit the remainder of the parts in the reverse order of removal.

1:13 Oil filter and relief valve

The oil filter element should be renewed at regular intervals. If the filter element is left in place it will eventually choke with dirt, though a balance valve is fitted to allow oil to bypass the filter. Oil pressure will drop as well as allowing dirty unfiltered oil to circulate in the engine and cause rapid wear.

Changing the element:

Release the filter bowl from the engine by undoing the centre bolt. On engines where the filter bowl is mounted uppermost a drain plug is fitted to the filter head so as to allow the oil to be drained out of the filter before removing the bowl.

Remove and discard the old element. Use a small pointed tool to pick out the rubber sealing ring from its recess in the filter head. Wash out the bowl in clean fuel. Fit the new element back into the bowl making sure that the small felt or rubber washer between it and the pressure plate is both in good condition and correctly in place.

Fit a new sealing ring back into the filter head, making sure that it is squarely in its recess and not twisted. Refit the filter bowl and tighten the centre bolt.

Start the engine and immediately check for leaks. One of the commonest causes of the filter leaking is that the sealing ring in the filter head has not been replaced. Stop the engine and check the oil level after it has been standing for several minutes. Approximately a pint will be required to replace the oil lost from the filter.

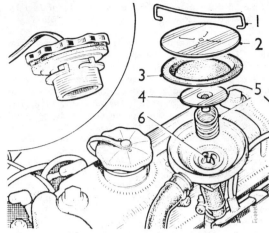

FIG 1:15   Closed-circuit breathing

Key to Fig 1:15   1 Spring clip   2 Cover
3 Diaphragm   4 Metering lever   5 Spring
6 Cruciform guides

Oil filter (later cars):

The disposable cartridge-type of filter is simply unscrewed by hand and discarded. The seal of the new cartridge should be smeared with engine oil before fitting and screwed in by hand.

Relief valve:

This is situated on the lefthand side rear of the engine block, under a domed hexagon nut. The nut is sealed by either two fibre washers or one copper washer.

The relief valve is not adjustable but it may still be a cause of drop in oil pressure. Remove the domed nut and withdraw the spring and valve cup. Clean out the seat in the block with a piece of hardwood. Tool 18G.69 is designed for regrinding the seat but it should only be used when the engine has been dismantled otherwise there is a danger of swarf, abrasive or chippings finding their way into the lubrication system.

Measure the free length of the relief spring and if it does not conform to the dimensions given in Technical Data it should be renewed. Renew the valve cup if this is worn.

Normally the oil pressure should lie between 50 to 80 lb/sq in (3.51 to 5.6 kg/sq cm) with the engine at normal road speeds and 10 to 25 lb/sq in (.7 to 1.7 kg/sq cm) at idling. The pressure will be less on a worn engine than a new one and will also drop if the strainer or filter elements are blocked.

1:14 Reassembling a stripped engine

Cleanliness is essential in all the reassembly operations and the parts should be as clean as possible before reassembly. The best way of cleaning metal parts is to use a trichlorethylene vapour bath, though this will remove paint as well. Washing in two changes of clean solvent, such as fuel, paraffin (kerosene) or other solvents is the next best method. Keep the working area clean otherwise dirt will only be picked up from the bench. Blow through all oilways.

It is advisable to renew all gaskets and seals, and scrape old gaskets and jointing material off before fitting new ones.

All dismantling and reassembly operations have been given in detail in the respective sections, so that it is simply a matter of tackling the tasks in a suitable sequence. First refit the crankshaft followed by the front bearer plate, camshaft and timing gear. The pistons and connecting rods are fitted next followed by oil pump and sump. The engine can then be stood upright and the tappets and cylinder head refitted. Refit the flywheel and clutch after which the gearbox can. be mated to the engine. Leave accessories such as water pump, distributor and oil filter to the last as they will only be in the way and are more prone to damage when fitted.

Liberally lubricate all bearing surfaces with clean engine oil. The torque load figures for the major components are given in the relevant sections and also listed in Technical Data.

Fill and check the levels of fluids in all the systems before starting the engine and also set the valve rocker clearances before starting the engine.

1 : 15 Valve rocker adjustment

Disconnect breather or vapour pipes as required. Free the throttle cable and remove the rocker cover by undoing the two screws securing it. Take care not to damage the cork seal under the rocker cover.

The method of adjusting the valve rockers is shown in **FIG 1 : 14**. The clearance must be set to .015 inch (.38 mm) with the engine cold and the tappet resting on the back of the cam opposite to the lobe.

Turn the engine until the appropriate valve is fully closed. Hold the adjusting screw with a screwdriver and slacken the locknut with a spanner as shown. Press down firmly on the screwdriver, so as to dissipate any oil film as well as taking up clearances, and insert a .015 inch feeler gauge between the valve stem and the rocker face. Note that if the rocker faces are worn the feeler gauge will bridge the depression and give a false reading. More accurate readings will be given using a DTI and measuring the movement, but worn rockers should be renewed. Turn the screwdriver until resistance is felt on the feeler gauge as it is moved. Hold the screwdriver still and tighten the locknut. Recheck the clearance in case the adjusting screw has turned with the locknut.

Ensuring that the tappets are on the backs of the cams . is best done by adjusting the rockers in the following order:

Adjust No. 1 rocker with No. 8 valve fully open
Adjust No. 3 rocker with No. 6 valve fully open
Adjust No. 5 rocker with No. 4 valve fully open
Adjust No. 2 rocker with No. 7 valve fully open
Adjust No. 8 rocker with No. 1 valve fully open
Adjust No. 6 rocker with No. 3 valve fully open
Adjust No. 4 rocker with No. 5 valve fully open
Adjust No. 7 rocker with No. 2 valve fully open

This series requires the minimum turning of the engine between each adjustment and it should be noted that the numbers in each line add up to 9 so constant reference to the table is not required.

Replace the rocker cover in the reverse order of removal, renewing the rubber seals under the screws or the cork gasket if either are damaged. Start the engine and allow it to run for several minutes before checking for oil leaks.

1 : 16 Crankcase ventilation

The fumes from the crankcase are drawn in through the carburetters and then burnt in the combustion chambers so as to prevent the emission of fumes from the crankcase. An oil separator is mounted on the timing case and on some systems it is connected directly to the inlet manifold, in which case a sealed oil filter cap is fitted to the rocker cover. This system will be shown in more detail in the next chapter. On other engines the oil separator is connected to the inlet manifold through a breather control valve as shown in **FIG 1 : 15**. Air is drawn in through a filter in the filler cap and the breather control valve partially closes at high induction vacuum to prevent excess air flowing through the engine.

The oil filler cap and filter on cars not equipped with evaporative loss control systems should be renewed every 12,000 miles or 12 months, whichever is the shorter.

At regular intervals the breather control valve should be dismantled and cleaned. Free the unit from the breather pipes, remove the spring clip 1 and take out the internal parts. Difficult deposits on the metal parts can be removed more easily if the metal parts are first boiled in water, after which any suitable solvent may be used. The diaphragm 3 must only be cleaned using detergent or methylated spirits. Never use any abrasive on any parts of the valve.

Reassemble and refit the valve. Check the operation with the engine running at idling speed. If the valve is working satisfactorily the engine will speed up by approximately 200 rev/min when the oil filler cap is removed.

1 : 17 Fault diagnosis

(a) Engine will not start

1 Defective ignition coil
2 Water on sparking plug leads or distributor cap
3 Loose wires or defective insulation in ignition circuit
4 Dirty, pitted or incorrectly set contact breaker points
5 Faulty distributor capacitor (condenser)
6 Too much choke
7 Too little choke
8 Faulty or jammed starter
9 Sparking plug leads incorrectly connected
10 Vapour lock in fuel pipes (hot weather only)
11 Defective fuel pump
12 Blocked petrol filter or carburetter jets
13 Leaking valves
14 Sticking valves
15 Valve timing incorrect
16 Ignition timing incorrect
17 Defective fuel pump

(b) Engine stalls

1 Check all the items in (a) except for 2, 8, 9, 15 and 16
2 Sparking plugs defective or gaps incorrectly set
3 Retarded ignition
4 Mixture too weak
5 Water in fuel system
6 Petrol tank vent blocked (note sealed cap is fitted to USA models)
7 Incorrect valve rocker clearance
8 Sticking air valve in carburetter

(c) Engine idles badly

1 Check 2 and 7 in (b)
2 Air leak at manifold joints
3 Carburetter jet blocked or out of adjustment
4 Air leak in carburetter
5 Over-rich mixture
6 Worn piston rings
7 Worn valve stems or valve guides
8 Weak exhaust valve springs

(d) Engine misfires

1 Check all of (a) except for 6, 7, 8 and 10. Also check 2, 3, 4 and 7 in (b)

(e) Engine overheats (see Chapter 4)

(f) Compression low

1 Check 13 and 14 in (a); 6 and 7 in (c)
2 Worn piston ring grooves
3 Scored or worn cylinder bores

(g) Engine lacks power

1 Check 4, 6, 12, 13, 14, 15, 16 and 17 in (a); 2, 3, 4, 7 and 8 in (b); 6 and 7 in (c). Also check (e) and (f)
2 Fouled sparking plugs
3 Leaking cylinder head gasket
4 Automatic advance not operating

(h) Burnt valves or seats

1 Check 13 and 14 in (a); 7 in (b). Also check (e)
2 Excessive carbon around valve seat and head

(j) Sticking valves

1 Weak valve springs
2 Bent valve stem
3 Scored valve stem or guide
4 Incorrect valve clearance
5 Gummy deposits on valve stem

(k) Excessive cylinder wear

1 Check 6 in (a) and check **Chapter 4** for possible causes of overheating
2 Lack of oil
3 Dirty oil
4 Piston rings gummed up or broken
5 Badly fitted piston rings
6 Connecting rods bent

(l) Excessive oil consumption

1 Check 6 and 7 in (c); 3 in (f) and also check (k)
2 Oil return holes in pistons blocked
3 Oil level too high
4 External oil leaks

(m) Main and big-end bearing failure

1 Check 2 and 3 in (k)
2 Restricted oilways
3 Worn journals or crankpins
4 Loose bearing caps
5 Extremely low oil pressure
6 Bent connecting rod

(n) Low oil pressure

1 Check 2 and 3 in (k); also check 2, 3 and 4 in (m)
2 Choked oil filter or oil strainer
3 Relief valve held open by dirt or worn seatings
4 Weak relief valve spring
5 Defective oil pressure gauge or transmitter

(o) Internal water leakage (see Chapter 4)

(p) Poor circulation (see Chapter 4)

(q) Corrosion (see Chapter 4)

(r) High fuel consumption (see Chapter 2)

(s) Engine vibration

1 Loose alternator bolts
2 Fan blades out of balance
3 Exhaust pipe mountings too tight
4 Mounting brackets not correctly fastened

NOTES

CHAPTER 2

THE FUEL SYSTEM

2:1 Description

All models have a fuel tank at the rear of the car and fuel is drawn from the tank by an electric AUF 300 or HP pump which feeds the fuel to the twin or single carburetter. Air cleaners are fitted to filter the incoming air into the engine so that microscopic particles of dust do not cause excessive wear to the carburetters or engine.

Certain areas have very stringent regulations concerning the emission of hydrocarbons and carbon monoxide into the atmosphere. The normal carburetters fitted to the standard engines do not control the mixture with sufficient accuracy to ensure that the emissions are within the legal limits and special carburetters are fitted instead. These special carburetters cannot be tuned by ear alone and require special equipment to ensure that they are in the correct mixture range.

Under conditions of engine overrun or deceleration the exhaust will contain excessive hydrocarbons and carbon monoxide. To cure this an air pump is fitted to the engine so that air is injected into the exhaust ports and the exhaust gases burn in this excess air so that the emissions are controlled. Under these conditions air is also injected into the intake manifold.

Fumes from the crankcase are drawn in with the air/fuel mixture and burnt as described in **Chapter 1, Section 1:16**. A further source of hydrocarbons is the fuel evaporating from the fuel tank and carburetter float chambers. The fuel tank and carburetter float chambers are sealed and connected by pipes to a carbon filled canister. Fuel evaporation is vented to atmosphere through this carbon filled canister, where the fuel content is absorbed by the carbon. When the engine is running, air is drawn through the canister in a reverse direction, purging

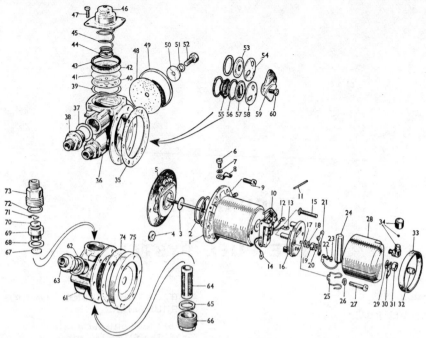

FIG 2:1   Fuel pump details

Key to Fig 2:1   1 Coil housing   2 Armature spring   3 Impact washer   4 Armature centralizing roller
5 Diaphragm and spindle assembly   6 Setscrew   7 Spring washer   8 Earth connector   9 Setscrew   10 Rocker mechanism
11 Rocker pivot pin   12 Terminal tag   13 Terminal tag   14 Earth tag   15 Terminal tag   16 Pedestal   17 Spring washer
18 Lead washer   19 Terminal nut   20 End cover seal washer   21 Contact blade   22 Washer   23 Contact blade screw
24 Capacitor   25 Capacitor clip   26 Spring washer   27 Pedestal screw   28 End cover   29 Shakeproof washer
30 Lucar connector   31 Nut   32 Insulating sleeve   33 Sealing band   34 Vent valve, AUF300 type   35 Gasket   36 Pump
body   37 Fibre washer   38 Outlet connection   39 Sealing washer   *40 Diaphragm plate   41 Plastic diaphragm barrier
*42 Rubber diaphragm   43 Rubber 'O' ring   *44 Spring end cap   *45 Diaphragm spring   **46 Delivery flow smoothing
device cover   47 Setscrew   48 Gasket   49 Inlet air bottle cover   50 Dished washer   51 Spring washer   52 Setscrew
53 Outlet valve   54 Valve cap   55 Filter   56 Sealing washer   57 Inlet valve   58 Valve cap   59 Clamp plate   60 Setscrew
HP type: 61 Pump body   62 Fibre washer   63 Outlet connection   64 Filter   65 Washer   66 Plug   67 Inlet valve
68 Thin fibre washer   69 Outlet valve cage   70 Outlet valve   71 Spring clip   72 Medium fibre washer   73 Outlet
connection   74 Gasket   75 Sandwich plate
                    * Early pumps   ** Later pumps

the carbon free from fuel. This mixture of air and fuel is then drawn into the engine where the fuel is burnt. So little fuel is involved that it does not alter the mixture strength.

For ease of reference this chapter has been subdivided into parts covering the different major components. Though there are many similarities care must be taken not to confuse instructions for the emission controlled carburetters with those fitted to standard engines, unless there is a deliberate cross-reference.

PART 1   THE FUEL PUMP

A SU AUF.300 or HP electrically-operated pump is fitted as standard and the details of this pump are shown in FIG 2:1. The early pump is fitted to the heelboard next to the front attachment of the rear righthand spring. The later pump is fitted in the luggage compartment.

2:2 Operation

When the ignition is first switched on there is no fuel pressure and the diaphragm 5 is held towards the body by the action of the spring 2. The contacts on the rocker

assembly 10 and contact blade 21 are closed, allowing current to pass through the solenoid in the coil housing 1. The solenoid draws in the diaphragm, creating suction in the chamber of the body 36 so that fuel is drawn in through the inlet, filter 55 and inlet valve 57. At the completion of the stroke the rocker mechanism 10 throws over, opening the contacts and isolating the solenoid. The diaphragm again moves out under the action of the spring 2, the inlet valve closes and the fuel in the chamber is forced out through the outlet valve 53 to the carburetter float chambers. At the end of the diaphragm stroke the rocker assembly again throws over, energizing the solenoid so that the cycle is repeated. This carries on until the carburetter float chambers are full and will accept no more fuel. The needle valves in the float chambers close and the fuel pressure rises until it balances the pressure of the return spring 2. The diaphragm stays in this position, with the contacts open, until sufficient fuel has been used to allow the diaphragm to reach the end of its stroke nearest the body, when the contacts can again close so that the solenoid is energized and a fresh charge of fuel is drawn into the chamber.

2:3 Testing

The pump can only be fully tested using an SU test rig, which checks both the pressure and the flow rate. However, the pump can still be functionally tested without the special test rig.

When the ignition is first switched on after the car has been standing for some time, the pump should be heard to operate rapidly at first and then to slow down as the carburetter float chambers fill. Eventually the pump should stop altogether and only operate for a single stroke at long intervals. If the pump continues to cycle then there is a defect in the system.

Disconnect the fuel line from the carburetter and hold it into a suitable container. Switch on the ignition and the pump should operate rapidly and regularly, producing a steady stream of fuel. In good conditions the pump should produce a flow of approximately 1 pint (Imperial) in 30 seconds. If the pump starts operating normally but then gradually slows down, it is likely that the vent to the fuel tank is blocked. On all fuel systems, removing the filler cap should allow the pump to speed up again if the vent is blocked.

The most likely causes of the pump failing to operate are given in the fault diagnosis at the end of this part.

2:4 Removal and replacement

The fuel tank should be drained or else the inlet pipe to the pump plugged, to prevent fuel from syphoning out of the tank when the pump is removed.

Disconnect the batteries, and then disconnect the earth and supply cables from the pump. Disconnect the breather, inlet and outlet pipes from the pump. Take out the two bolts securing the pump and free it from the car.

Replace the pump in the reverse order of removal, making sure that the breather pipes are refitted correctly and that they are secured by the T-pieces in the harness grommets on the boot floor.

From car No. 41002 disconnect the battery from inside the luggage compartment unscrew the retaining screws and remove the fuel pump guard. Slacken the clip retaining the pump in the support rubber. Disconnect the lead from the pump terminal. Disconnect the pipe unions from under the car. Disconnect the breather pipe and the earth connector and withdraw the pump from the support rubber.

To refit reverse the procedure ensuring that the pipe unions face upwards at an angle of 45° inclined to the centre line of the pump.

2:5 Dismantling

1 Remove the end cover 28. Free the capacitor 24 from its clip 25 and remove it and the contact blade 21 by unscrewing the 5.BA screw 23. Note the positions and attachments of the three leads 12, 13 and 14.
2 Remove the earth tag parts 6, 7 and 8. Use a well fitting screwdriver to remove the screws 9 and free the coil housing 1 from the pump body 36. Very carefully pull back the diaphragm 5 and check how it is held.
3 **Roller type diaphragm.** Hold the coil assembly over a cardboard box and unscrew the diaphragm assembly 5, anticlockwise, until the return spring pushes it free from the housing and the brass rollers 4 fall out into the box. Fully unscrew the diaphragm assembly.

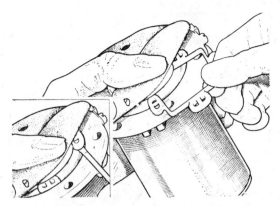

FIG 2:2 Fitting the armature guide plate. Inset shows the method of removing the guide plate

4 **Guide plate diaphragm.** Carefully turn back the edge of the diaphragm assembly and lever out the end lobes of the guide plate, as shown in **FIG 2:2**. Unscrew the diaphragm and remove it and the guide plate from the coil housing.
5 Remove the seal washer 20 and unscrew the nut 19. Use a sharp penknife to carefully cut away the old lead washer 18. Remove the two pedestal securing screws 27 and remove the earth tag 14 and capacitor clip 25. Tilt the pedestal assembly so that the terminal stud 15 can be withdrawn and then remove the pedestal assembly complete with the rocker assembly. The rocker assembly can be freed from the pedestal by pushing out the hardened steel pin 11. **Do not attempt to dismantle the coil housing 1 any further.**
6 **Do not dismantle the flow smoothing device unless a rig is available for testing the fuel pump delivery pressure after reassembly.** The flow smoothing parts are dismantled by taking out the screws 47 and 52.
7 Remove the valves and the valve caps from the pump body by taking out the screw 60 and removing the retaining plate 59. Carefully note the positions and directions of the valves so that they can be correctly reassembled.

2:6 Reassembly

Before reassembling the pump the parts should be inspected and cleaned.

Inspection:

1 Clean all the parts by brushing with either fuel or methylated spirits (denatured alchohol). Sometimes fuel evaporates leaving a stale-smelling gum which will coat the parts of the pump in contact with fuel with a substance resembling varnish. The brass and steel parts can be cleaned by first boiling them in 20 per cent caustic soda, dipping them in a strong nitric acid solution and finally washing them with boiling water. **Take great care as the chemicals are very dangerous.** Light alloy parts must not be given this treatment but should be soaked in methylated spirits

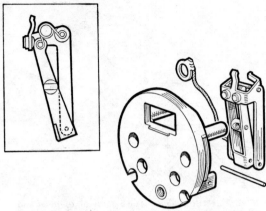

FIG 2:3 Refitting rocker assembly to the pedestal

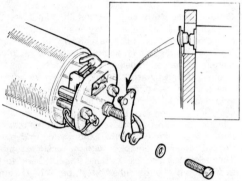

FIG 2:4 Correct position of contact blade

instead before scrubbing. The neoprene diaphragm should be inspected as the gum will attack neoprene.

2 Examine all the parts for cracks or fractures, and renew any that are damaged. Special points to check are around the rectangular hole in the pedestal mounting 16, the contact points, and the diaphragm 5. If the pump body 36 is deeply pitted then it must be renewed. Check the inlet and outlet valves by blowing and sucking through them. Do not use any abrasives to clean them and take great care not to scratch the plastic surface on the valve discs. Check that the tongue on the valve cage is not distorted and that it allows the valve approximately $\frac{1}{16}$ inch (1.6 mm) free lift.

3 Contact points that are dirty may be cleaned, using a strip of fine emerypaper. Check that the ball in the non-return valve fitted to the end cover is free to move and that the valve is unobstructed.

When the parts have been cleaned and checked they are reassembled as follows:

1 Refit the rocker assembly 10 to the pedestal 16 using the hardened steel pin 11. **Only the correct hardened steel pin made by SU may be used, non-hardened steel will wear rapidly.** With the inner rocker spindle in tension against the rear of the contact point, position the centre toggle so that the centre toggle spring is above the spindle on which the white rollers run, as shown in **FIG 2:3**. If the arms

catch on the pedestal legs, square them up using a pair of long-nosed pliers.

2 Refit the terminal stud 15, the wire terminal and parts, including the sealing washer 20 to the pedestal. Use a new lead washer 18 and refit the nut 19 so that its conical face is towards the lead washer. Resecure the pedestal assembly to the coil housing 1 using the screws 27, and not forgetting to replace the earth tag 14 and capacitor clip 25. Do not overtighten the screws 27 or the pedestal may crack, and hold the earth tag 14 to prevent it from rotating while tightening the screws.

3 Replace the armature spring with its largest diameter towards the coil housing. Make sure that the small neoprene impact washer is fitted into its recess in the armature housing, and refit the diaphragm by screwing into the threaded trunnion in the rocker assembly. Screw in the diaphragm until the rocker will not throw over, without allowing the armature to jam in the internal steps of the housing.

4 **Roller type.** Hold the coil housing with the rocker downwards. Turn back the edge of the diaphragm and replace the eleven brass rollers. Once the contacts have been adjusted and the diaphragm set, the diaphragm must be pressed and an adjusting fork slipped under the rockers so that they hold the diaphragm and prevent the rollers from falling out.

5 **Guide plate type.** Refer to **FIG 2:2** and refit the guide plate as shown. When the guide plate is in position then press the lobes into their recesses, starting on the centre lobes and finishing on the end pair.

6 Refit the contact blade 21 and set the contacts as described later. Once the setting is complete then carefully remove the contact blade.

7 Hold the coil housing horizontally in one hand and use the thumb of the other hand to operate the diaphragm. Unscrew the diaphragm until the rocker just throws over when actuated. From this position unscrew the diaphragm further until the securing holes are in alignment. Unscrew the diaphragm a further quarter of a turn (four holes). At this point fit the retaining fork under the rocker when rollers are fitted. The retaining fork is only there to prevent the rollers from falling out and it is not for applying any pre-tension to the diaphragm.

8 Reassemble the valves and their seals to the pump housing. The inlet valve recess in the body is deeper than that of the outlet valve, and the inlet valve and filter is fitted to the recess so that the tongue on the valve cage is outwards. The outlet valve is fitted with the cage tongue inwards to the body. If the inlet and outlet connections 38 have been removed then refit them using new fibre washers 37.

9 Refit the body to the coil housing, preferably using a new gasket 35. **No jointing compound may be used on the diaphragm.** Set the cast lugs on the coil housing to the bottom, align the holes, and tighten the screws 9 finger tight only. Refit the earth tag assembly. If the diaphragm is held in place by the retaining fork, then remove the retaining fork. Fully tighten the securing screws, tightening them evenly and diagonally.

10 Refit the contact blade 21 and the capacitor 24. Replace the end cover 28, sealing the join with the sealing ring 33 and waterproof tape.

Contact blade:

A limited degree of adjustment is provided for positioning the blade. It must be set so that its contacts are just above those on the rocker when the points are closed, as shown in **FIG 2:4**. The blade contacts must be square to the rocker contacts in the vertical plane.

When the points are open the contact blade must rest on the thin ridge at the edge of the rectangular opening in the pedestal. If it does not do so, release the screw and swing the contact blade to one side. Bend the blade slightly downwards, secure it correctly back in place and check again with the points open.

Contact gap:

Refer to **FIG 2:5**. Use feeler gauges to check that the contact blade lifts .035 ± .005 inch (.9 ± .13 mm) at A. If necessary bend the stop finger under the pedestal to bring about the correct lift.

Adjust the gap B so that it is .070 ± .005 inch (1.8 ± .13 mm) when the contact blade is pressed against the ridge on the pedestal. Adjustment is by carefully bending the blade.

2:7 Fault diagnosis

(a) Excessive burning or arcing on contact points

1 Defective capacitor
2 Leak wire in coil defective (necessitates renewal of complete coil housing)

(b) Little or no fuel delivery

1 Carburetter float chamber needle valve stuck closed
2 Air leaks in the system
3 Defective or dirty pump valves
4 Blocked fuel filters or pipelines
5 Blocked vent system
6 Dirty or incorrectly set contact points
7 Electrical supply failure
8 Defective pump diaphragm

(c) Noisy pump

1 Check 2, 3 and 4 in (b)
2 Loose mountings

(d) Pump operates continuously and rapidly

1 Check 2, 3, 4 and 8 in (b)
2 Float chamber needle valves stuck open
3 Heavy fuel leak
4 Very low fuel level in tank

If the fuel lines are blocked they may be cleaned out using compressed air, but the pump must first be disconnected from the pipelines otherwise the valves will be damaged.

PART 2   THE STANDARD CARBURETTERS

2:8 Operation of an SU carburetter

A sectional view of an HS4 carburetter is shown in **FIG 2:6**. The throttle butterfly on the right is connected to the accelerator pedal by a mechanical linkage and the feed tube 4 is connected to the float chamber so that the level of fuel in the jet is constant.

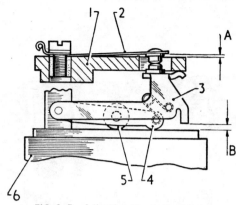

FIG 2:5   Adjusting the contacts gap

Key to Fig 2:5   1 Pedestal   2 Contact blade
3 Outer rocker   4 Inner rocker   5 Trunnion
6 Coil housing   A = .035 inch (.9 mm)
B = .070 inch (1.8 mm)

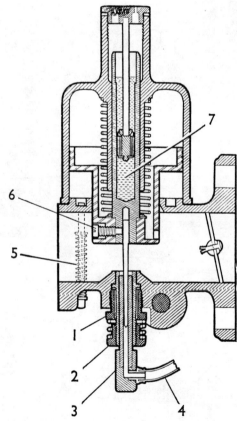

FIG 2:6   Sectioned HS4 carburetter

Key to Fig 2:6   1 Jet locking nut   2 Jet adjusting nut
3 Jet head   4 Feed tube from float chamber
5 Piston lifting pin   6 Needle securing screw
7 Oil damper reservoir

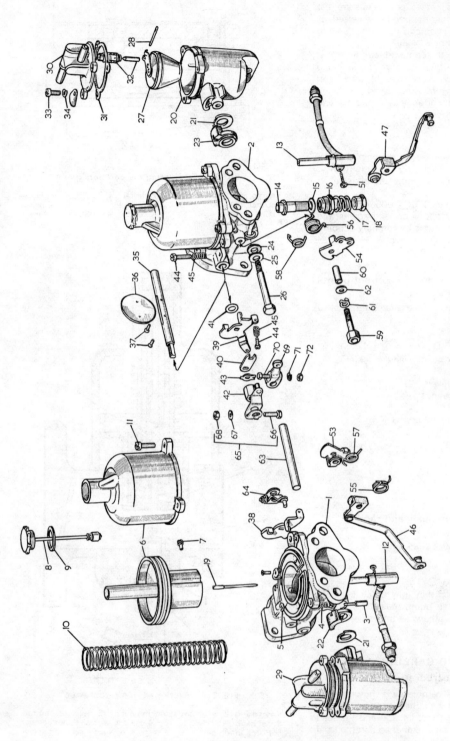

FIG 2:7   Carburetter details

Key to Fig 2:7
1 Front carburetter body   2 Rear carburetter body   3 Piston lifting pin   4 Pin spring   5 Pin circlip   6 Chamber and piston assembly
7 Needle locking screw   8 Cam and dampers assembly   9 Fibre cap washer   10 Red piston spring   11 Chamber to body screw   12 Front carburetter jet assembly
13 Rear carburetter jet assembly   14 Jet bearing   15 Brass jet bearing washer   16 Jet locking screw   17 Jet locking spring   18 Jet adjusting screw   19 Needle
20 Float chamber   21 Support washer   22 Rear carburetter rubber grommet   23 Rear carburetter rubber grommet   24 Rubber washer   25 Plain washer
26 Float chamber fixing bolt   27 Float assembly   28 Hinged lever pin   29 Front carburetter float chamber lid   30 Rear carburetter float chamber lid   31 Lid washer
32 Needle and seat assembly   33 Lid screw   34 Screw spring washer   35 Throttle spindle   36 Throttle disc   37 Disc screw   38 Front carburetter throttle return lever
39 Rear carburetter throttle return lever   40 Lost motion lever   41 Spacing washer   42 Lever nut   43 Nut tabwasher   44 Throttle stop screw   45 Throttle stop screw spring
46 Front carburetter throttle return lever   47 Rear carburetter pickup lever and link assembly   51 Link to jet screw   53 Front carburetter cam lever spring
54 Rear carburetter cam lever   55 Front carburetter pickup lever and link assembly   56 Rear carburetter pickup lever spring   57 Front carburetter cam lever
58 Rear carburetter cam lever spring   59 Pivot bolt   60 Pivot bolt tube   61 Pivot bolt spring washer   62 Distance washer   63 Jet connecting rod
64 Front carburetter lever and pin assembly   65 Rear carburetter lever and pin assembly   66 Lever bolt   67 Bolt washer   68 Bolt nut   69 Choke operating lever
70 Lever bolt   71 Spring washer   72 Nut

When the engine is running air is drawn through the carburetter. As there is a bridge in the intake below the air valve the airflow at this point is speeded up and the pressure decreased. This reduction in pressure draws fuel from the jet so that it mixes with the air. The pressure reduction is also transferred to the suction chamber above the air valve. The air valve will then rise to a position where the vacuum is balanced by the weight of the piston and the pressure of the return spring. If the throttle is opened and more air passes through then at first there will be an increased suction across the bridge and this will raise the air valve further to the new point of balance. Conversely if the airflow decreases the pressure will rise and the air valve will drop until the normal suction is restored.

As the weight of the piston and pressure from the return spring are virtually constant then the vacuum across the bridge is virtually constant and the air valve will rise proportionately to the air flow. The jet area is constant, but a tapered needle slides in the jet and is attached to the air valve. Consequently when the airflow is greatest the air valve will be at its highest and the effective area of the jet will also be greatest. Since the vacuum is constant the actual amount of fuel drawn through the jet will be larger. When the airflow is least then the air valve will be at the bottom and the effective area of the jet least, with consequently less fuel drawn through it. The amount of fuel is thus proportionate to the amount of air and the mixture strength is kept constant throughout the range.

For cold starts the jet head can be drawn downwards so that it operates over a narrower portion of the needle and a higher proportion of fuel is drawn in with the air.

The hydraulic damper fitted to the air valve serves the dual function of damping out rapid fluctuations and also acting as an accelerator pump. When the throttle is opened the damper causes the air valve to lag. The suction increases temporarily beyond its normal value and excess fuel for acceleration is then drawn through the jet.

2:9 Routine maintenance

The throttle and choke linkages and cables should be regularly checked for freedom of movement and pivot points lightly oiled.

At regular intervals unscrew the hexagonal damper plug from the top of each suction chamber and check the oil level in the damper. Only SAE.20 or SAE.30 engine oil may be used. On standard carburetters top up the level so that it is $\frac{1}{2}$ inch (13 mm) above the top of the hollow piston rod. Some carburetters are dustprooted (identifiable by a transverse hole in the neck of the suction chamber and no vent hole in the damper plug) and on these the oil level must be $\frac{1}{2}$ inch below the level of the hollow piston rod.

Air filters:

Periodically remove the casings and clean out loose dust and dirt. The paper elements may have loose dust and dirt brushed from their outsides of the dirt may be blown off using an airline. In both cases care must be taken to prevent dirt from passing to the clean side of the filter.

The elements must be renewed before they are choked as dirt cannot be cleaned out of the paper. Remove the

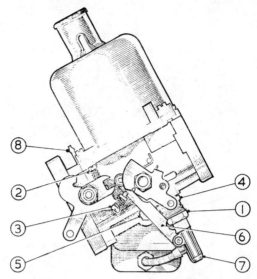

FIG 2:8 Carburetter external details

Key to Fig 2:8   1 Jet adjusting nut   2 Throttle stop screw
3 Choke or fast-idle screw   4 Jet locking nut
5 Float chamber securing nut   6 Jet link   7 Jet head
8 Vacuum ignition take-off

complete filters from the engine and then take off the base plates, discarding the old elements. Clean all the parts thoroughly before reassembling them with new elements and refitting them.

2:10 Removing and replacing

1 Disconnect the fuel supply pipe from the rear carburetter. Disconnect the overflow, or vapour, pipes from the carburetter float chambers.
2 Disconnect the mixture control and throttle cables completely from the carburetters. Disconnect the throttle return springs. Pull off the vacuum pipe to the distributor from its connection on the rear carburetter.
3 Remove the two nuts securing each carburetter flange to the manifold and remove both carburetters together complete with their air cleaners.

Refit the carburetters in the reverse order of removal, checking and resetting the throttle linkage if required. Before refitting the carburetters their flanges should be checked and any distortion or high spots rectified, either by lapping or very careful filing.

2:11 Slow-running adjustments and synchronization (SU carburetters)

The details of the carburetters are shown in FIG 2:7 and the adjustment points and external parts are shown in FIG 2:8.

It is useless to try tuning twin carburetters if the engine is in poor condition or the ignition timing is incorrect, so any faults in these should be rectified before tuning the carburetters.

1 If the tuning is completely out then first roughly set the carburetters. Refer to FIG 2:8. Turn the throttle stop screws 2 until they are just clear of their stops and then

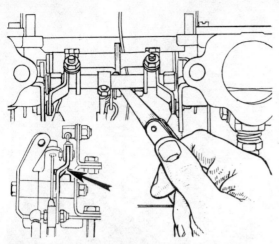

FIG 2:9 Adjusting the throttle linkage. Inset shows the position of the feeler gauge on automatic transmission models

screw them back in $1\frac{1}{2}$ turns. Either remove the suction chamber and air valve assemblies, or else remove the air cleaners. Turn each jet adjusting nut 1 up until the jet head 7 is flush with the bridge piece in the air intake. Replace the parts removed. Turn the jet adjusting nuts down by two complete turns (12 flats).

2 Slacken the pinch bolt on one of the coupling levers so that the two carburetter throttle spindles are free to rotate independently. Start the engine and allow it to run until it has reached its normal operating temperature. Disconnect the mixture control cable. Slacken the two pinch bolts to free the choke actuating lever and unscrew the two fast-idle screws 3 so that they are well clear of their cams.

3 Listen at each air intake in turn using a piece of rubber tube, and adjust the throttle stop screws 2 until the hiss in each air intake is equal to the other and the engine is running at 500 rev/min.

4 Check the mixture at each carburetter by lifting the piston of the air valve $\frac{1}{32}$ inch (.75 mm) either using the lifting pin or a long thin screwdriver through the air intake. If the engine speed rises then the mixture is too rich while if the engine stops or loses speed then the mixture is too weak. Adjust the mixture strength by turning each adjusting nut a flat at a time in the required direction. Screwing the nut up the carburetter will weaken the mixture and down will enrich the mixture. Check each carburetter in turn as they are interdependent.

5 The mixture for a carburetter is correct when the engine momentarily increases speed when the piston is lifted. A further indication is the exhaust note, which will be regular and even. A rich mixture causes black smoke and a rhythmical misfire, while a weak mixture gives a splashy type of misfire only. As the mixture strengths are altered the engine may vary in speed and it should be adjusted back to 500 rev/min by turning the adjusting screws 2 by equal amounts.

6 Refer to **FIG 2:9**. Slacken both pinch bolts so that the throttle levers are free. On manual gearbox models put a .12 inch (.3 mm) feeler gauge between the throttle shaft stop and the choke interconnecting rod

as shown. On automatic transmission models put a .020 inch (.5 mm) feeler gauge between the throttle lever and the stop as shown in the inset. Lightly press each throttle lever down until its pin rests on the lower fork of the lever attached to the throttle spindle. Tighten the pinch bolts in this position and remove the feeler gauge.

7 Press the jet heads firmly up against the adjusting nuts and reconnect the choke cable with a very small amount of slack. Start the engine and pull out the choke control until the carburetter jets are just about to move. The control should be out a minimum of $\frac{1}{4}$ (6 mm). Adjust the fast-idle screws until the engine is running at a speed of 1000 rev/min when hot. Make sure that there is some clearance between the screws and the cams when the choke control is fully returned.

2:12 Carburetter faults

The dismantling of the various parts of the SU carburetter will also be given in this section as this will be required for curing the faults. By following through this section the complete carburetter can be dismantled and reassembled.

Sticking air valve:

This can cause difficult starting and poor response. Remove the air cleaner and unscrew the damper assembly 8 from the carburetter. Raise the piston using a pencil through the air intake and allow it to fall under its weight. The piston should fall freely and hit the bridge in the air intake with a definite click.

If the piston does not move freely then there is a fault. Undo the screws 11 and carefully lift off the suction chamber 6. Remove the spring 10 and withdraw the piston 6 complete with the needle 19. **Take great care not to damage or drop any of these parts.**

Wash the suction chamber and piston assembly with clean fuel or methylated spirits. Do not use any form of abrasive on them. Lightly oil the outside of the ground hollow piston rod and insert the piston back into the suction chamber. Take care not to allow any oil onto the rim of the piston or inside the suction chamber. The piston should move freely in the suction chamber with a small constant clearance between it and the inside of the chamber. If the rim does contact the suction chamber then the chamber has been dropped and become distorted. The only cure is to renew the assembly 6.

Check the needle 19 as if this is bent the air valve will stick. To renew the needle slacken the clamp screw 7, withdraw the old needle 19 and refit a new needle of the correct size (see Technical Data) so that the shoulder on the shank is flush with the face of the piston.

Refit the piston, taking care on entering the needle into the jet head, replace the spring and refit the suction chamber. Check that the piston now falls freely under its own weight. If the piston does not fall freely then the jet requires centralizing (see **Section 2:13**). If a new needle has been fitted then the jet must be recentralized.

Top up the damper to the correct level with oil and then refit the damper.

Jet blocked:

To remove the jet first take out the screw 51 which holds it to the choke linkage and then unscrew the pipe union at the float chamber. The jet assembly 12 or 13 can then be withdrawn from the carburetter.

The jet bearing 14 can be removed after taking off the adjusting nut 18 and spring 17 and then undoing the nut 16.

The parts are replaced in the reverse order of removal. Use a thin smear of petroleum jelly on the jet itself as lubrication. Whenever the nut 16 has been slackened or removed then the jet must be recentralized (see **Section 2:13**).

Flooding or fuel starvation:

If there is fuel starvation on both carburetters then the fuel pump and fuel lines should be checked by disconnecting the line from the carburetter and switching on the pump. Provided that these are satisfactory then the fault most likely lies in the float chamber.

Disconnect the fuel lines from the float chamber top. Remove the top by taking out the three screws 33 and washers 34. Check that the float 27 is undamaged and free from fuel. Invert the top and withdraw the pin 28 to free the float.

Withdraw the needle of the assembly 32 and blow through the inlets to remove any dirt. Wipe the needle clean and examine it. If the tapered seat on the needle is worn to a step then the complete assembly 32 must be renewed.

Clean any sediment out of the float chamber. The chamber is secured to the carburetter by the bolt 26 and the union on the jet fuel line. Take note of the position of all sealing washers and grommets so that the float chamber can be correctly refitted.

Reassemble the float chamber top in the reverse order of dismantling. Check that the fuel level is correct. Invert the top and lay a $\frac{1}{8}$ to $\frac{3}{16}$ inch (3.18 to 4.76 mm) test bar or suitable drill shank under the float, as shown in **FIG 2:10**. Carefully bend the float lever so that the angle between the straight portion and its hinge allows the float to rest on the test bar when the needle valve is fully shut.

Refit the top of the float chamber using a new gasket 31 if the old one is damaged.

Air leaks around throttle spindle:

These will cause difficulty in tuning the carburetters and erratic slow-running. To rectify, the carburetter must be removed from the engine.

Remove the throttle linkage. Take out the two screws 37 and turn the spindle 35 so that the throttle butterfly 36 can be slid out. The spindle 35 can then be renewed. If there is still excessive wear then the carburetter must be exchanged for a new or reconditioned unit.

2:13 Centralizing the jet (SU carburetters)

Remove the air cleaner and damper. Check that the piston falls freely under its own weight and hits the bridge with an equal noise when the jet is at its highest position as well as at its lowest position. A difference in noise indicates that the jet is not centralized. Centralizing can be carried out with the carburetter fitted but it is easiest if the carburetter has been removed from the engine.

Remove the damper. Disconnect the jet fuel line from the float chamber and remove the screw 51. Withdraw the jet from the carburetter and take off the adjusting nut 18

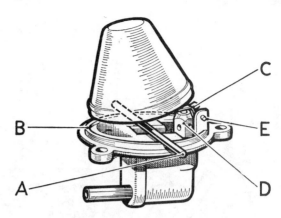

FIG 2:10   Checking float chamber fuel level

Key to Fig 2:10   **A** $\frac{1}{8}$ to $\frac{3}{16}$ inch (3.18 to 4.76 mm)
dia. bar   **B** Machined lip   **C** Float lever resetting point
D Needle valve assembly   **E** Hinge pin

and its spring 17. Replace the jet and loosely reconnect its flexible tube to the float chamber. The reconnection of the tube is only to ensure that the jet will always be replaced in the same angular position in the bearing.

Slacken the locking nut 16 until the jet bearing 14 can just be rotated with the fingers. Press the jet assembly 13 up to its highest position and use a pencil to press the air valve piston down onto the bridge. Tighten the nut 16 in this position. Lift the piston and check that it falls freely, hitting the bridge with a soft metallic click. If the piston does not fall freely, repeat the centralzing procedure. If the piston cannot be made to fall freely, check for other causes of the piston sticking (see **Section 2:11**).

2:14 Fault diagnosis

(a) High fuel consumption

1 Carburetters out of adjustment
2 Fuel leakage
3 Sticking carburetter controls
4 Dirty air cleaners
5 Float chamber flooding
6 Excessive engine temperature
7 Brakes binding
8 Tyres under-inflated
9 Idling speed too high
10 Car overloaded

(b) Poor idling

1 Check 3, 4 and 5 in (a)
2 Incorrect air/fuel mixture strength
3 Slow-running screws incorrectly adjusted
4 Worn throttle spindles
5 Air valve sticking

PART 3   THE EMISSION CONTROL CARBURETTERS

Earlier models incorporated SU carburetters similar to the standard version described in **PART 2**. It is recommended, however, that these are tuned at 12,000 mile intervals and that new seals, jet needles and float needle

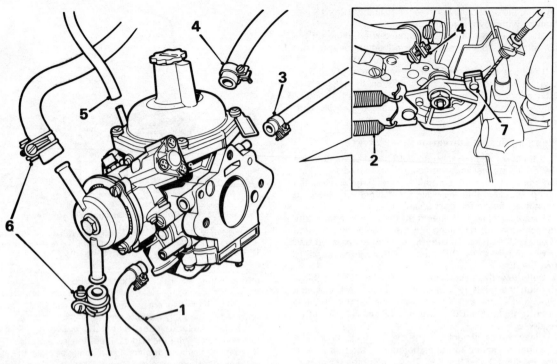

FIG 2:11   The Zenith carburetter installation

Key to Fig 2:11   1 Fuel inlet pipe   2 Throttle return spring   3 Adsorption canister pipe   4 Crankcase breather pipe
5 EGR valve pipe   6 Coolant hose   7 Throttle quadrant

valves are replaced at 48,000 miles. Such attention is essential to maintain the high standard of efficiency demanded by emission control regulations.

Emission control regulations:

With regard to operation, routine maintenance, removal and replacement of SU carburetters, all details are contained in **PART 2**.

The Zenith carburetter, Zenith 175 CD 5T:

This carburetter is designed specially for emission control models produced from 1976 onwards. It is a single unit, constant depression, side draught carburetter embodying an automatic choke (fuel enrichment) device.

Routine maintenance is confined to checking the condition of the air valve diaphragm and topping up the dashpot as described later in this section.

It is strongly advised that neither adjustment nor tuning is carried out on emission control carburetters without the use of an accurate tachometer and also an exhaust gas (CO) content analyser. If these instruments are not available, or are not fully understood, the vehicle should be referred to a garage possessing the right equipment and expertise.

Removing the Zenith carburetter:

1 Remove the air cleaner and refer to **FIG 2:11**. Disconnect the six hoses shown after labelling them to avoid confusion when refitting. When removing the

two coolant hoses 6, some coolant should be drained out of the radiator until the level is below that of the two hoses 6, otherwise a little coolant will be lost.

2 Disconnect the two throttle return springs 2, shown in the inset of **FIG 2:11**. Unscrew the locking and adjustment nuts which secure the throttle cable outer casing to the supporting bracket, and then detach the cable from the throttle quadrant by freeing the cable and pulling out the end barrel to detach the cable from the quadrant.

3 Unscrew the four nuts and washers securing the carburetter to the inlet manifold, and remove the carburetter.

Dismantling the Zenith carburetter:

Refer to **FIG 2:12**.

1 Unscrew and remove the damper 1 from the top of the carburetter.

2 Note the position of the carburetter top cover 7 relative to the body, unscrew the four screws, remove the top cover and collect the spring 8.

3 Pull out the air valve assembly 9 complete. Store the assembly so as not to damage the diaphragm 10 or the needle protruding from the base of the air valve piston 2.

4 Pull out the bottom plug 3 and allow fuel to drain out of the float chamber into a suitable container. Collect the plug sealing ring and store it with the plug.

5 Invert the carburetter, remove the six screws securing

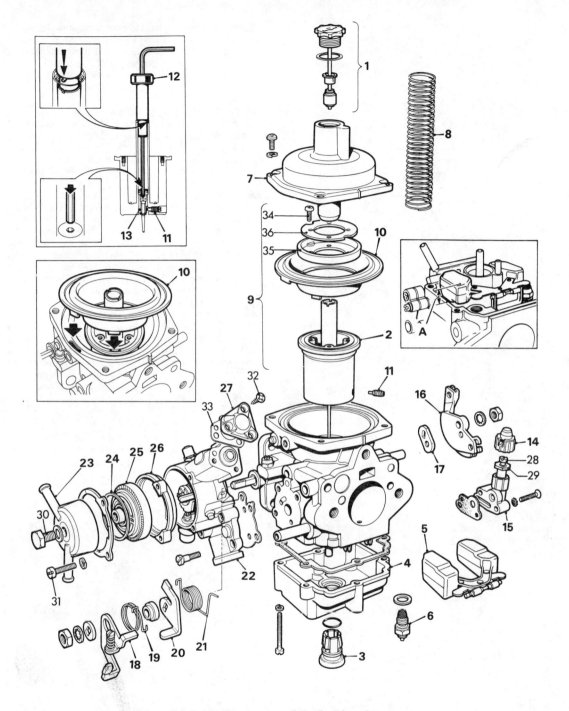

FIG 2:12 Components of the Zenith carburetter

Key to Fig 2:12 1 Damper   2 Air valve piston   3 Float chamber plug   4 Float chamber   5 Twin floats   6 Float needle valve   7 Top cover   8 Spring   9 Air valve assembly   10 Diaphragm   11 Grubscrew   12 Adjusting tool S353   13 Needle housing   14 Idle air regulator sealing cover   15 Idle air regulator   16 Throttle quadrant   17 Locating plate   18 Automatic choke outer lever   19 Return spring   20 Inner lever   21 Return spring   22 Automatic choke unit   23 Water jacket   24 Sealing ring   25 Heat mass   26 Insulator   27 Vacuum kick piston cover   28 Fine-idle adjustment screw   29 Coarse idle adjustment nut
A = .625 to .672 inch (15.87 to 17.07 mm)

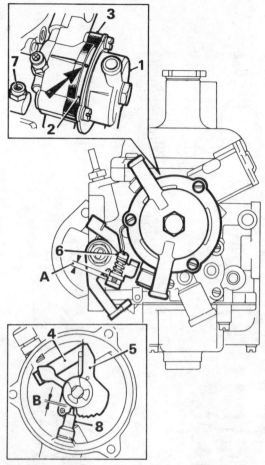

FIG 2:13 Checking and adjusting the automatic choke settings

Key to Fig 2:13 1 Water jacket   2 Heat mass
3 Insulator   4 Vacuum kick piston rod   5 Fast-idle cam
6 Idling speed adjustment screw   7 Throttle stop screw
8 Fast-idle pin   A = $\frac{3}{32}$ inch (2.4 mm)   B = .025 inch
(.64 mm)

the float chamber 4 to the carburetter body and remove the float chamber. Collect the float chamber gasket if it becomes detached.

6 Remove the twin floats 5 by freeing their pivot pin from the supporting bracket.

7 Unscrew and remove the float needle valve 6 together with its washer.

8 Remove the two screws which attach the idle air regulator 15 to the carburetter body, and remove the regulator. Do not detach the cover 14, if fitted, or alter the setting of the fine-idle screw 28 or coarse-idle nut 29. Collect the idle air regulator gasket should it become detached.

9 Unscrew the nut which secures the throttle quadrant 16 (see also **FIG 2:11**). Pull off the throttle quadrant 16 and the locating plate 17.

10 Unscrew and remove the nut, washer and spacer

which secure the choke lever assembly 18 to 21. Detach the outer lever 18 complete with its return spring 19. Pull off the bush and the inner lever 20 complete with its return spring 21.

11 Remove the screws which secure the automatic choke unit 22 and detach the unit complete with gasket.

12 Place the choke unit on the bench, unscrew the central bolt 30 and remove the water jacket 23. Collect the water jacket sealing ring 24. Unscrew the three screws 31 and remove the heat mass 25 and insulator 26. Unscrew the three small screws 32 and remove the vacuum kick piston cover 27 together with the gasket 33.

13 Remove the four screws 34 securing the air valve diaphragm 10 to the air valve piston 2. Remove the diaphragm, nylon spacer 35 and retaining ring 36.

14 To remove the needle from the air valve piston it will be necessary to use the tool S353 shown in the top lefthand inset of **FIG 2:12**. This tool must also be used when resetting or adjusting the fuel mixture during tuning operations. Loosen the grub screw 11 by a few turns, insert the tool as shown, hold the outer portion to prevent the air valve piston from turning, and turn the inner spindle (hexagon key) by two or three turns counter-clockwise. The needle housing will then become exposed at the bottom of the air valve piston. Remove the grub screw 11 and pull out the needle. Note how the needle is fitted (biased away from the engine). The needle adjuster in the air valve piston is a fixed assembly and no attempt should be made to remove it.

Inspection and overhaul:

Clean all components in methylated spirit, fuel or an approved solvent and allow them to dry. If the diaphragm is slightly distorted but not punctured, it may be left in a

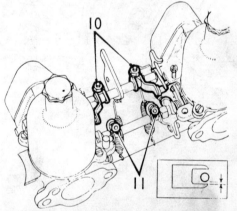

FIG 2:14 Throttle and jet interconnection clamping bolts. Inset shows the clearance between the pin and fork at idling speed

Key to Figs 2:14, 2:15 and 2:16   1 Jet adjusting nuts
4 Fast-idle adjusting screws   5 Throttle adjusting screws
7 Jet adjustment restrictors   8 Choke inner cable
9 Jet levers   10 Throttle lever clamp nuts
11 Jet control interconnection clamp nuts

cool place for about an hour where it will assume its original shape, after which it can be refitted.

Examine all components for wear, scoring, damage or deterioration. The best method is to renew the diaphragm, needle and seat, all the gaskets, float chamber needle valve, and all sealing 'O' rings.

Inspect the choke unit springs and levers for wear or distortion. Renew the levers if their locating holes have become enlarged or worn, causing free play when the levers are fitted.

Check the throttle quadrant and the butterfly valve. Check also the butterfly spindle and its bore in the carburetter body. Renew the spindle if worn, or the carburetter body if the bore is enlarged (the fuel mixture cannot be set accurately if either the spindle or bore are worn).

Examine the floats for damage or punctures. Rubber floats must be perfectly smooth along their entire surfaces, as even the slightest cracks will become porous, admitting fuel into the floats and rendering them useless. A fairly accurate method of checking the floats for punctures is to suspend them in a container full of water. Heat the water and observe the floats. If the floats are punctured, small air bubbles will emerge as the temperature of the water rises causing air inside the floats to expand and escape through the punctures.

Finally, use low pressure compressed air (such as air from a tyre pump) to blow through all ports, orifices and drillings to clear any obstructions that may exist.

Reassembling the Zenith carburetter:

This is a reversal of dismantling, noting the following:

Invert the carburetter body, refit the needle valve and washer. Refit the floats noting that the supporting metal plate is positioned towards the outside of the float chamber. Check the float level as shown in the righthand inset of **FIG 2:12** by measuring distance A between the float chamber face and the highest point on each float. The floats should be parallel and the correct distance A should be .625 to .672 inch (15.87 to 17.07 mm). If the floats are not parallel, bend the metal plate between them as necessary until they are parallel, i.e. until distance A is the same for both floats. The correct distance can be obtained by bending the metal tag which bears against the needle of the needle valve, provided that the tag bears squarely against the needle and not at an angle.

When refitting the diaphragm to the air valve piston, refer to the lower lefthand inset of **FIG 2:12** and locate the lower tag in the piston slot as shown by the righthand arrow. Refit the diaphragm nylon spacer and retaining ring and tighten the four retaining screws 34.

Check that the needle is of the correct type. A standard needle, No. 45G, is fitted, but cars equipped with a catalytic converter (after-burner) in the exhaust system use a 45H needle. Removing the needle is described earlier in this section. Refit the needle, positioning it in the air valve piston so that it is biased away from the engine side of the carburetter. Refit, but do not tighten, the needle securing grub screw, use the tool shown in **FIG 2:12** and turn the needle adjuster by two or three complete turns clockwise until the needle housing is retracted into the piston and then tighten the grub screw to secure the needle.

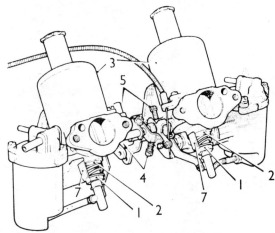

FIG 2:15   Carburetters installed

Refit the air valve piston, correctly locating the diaphragm outer tag so that it fits in the slot provided in the carburetter body as shown by the lefthand arrow of the lower lefthand inset (**FIG 2:12**).

Refit the spring and the top cover, ensuring that the offset casting in the neck faces towards the air cleaner side of the carburetter. Refit and tighten the four top cover screws. Check that the air valve piston moves freely throughout its full travel by pushing it up fully with a finger inserted through the air intake. The piston should fall steadily and smoothly when released, and should contact the bridge (bottom end) with an audible click. Should the fall be jerky or incomplete, try loosening the top cover screws, tapping the cover to centre its position, retighten the screws and recheck the piston movement. Should the piston movement remain jerky or difficult, remove the air valve assembly and examine the needle for bending or distortion. Use a new needle as a substitute, refit the piston and recheck the piston movement. If this improves then the original needle is slightly bent and must be discarded.

Refit and adjust the automatic choke unit as follows:

Refer to **FIG 2:12**. Refit the choke unit 22 using a new gasket and secure the unit with the retaining screws. Hold the throttle butterfly in the fully open position while carrying out the next adjustment. Refer to **FIG 2:13**. Rotate the operating lever several times to check the vacuum kick piston and rod 4 for full and free operation. Check also that the fast-idle cam 5 and the thermostat lever are free on their pivot. Move the cam away from the thermostat lever and then release it. The cam should return to the lever by the action of the return spring. Ensure that the cam remains in contact with the lever when the latter is rotated.

Release the throttle butterfly. Set the gap between the choke and throttle levers as shown at A in **FIG 2:13**. A should be set to $\frac{3}{32}$ inch (2.4 mm) by turning the idle speed adjusting screw 6.

Refer to the insets of **FIG 2:13** and adjust the throttle stop screw 7 to obtain a clearance of .025 inch (.64 mm) between the end of the fast-idle pin 8 and the cam as shown at B. When the correct clearance B is obtained,

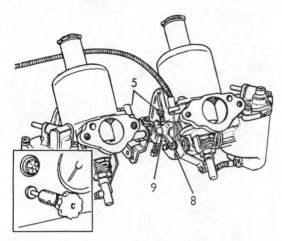

FIG 2:16   Adjusting the choke cable

secure the throttle stop screw 7 by tightening the locknut fitted around it.

Refit the heat mass and insulator so that they are aligned as shown by the arrow (top inset, **FIG 2:13**). The mark on the heat mass 2 must align with the mark on the choke body. Refit and tighten the three retaining screws to 8 to 10 lb inch (.092 to .115 kgm).

Refit the water jacket, together with its sealing ring, and position it correctly so that the pipe connections are as shown in **FIG 2:13**. Secure the water jacket with the central bolt.

Refit the remaining components in the reverse order of dismantling. Refit the carburetter, using a new flange gasket and reversing the removal procedure.

Push the air valve piston fully up and fill the hollow piston rod with fresh engine oil to a level $\frac{1}{4}$ inch (6 mm) below the top of the rod. Release the piston and refit the damper.

Tuning the Zenith carburetter:

It must be stressed that accurate tuning cannot be carried out without the use of a tachometer and an exhaust gas analyser to monitor the percentage of carbon monoxide (CO) in the exhaust gases. If the operator is not a skilled motor mechanic, and in the absence of the instruments mentioned, the car should be handed over to a fully equipped garage for tuning to be carried out. However, tuning may commence once the ignition is set correctly (spark plugs, contact points and timing), and the valve running clearances adjusted as specified in **Technical Data**. It must also be pointed out that tuning is useless unless the mechanical condition of the engine (crankshaft, timing chain, pistons, piston rings and valves) is such that they are all satisfactory and operating efficiently.

1 Remove the air cleaner. Check that the throttle linkage operates fully and smoothly. Check that the correct needle is fitted and that the air valve piston operates smoothly as described previously under 'Reassembling the Zenith carburetter'.

2 Refit the air valve piston, spring and carburetter top cover, locating the latter so that the offset casting in

the neck is towards the air cleaner side. Remove the damper and top up with fresh engine oil as detailed earlier.

3 Refit the air cleaner and run the engine until it attains normal operating temperature.

4 Refer to **FIG 2:19** and disconnect the hose from the air pump to the air manifold. Plug the free end of the disconnected hose.

5 Disconnect the adsorption canister pipe 3 (**FIG 2:11**).

6 Connect an accurate tachometer if the car is not fitted with one. Increase the engine speed to 2500 rev/min and hold it at this speed for 30 seconds to clear the sparking plugs and combustion chambers of excess carbon deposits built up during idling. This procedure should be repeated every three minutes during the tuning operation, otherwise an accurate CO reading cannot be obtained.

7 Release the throttle, allow the engine to idle and adjust the idling speed to the normal specified speed of 850 rev/min.

8 Connect an exhaust gas analyser in accordance with the manufacturer's instructions. At idling, the CO percentage of the exhaust gases should be $5\frac{1}{2}\% \pm 1\%$. If the analyser reading is outside these limits, adjust the fine-idle screw shown at 28 in **FIG 2:12**. (The fine-idle screw may sometimes be sealed with the cover 14.) Remove the cover by pulling it upwards to expose the screw. Turn the fine-idle screw slowly, a little at a time but do not disturb the setting of the coarse idle nut 29. Turning the screw clockwise will increase the CO content and counter-clockwise will decrease it.

9 If the correct CO percentage cannot be obtained using the screw, reposition the fine-idle screw in the mid-point of its range. This is obtained by turning the screw clockwise to the limit of its range and then turning it back two-and-a-half turns. Remove the damper from the top of the carburetter and use the tool No. S353 as shown in **FIG 2:12**. Insert the tool as shown so that the lugs cast in the outer sleeve fit into the slots at the top of the hollow piston rod. Fit the spindle (hexagon key) of the tool into the needle adjuster at the bottom of the air valve piston. Hold the outer sleeve firmly to prevent the piston from rotating and damaging the diaphragm when the spindle is turned.

10 Turn the spindle clockwise to enrich the fuel mixture and obtain a higher CO concentration, or counter-clockwise to weaken the mixture. Continue turning slowly until the correct setting is obtained as read on the exhaust gas analyser. Do not forget to stop tuning and increase the engine speed to 2500 rev/min for 30 seconds once every three minutes for the reasons described earlier.

11 From this point onwards, minor variation in the CO content can be obtained, using the fine-idle screw and coarse idle nut 28 and 29 (**FIG 2:12**) until a figure of $5\frac{1}{2}\% \pm 1\%$ is obtained. Turning the coarse idle nut clockwise will enrich the mixture (increase the CO content) and counter-clockwise will weaken it.

12 When the correct reading is obtained, fill the air valve piston rod with fresh engine oil to a level $\frac{1}{4}$ inch (6 mm) below the top of the rod, and refit the damper. Recheck the CO percentage and, if necessary, adjust

using the fine-idle screw. Refit the cap to seal the fine-idle screw and coarse idle nut.

Note that if it is not possible to obtain the correct CO percentage following the adjustment detailed, the carburetter must be overhauled or renewed. Overhauling the carburetter is detailed earlier in this section.

13 On completion, unplug and reconnect the air manifold hose. Reconnect the adsorption canister pipe, increase the engine speed to 2500 rev/min for 30 seconds and then re-adjust the idling speed to the normal 850 rev/min.

2:16 The SU carburetters

Tuning:

Before carrying out any adjustments the engine must be at its normal working temperature and the sparking plugs cleared. Start the engine and run it at a fast-idle speed. Let the engine run for five minutes after the thermostat valve has opened, detected by the radiator header tank heating up. When the engine is hot, run it at 2500 rev/min for one minute and then throttle back to normal idling. After every three minutes at idling, the engine must again be speeded up to 2500 rev/min for one minute, and the checks carried out in the three minute periods at idling.

1 Remove the dampers and top up the damper oil well to the correct level and then replace the dampers.

2 With the engine running, check that the idling speed is 900 rev/min and that the engine is running smoothly. Use a balance meter to check that the airflows through the carburetters are equal. Provided that this operation is satisfactory, operation 3 can be ignored.

3 If operation 2 is unsatisfactory stop the engine and remove the air cleaners. Slacken the clamping nuts 10 on the throttle spindles and the clamping nuts 11 on the jet control interconnection, shown in **FIG 2:14**. Restart the engine and adjust the throttle adjusting screws 5 (shown in **FIG 2:15**) on both carburetters until the idling speed is correct at 900 rev/min and a balance meter shows that the airflow through both carburetters is equal. If balance cannot be obtained check the system for air leaks.

4 If the engine still runs unevenly reset the mixture as detailed later.

5 Tighten the clamp nuts 10 so that there is $\frac{1}{32}$ inch end float on the interconnection rod and the gap between the link pin and lower edge of the fork, shown in the inset in **FIG 2:14**, is .012 inch on both carburetters. Set the jet levers at their lowest position and tighten the clamp nuts 11 so that the jets move simultaneously.

6 Increase the engine speed to 1500 rev/min and again check the carburetter synchronization with a balance meter. Readjust the throttle levers if required so that the carburetters are balanced both at idling (900 rev/min) and at 1500 rev/min.

7 Adjust the position of the choke cable 8, shown in **FIG 2:16**. so that there is approximately $\frac{1}{16}$ inch (1.6 mm) free movement on the control before the cable starts to pull on the jet levers 9. Pull the control out until the jets are just about to move. Use a balance meter and adjust the fast-idle screws 4 (see **FIG 2:15**) until the engine speed is between 1300 and 1400 rev/min.

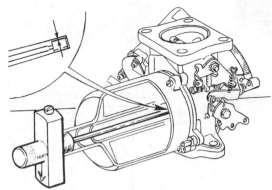

FIG 2:17   Centralizing the jets on AUD.265 carburetters

Mixture strength:

The mixture strength must be checked using an exhaust gas analyser.

Normally the restrictor 7 limits the amount of adjustment (within close tolerances), that is available on the jet adjusting nuts 1 and the engine should be set to run evenly within those limits. After the mixture has been reset it will most likely be necessary to synchronize the carburetters and reset the idling speed again.

When a reading is to be taken using the exhaust gas analyser, gently tap the neck of each suction chamber 3 with a light non-metallic object.

If the carburetters have been dismantled, the basic setting of the jet adjusting nuts is 14 flats down from the position where the jet is flush with the bridge in the air intake. From 1971 models the basic setting is 12 flats down.

With the engine hot and cleared, proceed as follows:

1 Turn both nuts 1 up or down by equal amounts until the engine idling speed is highest. Turn both nuts up (weaken) together and by equal amounts until the engine speed just starts to fall and then turn both nuts down (enrich) by one flat.

2 Use a balance meter to synchronize the carburetters and adjust the idling speed to 900 rev/min.

3 Use an exhaust gas analyser and check that the maximum CO emission does not exceed 4.5 per cent. If the reading is excessive, adjust both nuts equally by the minimum required to bring the CO emission within limits. If the adjustment required exceeds two flats then the test equipment should be checked.

4 Securely hold the adjusting nuts 1 and turn the restrictors 7 until the large vertical tag contacts the carburetter body on the lefthand side when viewed down the air intake. Bend down the small tag until it contacts the adjusting nut and locks to it. Mark both the small tag and the flat that it contacts with a small spot of paint for identification.

5 Carry on tuning and setting the carburetters.

Servicing:

These carburetters are of very similar design to the standard carburetters and the instructions in **Section 2:11** are partially applicable, though the following points must be noted.

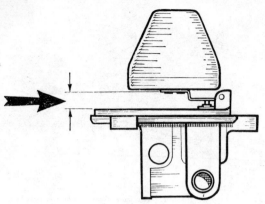

FIG 2:18   Float chamber fuel level

Piston and suction chamber:

Before removing these the suction chamber should be marked so that it can be replaced in the same position on the carburetter. Do not allow the suction chamber to tilt when it is being drawn off.

Wash the parts in clean fuel or methylated spirits (denatured alchohol) and fit the damper and piston back into the suction chamber, omitting the spring. Fit a large washer to one of the securing lugs of the suction chamber, using a nut and bolt so that the piston cannot come out of suction chamber. Plug the two transfer ports in the bottom face of the piston with small rubber plugs. Hold the assembly vertically upwards by the piston so that the suction chamber slides fully down onto it. Invert the assembly and note the time that it takes the suction chamber to fall through the full piston travel and hit the washer fitted. If the time taken is outside the limits of 5 to 7 seconds, dismantle the parts and make sure that they are absolutley clean and then reassemble them and repeat the test. If the time limits are still not met, a new suction chamber and piston assembly must be fitted.

AUD.265 fixed needle type SU carburetter:

The needle is secured to the piston by a locking screw which must be renewed at the same time as the needle. **Under no circumstances may a spring-loaded type of needle and shorter screw be fitted in place of the fixed type of needle or vice-versa.** Fit the needle so that the lower edge of the needle shoulder is flush with the bottom face of the piston. Fit the assembly back into the suction chamber and spin the piston to check that the needle is concentric.

A special tool, as shown in **FIG 2:17**, must be used to centralize the jet. Remove the jet and take off the restrictor, jet adjusting nut and spring. Refit the jet, loosely connecting its flexible pipe to the float chamber and press it up to the top of its range of movement. Slacken the jet bearing securing nut. **Lay the carburetter down onto its intake flange and do not remove it from this position until the jet is centralized and the jet bearing secured.** Screw the tool fully into the carburetter and then unscrew it until the etched arrow points towards the intake as shown. Carefully tighten the jet bearing securing nut, checking

that the jet is not binding in the bearing as the jet is drawn in and out. Remove the tool and withdraw the jet. Refit the parts removed. When connecting the jet flexible pipe to the float chamber, ensure that the tube projects a minimum of $\frac{3}{16}$ inch (4.8 mm) beyond the gland and only tighten the nut sufficiently to compress the gland. **Overtightening can cause leaks.**

Spring-loaded needle type SU carburetter:

Remove the guide locking screw from the piston and withdraw the complete needle assembly. Withdraw the needle from the guide and remove the spring from the needle.

New needles are fitted complete with the shouldered spring seats, and no attempt should be made to alter the position of the seat.

Some guides will have a pipe to ensure correct centralization of the needle and they must be positioned so that their lower faces are flush with the lower faces of the pistons, and so that the etched mark on the lower face of the guide is adjacent to, and in line with, the mid point between the transfer ports in the piston face.

Other guides will have a flat machined on them. The locking screw must act squarely onto this face otherwise it will protrude from the piston. In both cases renew the locking screw when fitting new needles.

The jet fuel tube attachment to the float chamber is the same as on AUD.265 carburetters.

Float chamber:

The needle valve assembly is fitted with a needle which has a spring-loaded plunger to damp out vibrations.

The correct level is when the gap arrowed in **FIG 2:18** lies between $\frac{1}{8}$ to $\frac{3}{16}$ inch.

Throttle spindles and butterflies:

The butterflies are oval, so care must be taken when they are being removed otherwise they will jam in the bores. When refitting the butterflies make sure that the countersinks in the spindles face outwards and refit the butterfly so that the limiting valve is at the bottom and the head of the valve facing the engine. Take great care to centralize the butterfly and make sure that there is a clearance between the throttle lever and carburetter body when the throttle is closed.

PART 4   EXHAUST PORT AIR INJECTION

This is only fitted to emission controlled engines destined for the USA market.

2:17 Description

The layout of the parts is shown in **FIG 2:19**. The air pump 5 is driven by a belt from the engine. An integral relief valve 6 limits the air pressure produced by the pump, and air is drawn into the system through an air filter 4.

Air is blown into each exhaust port through the air manifold 1 and the check valve 3 is fitted to prevent high-press exhaust gases from blowing back into the pump.

The gulp valve 9 allows extra air from the pump to pass into the inlet manifold, so as to weaken the mixture, on overrun or throttle closure. A pipe from the inlet manifold

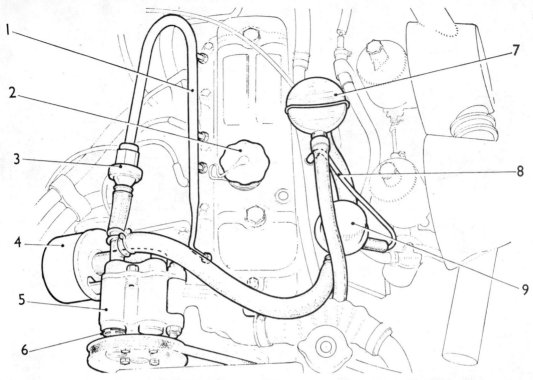

FIG 2:19 Typical emission control system

Key to Fig 2:19   1 Air manifold   2 Filtered oil filler cap   3 Check valve   4 Emission air cleaner   5 Air pump
6 Relief valve   7 Crankcase emission valve   8 Vacuum sensing tube   9 Gulp valve

connects to the underside of the diaphragm in the gulp valve so that the valve will open on sudden increases in manifold suction.

2:18 Routine mantenance

Renew the element in the air filter 4 at regular intervals. Check the driving belt tension at regular intervals. The tension should be such that the total deflection of the belt, midway between the pulleys at the longest run, should be $\frac{1}{2}$ inch with moderate hand pressure. The pump is supported on a pivot bolt and a slotted adjusting link. Slacken the securing nuts and bolts and pull the pump by hand until the belt tension is correct. Hold the pump in place and tighten all three bolts.

2:19 Testing

Air pump:

1 Disconnect the hose between the air pump 5 and gulp valve 9 at the gulp valve and plug the end of the hose securely. Disconnect the supply hose from the pump at the check valve 3 and securely connect a pressure gauge to the hose.
2 Start the engine and run it at 1000 rev/min. The gauge should register a pressure of not less than 2.75 lb/sq in. If the pressure is low stop the engine and fit a new element to the air filter 4, and repeat the test.
3 If the pressure is still low, then stop the engine and

temporarily blank off the relief valve outlet 5. If, on test, the pressure is now satisfactory then the relief valve is defective and will have to be renewed. If the pressure is still low then the pump will have to be repaired.

Relief valve:

1 Provided that the pump is satisfactory, connect a gauge into the circuit as described in operation 1 of testing the pump.
2 Make a temporary duct over the relief valve out of masking tape, so that any air out of the relief valve will be ducted upwards and can be detected. **Never place a finger between the pulley and relief valve to check if air is flowing out of the relief valve.**
3 Start the engine and gradually increase its speed until a flow of air can be detected coming from the relief valve. The gauge should read 4.5 to 6.5 lb/sq in. If the reading is outside these limits the relief valve is defective and must be renewed.

Check valve:

1 Disconnect the air supply hose. Hold the manifold 1 and unscrew the check valve 3 from it.
2 Blow, **by mouth only,** through the check valve in both directions. Air should pass through the valve only when blowing from the supply hose connection, and

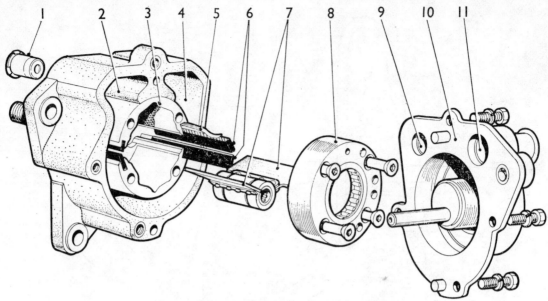

FIG 2:20 Air pump details

Key to Fig 2:20   1 Relief valve   2 Inlet chamber   3 Rotor   4 Outlet chamber   5 Spring   6 Carbons
7 Vane assemblies   8 Rotor bearing end plate   9 Outlet port   10 Port end cover   11 Inlet port

if it blows in the reverse direction then the valve is
faulty and must be renewed.
3 Refit the valve in the reverse order of removal.

Air manifold and injectors:

1 Disconnect the air manifold from the cylinder head.
Slacken the supply hose connection at the check valve
3 and rotate the manifold and check valve about the
hose. Retighten the connection.
2 Start the engine but **do not let it increase speed
beyond idling.** Check that air is blowing from all four
of the manifold outlets. If a manifold outlet is blocked,
use an airline to clear it.
3 Check that exhaust gases are blowing from the four
cylinder head connections. If an injector is blocked,
turn the engine until the exhaust valve for that injector
is shut. Use a $\frac{1}{8}$ inch drill in a hand-brace, **never power
tool,** and drill through the injector bore. Use an airline
to blow away loose carbon chippings.
4 Slacken the connection and rotate the manifold into
position. Remake the connections.

Gulp valve:

1 Disconnect the air supply hose to the gulp valve at the
pump connection. Fit a T-piece into the end of the hose
and fit a vacuum gauge onto one arm of the T-piece.
2 Start the engine and run it at idling speed. Put a thumb
over the third arm of the T-piece and check that the
gauge shows no reading for 15 seconds. If the gauge
registers vacuum in this time then the gulp valve is
defective and must be renewed. Release any vacuum
by taking off the thumb from the arm.
3 With the thumb over the arm again, snap the throttle
wide open. The gauge should immediately show a
vacuum. Repeat the test several times, releasing the

vacuum between each test. If the gauge does not
register vacuum then the gulp valve is defective and
must be renewed.
4 Remove the T-piece and gauge and reconnect the
hose to the pump.

Limit valves:

These are fitted onto the carburetter throttle butterflies
to ensure that the mixture is at a burnable ratio during
high inlet manifold depression.
1 Disconnect the gulp valve sensing pipe from the inlet
manifold and fit a vacuum gauge to the connection on
the manifold.
2 When the engine is hot, run it up to a speed of 3000
rev/min and quickly release the throttle. The gauge
reading should immediately rise to 20.5 to 22 in. Hg. If
the gauge reading falls outside these limits then the
limit valves are defective, and new throttle butterflies
must be fitted to the carburetters.
3 Remove the gauge and reconnect the gulp valve
sensing pipe.

2:20 The air pump

The details of the pump are shown in **FIG 2:20**.

Removal:

Disconnect the hoses and slacken all the securing nuts
and bolts. Press the pump inwards and remove the driving
belt from the pulley. Free the adjusting link, support the
pump and remove the long pivot bolt.
Refit the pump in the reverse order of removal, making
sure that the driving belt tension is correct.

Relief valve:

To change the relief valve the pump must be taken out of the engine and the driving pulley removed. Use a long ½ inch diameter drift through the outlet port to drive out the old relief valve 1.

Fit a new copper seating valve to the relief valve and push the relief valve partially into place by hand. Use a tool made up as shown in **FIG 2:21** to drive the relief valve into place so that copper seal is held firmly between the pump and valve without actually compressing the seal.

Dismantling:

1 Take out the securing bolts and carefully remove the port end cover 10.
2 Remove the four socket-headed screws and take off the end plate 8.
3 Lift out the vane assemblies 7 and remove the carbon and spring assemblies 5 from the rotor 3.

Servicing:

1 Wipe the inside parts with non-fluffy cloth. Clean all the bearings and repack them with Esso 'Andok' 260 lubricant.

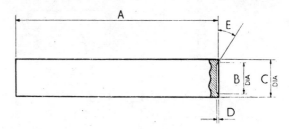

FIG 2:21   Dimensions of tool for refitting relief valve to pump

Key to Fig 2:21   A = 5 inch   B = .986 inch   C = 1.062 inch   D = .05 inch   E = 30 deg.

2 Renew worn or damaged vanes. Fit new carbons, using the old springs if they are still serviceable. All carbons are fitted with the chamfered edges to the inside and it should be noted that the slots for the carbons and springs are deeper than the others.
3 Reassemble the pump in the reverse order of dismantling, using a little Locktite under the heads of the rotor bearing end plate securing screws.

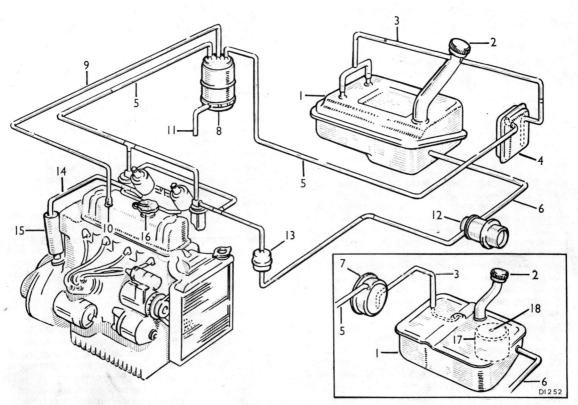

FIG 2:22   Schematic layout of evaporative loss control system

Key to Fig 2:22   1 Fuel tank   2 Sealed fuel filler cap   3 Expansion/vapour line   4 Expansion tank   5 Vapour pipe   6 Fuel pipe   7 Separation tank   8 Adsorption canister   9 Purge line   10 Restricted connection   11 Air vent   12 Fuel pump   13 Fuel line filter   14 Breather pipe   15 Oil separator   16 Sealed oil filler cap   17 Capacity limiting tank   18 Air lock bleed

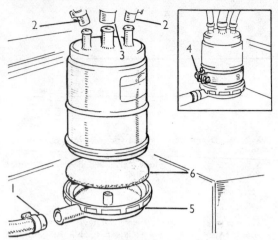

FIG 2:23 The early type adsorption canister air filter pad

Key to Fig 2:23   1 Air vent tube   2 Vapour pipes
3 Purge pipe   4 Canister securing clip   5 End cap   6 Air filter pad

PART 5   EVAPORATIVE LOSS CONTROL

This system is only fitted to cars destined for the USA market.

2:21 Description

The schematic layout of the system is shown in **FIG 2:22**, and it is accurate enough for the actual pipes to be identified. The tank fitted to MGB's is of the type shown in the inset where the limiting tank 17 is filled with air and ensures that there is always space for expansion if the fuel tank is fully filled.

Both the engine and the fuel tank vent through the air vent 11 on the adsorption canister 8 and when the engine is not running then the fuel fumes from the carburetters and fuel tank are adsorbed by charcoal granules. Air being drawn back into the system is cleaned by a filter pad in the base of the adsorption canister.

When the engine starts, the fumes from the crankcase are drawn in through the intake manifold and burnt in the combustion chambers. Air to the engine crankcase is drawn through the adsorption container and purges the charcoal granules of the fuel fumes. Normally the fuel fumes are not sufficient to affect the mixture strength but some engines may be fitted with a temperature compensator device. This device bleeds extra air into the manifold to weaken the mixture to compensate for the fuel fumes and higher rate of fuel flow in high ambient temperature conditions.

When the engine is running, air to replace the fuel used in the petrol tank is also drawn in through the adsorption canister.

The system depends on both the fuel filler cap 2 and oil filler cap 16 being efficiently sealed, so these must always be correctly replaced.

2:22 Routine maintenance

1 Renew the fuel line filter 13 (if fitted) at 12,000 mile intervals. The unit is sealed and cannot be cleaned.

2 Renew the air filter pad 6, shown in **FIG 2:23**, at 12,000 mile intervals on models prior to 1973 only.

3 The complete adsorption canister must be renewed at 24,000 mile intervals. **If at any time the canister is contaminated with liquid fuel it must be renewed immediately.** Liquid fuel cannot be purged out by blowing through clean air.

4 Regularly examine the filler caps and check that they seal efficiently. At the same time examine all hoses and their connections for leaks or defects.

2:23 Leak testing

1 Check that there is at least one gallon of fuel in the fuel tank. Switch on the ignition and leave it on for one minute so as to fully prime the carburetters. Switch off the ignition.

2 Disconnect the fuel tank vent pipe from the adsorption container. Connect a T-piece having a Schrader inflation valve on one arm and a pressure gauge on another arm to the vent hose.

3 Use a typre pump to inflate the system through the Schrader valve to a pressure of 1 lb/sq in. **This pressure must not be exceeded at any time.**

4 Check that the system holds pressure and does not drop more than .5 lb/sq in within 10 seconds. If the system does not hold pressure check through for leaks, starting with the fuel filler cap as the most likely defect.

5 Reinflate the system and check that the pressure drops immediately the fuel filler cap is removed.

6 Remove the T-piece and reconnect the vent hose to the adsorption canister.

2:24 HIF type carburetters

The type HIF (Horizontal Integral Float Chamber) carburetter is a new concept in the SU carburetter range, designed primarily to meet the requirements of exhaust emission control systems. It functions similarly to previous SU carburetters inasmuch as it uses a variable choke and a constant depression principle to achieve a precise induction of mixture. The float chamber is contained in the body of the carburetter instead of, as in previous designs, an external part interconnected by a supply tube. The cold-start system also differs from the earlier designs, insomuch as the fuel is drawn from a separate jet and not from the main jet by operating the jet tube. Jet centralizing is unnecessary and is in fact strictly advised against, as the mixture setting is adjusted at the factory and then sealed. An exploded view of the HIF is shown in **FIG 2:24**.

The float chamber:

Refer to **FIG 2:25**. The float chamber is contained in the main body of the carburetter, access to it is gained by removing the coverplate 9. The concentrically moulded float 2 surrounds the jet tube and pivots on a spindle 6 which screws into the body casing.

The fuel enters the chamber through the supply pipe 7 into the side of the carburetter to the needle valve assembly 8. The needle is spring-loaded to prevent vibrations unseating it off the valve. As the fuel level increases in the float chamber, fuel enters through an opening in the jet head 3 and rises up the jet tube with the level in the float chamber. The supply is cut off, at a predetermined level, by a tag in the float bearing upwards on the needle and closing the valve.

Mixture adjustment:

Unlike previous types of SU carburetters the jet tube is not pulled down the jet needle to provide a cold starting mixture, although it does move vertically to provide a correct mixture adjustment. This is done automatically by a compensating bi-metal spring 1, or manually, by working the mixture adjustment screw 4 to find the correct setting.

The bi-metal blade 1 is pierced and shaped to accept the jet head 3. The shape of the jet head is so designed that any movement of the bi-metal spring is transmitted directly to it, thus moving it in the vertical plane.

A spring-loaded retaining screw 5 secures the bi-metal spring and the right-angled adjusting lever to the carburetter body. This attachment is designed to allow the adjusting lever to pivot on the outer edge of its short

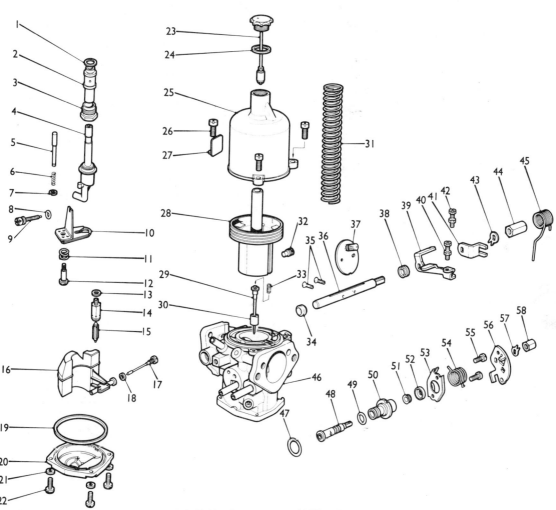

FIG 2:24   Components of HIF carburetter

Key to Fig 2:24   1 Jet bearing washer   2 Jet bearing   3 Jet bearing nut   4 Jet assembly   5 Lifting pin   6 Lifting pin spring   7 Circlip   8 Adjusting screw seal   9 Jet adjusting screw   10 Bi-metal jet lever   11 Jet spring   12 Jet retaining screw   13 Needle seat washer (if required)   14 Float needle seat   15 Float needle   16 Float   17 Float pivot   18 Pivot seal   19 Float chamber cover seal   20 Float chamber cover   21 Spring washer   22 Cover screw   23 Piston damper   24 Damper washer   25 Suction chamber   26 Chamber screw   27 Identity tag   28 Piston   29 Jet needle   30 Needle guide   31 Piston spring   32 Needle retaining screw   33 Needle spring   34 Throttle spindle seat   35 Throttle disc screws   36 Throttle spindle   37 Throttle disc   38 Throttle spindle seal   39 Throttle actuating lever   40 Fast idle screw and nut   41 Throttle lever   42 Throttle adjusting screw and nut   43 Tab washer   44 Retaining nut   45 Throttle spring   46 Body   47 Cold start seal   48 Cold start spindle   49 O-ring   50 Cold start body   51 Spindle seal   52 End cover   53 Retaining plate   54 Cold start spring   55 Retaining screw   56 Fast idle cam   57 Tabwasher   58 Retaining nut

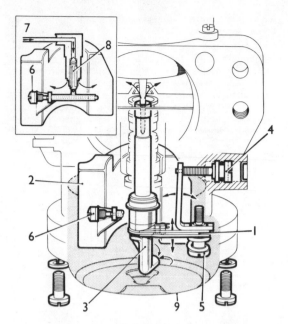

FIG 2:25   Details of float chamber

Key to Fig 2:25   1 Bi-metal assembly   2 Concentric float
3 Jet head   4 Jet adjusting screw   5 Bi-metal pivot screw
6 Float fulcrum screw   7 Fuel inlet   8 Needle valve
9 Bottom coverplate

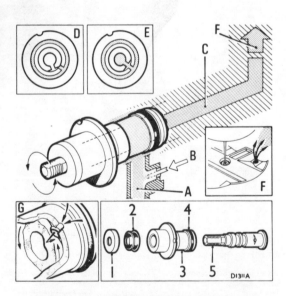

FIG 2:26   Cold start enrichment device

Key to Fig 2:26   1 End seal cover   2 End seal
3 Starter valve body   4 O-ring   5 Valve spindle
A Fuel supply   B Air bleed   C Fuel delivery to jet bridge
D Commencement of enrichment   E Maximum enrichment
F Enrichment outlet   G Fuel flow through valve

arm and at the same time place a load on the adjusting screw 4 with its long arm.

The jet adjusting screw 4 is sealed by a plug in the screw-head orifice. To lower the jet and enrich the mixture the screw is turned inwards. To weaken the mixture the screw is turned outwards. Replace the sealing plug. **It must be stressed that the adjusting screw should not be tampered with unnecessarily, nor without the necessary equipment to measure the exhaust emission, otherwise the toxic elements will be uncontrolled and will contravene the statutory requirements.**

Fuel temperature compensator:

The bi-metal spring device alters the jet tube position to compensate for viscosity changes in the fuel, caused by varying temperatures. When the fuel temperature rises, the viscosity is lowered and without the compensating device would allow more fuel to flow through the jet orifice. The bi-metal spring, immersed in the fuel in the float chamber, reacts to the changes in fuel temperature and actuates the jet tube in the vertical plane to weaken or enrich the mixture to the prevailing fuel temperature.

From this, it will now be understood that altering the adjustment screw will also effect the jet positions, when it is compensating for changes in the fuel viscosity. The temperature compensating device allows the carburetters to have the mixture control pre-set at the factory and sealed, it should not require any further adjustment. The effect is to improve the drivability and at the same time control the exhaust emission over a wide range of temperatures, from cold starting to warm-up.

Cold starting device:

The additional mixture required for cold starting is supplied separately to that from the main jet. The starting device is in the form of a rotary valve (see 3 in **FIG 2:26**), which is positioned in the side of the float chamber and fuel is fed to it from the float chamber through the passage **A**. An air bleed **B** is situated in the

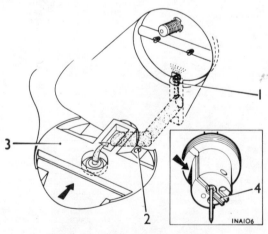

FIG 2:27   Bypass emulsion system

Key to Fig 2:27   1 Bypass emulsion outlet   2 Cold start enrichment outlet   3 Carburetter bridge   4 Slot in piston

feed passage. The fuel enters the passage **A** when the engine is stopped and rises only as high as the level in the float chamber, which is below the air bleed **B**.

When the choke is operated, the inner spindle 5 is revolved inside the valve 3, the spindle is bored out at one end and has a single entry hole drilled in its side. The drilled hole, which has a tapered groove on both sides, aligns with a communicating passage inside the valve body (see inset **E**). When the engine is turned over for starting a depression is transmitted from the outlet hole **F** through the spindle bore and valve body to the feed passage **A**. Fuel is drawn from the feed passage into a cavity between the rotary valve and the carburetter body with air from the air bleed, seals 2 and 4 prevent leakage to atmosphere. This emulsified mixture is channelled through the communicating passage in the valve body and through the drilled hole into the bore of the spindle. From the bore of the spindle it passes through the channel **C** into the carburetter outlet **F**.

The varying depth of the grooves in the spindle, the ones on each side of the drilled hole, ensure that the device is progressive. Inset **D** shows the position of the drilled hole and grooves as the spindle is starting its rotation in the valve body, as it is rotated further by the action of the cold-starter lever (see 56 in **FIG 2 : 24**), a progressively larger passage is exposed until the maximum enrichment position is reached as shown in inset **E**. The flow through the valve body is shown in inset **G**.

Emulsion system during part-throttle openings:

The function of this system is to deliver a quantity of mixture in a perfectly emulsified condition at small throttle openings. It consists of a small-bore passageway, which leads from a duct adjacent to the main jet orifice, to a discharge point (see 1 in **FIG 2 : 27**), in the air induction port and aligned to a cut-out on the edge of the throttle valve. A slot 4 in the base of the piston guides the fuel into the duct and passageway orifice.

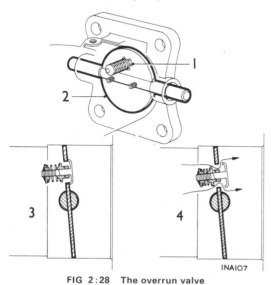

FIG 2 : 28   The overrun valve

Key to Fig 2 : 28   1 Overrun valve   2 Throttle butterfly disc
3 Overrun valve closed   4 Overrun valve open

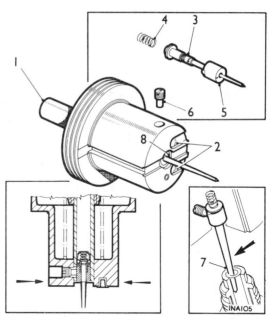

FIG 2 : 29   The spring-loaded jet needle

Key to Fig 2 : 29   1 Piston rod   2 Transfer holes
3 Jet needle   4 Needle spring   5 Needle guide
6 Needle locking screw   7 Needle biased in jet   8 Etch mark

At small throttle openings the mixture is drawn through the bypass, in preference to the normal induction, and discharged at the high depression point near the edge of the throttle valve. Due to the relatively small area, the velocity of the mixture is greater than it would be if drawn through the carburetter body, therefore the breakdown is much more complete.

The overrun valve:

Referring to **FIG 2 : 28** the overrrun valve consists of a spring-loaded plate valve located in the throttle valve disc. Its purpose is to improve the fuel combustion at high manifold depression, such as overrun at closed throttle, by slightly reducing the depression and supplying a correct quantity of emulsified fuel. The method is shown in 3 and 4 of the illustration. This helps to maintain correct combustion and prevents excessive hydrocarbon emission being produced under high manifold depression conditions. The valve is not fitted to standard carburetters.

Spring-loaded jet needle:

The jet needle of the HIF carburetter is spring-loaded and biased towards a pre-determined position in the jet orifice (see **FIG 2 : 29**). The quantity of fuel discharged is affected by the shape, size and position of the metering orifice. By maintaining these specifications in the HIF the repetition of emission values, from one vehicle to another, is achieved. The shoulder of the needle 3 abuts to a protrusion formed on the needle guide 5. Under the pressure of a spring 4 the needle is held permanently

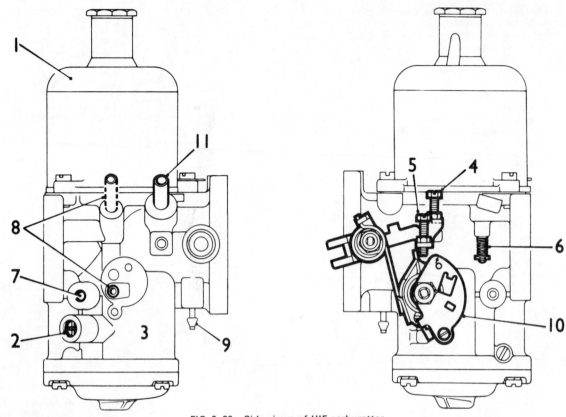

FIG 2:30 Side views of HIF carburetter

Key to Fig 2:30   1 Piston/suction chamber   2 Jet adjusting screw   3 Float chamber   4 Throttle adjusting screw   5 Fast-idle adjusting screw   6 Piston lifting pin   7 Fuel inlet   8 Vent tube (alternative positions)   9 Auto ignition connection   10 Cold start enrichment lever (cam lever)   11 Crankcase ventilation tube

in one position, relative to the air flow. The direction of this bias 7 being either to the inlet or the outlet side of the carburetter. Because of this, no jet centring is required and a non-centring jet bearing is fitted.

To ensure correct fitting the needle guide 5 has an etched alignment mark 8.

2:25 Tuning HIF carburetters

Before tuning the carburetters it is essential to check and adjust beforehand, the valve clearances, sparking plug condition, contact breaker condition and the ignition timing and automatic advance mechanism. Also it is quite pointless trying to tune the carburetters if the engine is in a badly worn condition.

The HIF carburetters are balanced at the factory to provide an efficient engine performance with pollution control. Under no circumstances may they or their components be interchanged with others from normal carburetters. The jet adjusting screws also, have been preset at the factory and the screw orifices sealed. They should not require any other adjustment except through the normal procedure of balancing and tuning after the carburetters have been overhauled. It is for these conditions only that the following instructions are given.

1 Remove the air cleaners. Check the throttle linkages for correct operation and make sure they are not sticking.

2 Refer to **FIG 2:30** and unscrew the throttle adjusting screws 4 on both carburetters until they are just clear of the throttle levers. In this condition they should be touching the levers but applying no pressure. Now turn the screws clockwise one turn.

3 Raise the piston with the lifting pin 6, release it quickly and listen for an audible 'clonk' as the piston drops onto the jet bridge. If the piston sticks, the suction chamber and piston should be removed and cleaned with methylated spirits. Read operation 4 before refitting them.

4 Lift the piston again and looking through the air intakes make sure that the top of the jet tube is flush with the level of the jet bridge as shown by the arrow. in **FIG 2:31**. If it is not possible to see through the air intakes, remove the suction chamber and piston assembly.

5 Remove the plugs from the jet adjusting screw orifices 2 in **FIG 2:30**, and turn the screws to align the jet tubes to the condition described in operation 4, or as high as possible without exceeding the bridge height. A clockwise rotation will lower the jet tube

and an anticlockwise rotation will raise it. If it is not possible to lift both or one, high enough, it is essential that they are both set in identical positions relative to the jet bridge.

Check that the jet needle shank on each piston is flush with the bottom of the piston as shown in **FIG 2:31**.

6 Having achieved a correct jet tube setting, now turn the jet screws clockwise, two full turns.

7 Refer to **FIG 2:30** and turn the fast-idling screw 5 on each carburetter anticlockwise, until it is well clear of the cam.

8 If the suction chamber and piston assembly were removed, refit them and make sure the piston falls freely on the jet bridge by using the lifting pin. Top up the piston damper reservoir as described in **Section 2:9**.

9 The carburetters are now set to give a basis to work on and run the engine satisfactorily through the process of tuning. It is important that during the tests a thoroughly reliable tachometer is connected to the engine, the cars revolution counter is not reliable enough for this type of test. A balancing meter will also be required.

If vehicles are subject to emission control laws, an approved gas analyser must be connected to the engine in accordance with the manufacturers instructions.

10 Start the engine and run it at a fast idle speed until it reaches normal working temperature, then continue to run it for a further five minutes. Increase the speed to 2500 rev/min and hold it for 30 seconds. Repeat this 30 second clearing operation every 3 minutes during the test.

11 Connect the gas analyser and the carburetter balancing meter in accordance with the maker's instructions.

12 Refer to **FIG 2:32** and slacken the clamping bolts on the throttle spindle and cold start interconnections.

13 Lightly tap the neck of each suction chamber with a non-metallic instrument, such as the handle of a screwdriver during the procedure and before taking a reading on the tachometer and analyser.

14 Start the engine and turn the jet adjusting screws (inwards to enrich and outwards to weaken) equally on each carburetter, until the tachometer registers the fastest speed. Now turn both screws an equal proportion outwards until the engine speed just commences to fall, then turn them inwards until the maximum speed is regained. Throughout these adjustments the carburetter balance should be maintained.

Check the percentage CO reading on the gas analyzer to ensure that it is within the limits specified that is, not more than 3 per cent. If so, readjust the jet screws by the minimum amount necessary to bring it within the limits. If an adjustment in excess of a $\frac{1}{2}$ turn is needed to do this, the carburetters are suspect and must be overhauled.

15 Refer to **FIG 2:32** and tighten the clamp bolts on the throttle spindle interconnection so that a clearance of .012 inch (.30 mm) exists between the link pin and the lower inside edge of the fork (see inset in **FIG 2:14**). Ensure that there is approximately $\frac{1}{32}$ inch (.79 mm) end float in the interconnecting rod.

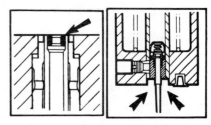

FIG 2:31 The jet must be flush with the level of the bridge (left). The needle shank must be level with the underside of the piston (right)

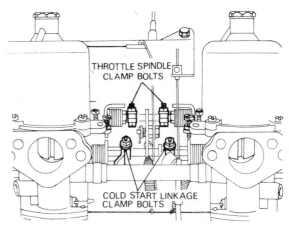

THROTTLE SPINDLE CLAMP BOLTS

COLD START LINKAGE CLAMP BOLTS

FIG 2:32 Clamping bolts of the throttle spindle and cold start interconnections

16 Run the engine at 1500 rev/min to check the reconnection and note the reading on the balancing meter. Alter the clearance on the throttle spindle interconnection to obtain an even balance.

17 Refer to **FIG 2:30** and make sure the fast-idle cams 10 are abutting their respective stops. Refer to **FIG 2:32** and tighten the clamp bolts on the cold start interconnection so that the cams begin to move simultaneously when the lever is operated. Make sure there is $\frac{1}{16}$ inch (1.5 mm) free movement in the operating cable before the cable activates the cams.

18 Refer to **FIG 2:33** and operate the fast-idling cams through the control until the arrow on the cam is positioned under the fast idler screw of each carburetter. Using the balancing meter and the tachometer turn the fast idle screws to achieve between 1300 and 1400 rev/min. Release the choke control and check also the normal idling speed, that is, 850 rev/min. Remove the test equipment and refit the air cleaners.

2:26 Dismantling the HIF

1 Detach the carburetters from the engine.

2 Thoroughly clean the carburetters on the outside. Work on one carburetter at a time and ensure that it is a clean working area, if possible with access to an air pressure line. Have a foot pump available if this is not possible.

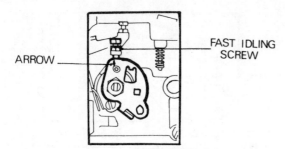

FIG 2:33   Setting the fast-idling position

3 Refer to **FIG 2:24** and remove the piston damper 23 and washer 24. Pour out the surplus oil in an old container. Unscrew the four screws 26, remove the identity tag 27 and lift off the suction chamber 25. Lift it off evenly without tilting it. Remove the spring 31 and lift out the piston assembly 28, 29, 30, 32 and 33. Place the piston and jet needle in a safe, clean place.

4 Mark the position of the coverplate 20 in relation to the body 46. Unscrew the screws 22 and lift off the cover 20 and seal 19. Collect the washers 21.

5 Take out the sealing plug and remove the jet adjusting screw 9 complete with O-ring 8. Take out the jet retaining screw 12 complete with spring 11. Withdraw the jet 4 complete with the jet lever 10. Separate the lever from the jet and lay them on one side in a clean, safe place.

6 Take out the float pivot 17 and collect the fibre washer 18. Lift out the float 16.

7 Take out the float needle 15, unscrew the needle seat 14 and collect the washer 13 (if fitted).

8 Unscrew the jet bearing nut 3 and withdraw the bearing 2 complete with washer 1.

Removing starter spindle:

9 Make a note of the location in which the ends of the cold start spring 54 are situated. Unscrew the retaining nut 58 and take off the lockwasher 57.

10 Hold the spring 54 towards the body of the carburetter and prise off the fast idle cam 56. Remove the spring.

11 Remove the screws 55 and the retaining plate 53. Extract the starter unit assembly 52, 51, 50, 49 and 48 complete with gasket 47. Place it in a clean, safe place.

Removing throttle spindle:

12 Make a note of the location of the legs on the spring 45. Release the tension and remove the spring. Unscrew the nut 44 and collect the lockwasher 43. Take off the throttle lever 41 and the actuating lever 39.

13 Unscrew the screws 35, open the throttle and observe that the disc 37 is oval, carefully take off the disc and avoid damaging the overrun valve, if it is fitted. Extract the throttle spindle 36 and pull off the seals 34 and 38.

Inspection:

14 Pick up the cold start spindle assembly and withdraw the valve spindle 48, remove the O-rings 49, seal 51 and dust cap 52.

15 Examine all the rubber seals, O-rings, fibre washers and gaskets for deterioration and renew them where necessary. Renew the fibre washers and the cover gasket 19 whatever their condition.

16 Examine the throttle spindle and its bearings for wear and also the float needle and seating.

17 Clean the carburetter body and parts with methylated spirits or petrol. Use an air-line to dry them off, injecting the air through the various passages and orifices. Examine the body for cracks and check the security of the brass connections and the piston key.

18 Do not disturb the jet needle 29, unnecessarily, but if it must be removed, take out the securing screw 32. Take care not to lose the spring 33. If the needle is to be renewed, refer to **Technical Data** for the correct type.

   Use a new retaining screw 32 to secure the needle. Refer to **FIG 2:29** and make sure that the etch mark 8 on the needle guide 5 aligns correctly between the piston transfer holes 2. The guide must also abut, with its protrusion, onto the shoulder of the needle. After fitting it in the piston, check that the shoulder of the needle is level with the bottom face of the piston (see **FIG 2:31**).

Reassembly:

19 Reverse the instructions given, 3 to 13, to reassemble the carburetter, noting the following points.

20 The throttle spindle 36 is fitted with the threaded end located at the piston lifting pin (5) side of the body. Fit the throttle disc 37 so that the overrun valve (if fitted) is at the top of the bore and the spring towards the inside when the throttle is closed. Fit new retaining screws 35 and make sure the disc closes properly before finally tightening the screws. Position the end

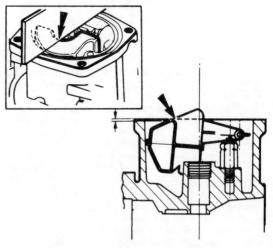

FIG 2:34   Checking the float level

seals 34 and 38 so that they are just below the spindle housing flange.

21 The starter unit valve 50 is fitted with the cut-out towards the top in line with the upper screw hole in the retaining plate 53. The plate is positioned with the slotted flange towards the throttle spindle.

22 After fitting the float and valve, check the float level dimension. Refer to **FIG 2 : 34**, invert the carburetter and place a straightedge across the base flange. In this position the float is holding the needle valve closed and a gap of between .02 and .06 inch (.5 to 1.5 mm) should exist between the bottom of the float and the straightedge (arrowed). To obtain this dimension bend the needle operating arm very carefully.

23 Ensure that the small diameter of the jet adjusting screw 9 engages with the slot in the adjusting lever 10 and adjust the jet assembly 4, with the screw, so that the top of the jet is flush with the level of the jet bridge (see **FIG 2 : 31**).

24 Refit the carburetters and tune them to the instructions given in **Section 2 : 25**.

2 : 27 Fault diagnosis, emission control systems

(a) Backfire in exhaust system

1 Leak in exhaust system
2 Leak in intake system
3 Faulty gulp valve
4 Faulty throttle disc and limit valve

(b) Hesitation after sudden throttle closure

1 See 2 and 3 in (a)
2 Low damper oil level

(c) Erratic operation

1 See 2 and 3 in (a)
2 Restricted air supply to adsorption canister

(d) Stalling or erratic idling

1 See 2, 3 and 4 in (a) ; 2 in (b)
2 Carburetter settings incorrect
3 Carburetter suction chamber faulty

(e) Overheated hose, air pump to check valve

1 Check valve faulty
2 Air pump faulty

(f) Noisy air pump

1 Belt tension incorrect
2 Pulleys damaged, loose or misaligned

(g) High exhaust system temperature

1 Ignition timing incorrect
2 Choke setting incorrect
3 High fast-idle speed
4 Air injector faulty
5 Air pump relief valve faulty

(h) Excessive enrichment required to correct exhaust emission readings

1 Air leak into crankcase
2 Crankcase control valve diaphragm faulty on early cars
3 Breather hose or connections leaking on later cars

(j) Fuel leakage

1 Fuel pipe or vapour ventilation system fracture
2 Filler cap not sealing
3 Fuel filler tube or tank leak

(k) Fuel starvation

1 See 2 in (c)
2 Vapour line between tank and adsorption canister obstructed
3 Faulty fuel pump

(l) Engine runs after ignition is switched off

1 Fuel grade too low
2 Ignition retarded
3 Idle speed too high
4 Weak fuel mixture

NOTES

CHAPTER 3

THE IGNITION SYSTEM

3 : 1 Description

Most models covered by this manual use a Lucas 25.D4 distributor which incorporates automatic timing control by a centrifugal mechanism and a vacuum operated unit. The distributor is fitted with a micrometer adjusting screw so that the ignition point can be accurately set to allow for different grades of fuel or changes in the engine condition. Later models, up to 1976, are fitted with a Lucas 45D4 distributor, similar in design to the 25D4 with the exception of the micrometer adjuster which is eliminated.

Models equipped with a single Zenith carburetter are also fitted with the Lucas 45D4 distributor, but the latest models (destined to certain areas with emission control regulations) equipped with this type of carburetter and having a catalytic converter (after-burner) in the exhaust system are fitted with an electronic distributor, Lucas 45DE4, which is fully detailed at the end of **Section 3 : 4**.

The centrifugal advance mechanism is incorporated between the distributor cam and the distributor shaft. As the engine speed increases two small spring-loaded weights are thrown outwards by centrifugal action and turn the cam so as to advance the ignition. The vacuum unit is connected to the inlet manifold by a small-bore pipe so that the unit senses manifold depression. As the manifold pressure drops at high loads and wide throttle openings, such as hill-climbing, the unit rotates the base plate of the contact breakers about the cam so as to advance the ignition.

The contact breakers open and close under the action of the cam. This pulsating voltage generates a high voltage in the secondary coil of the ignition coil and the high voltage is fed back to the centre of the distributor cap by an HT lead. The rotor arm directs the HT voltage to the appropriate sparking plug where the air/fuel mixture in the cylinder is ignited.

3 : 2 Routine maintenance

The distributor details are shown in **FIG 3 : 1**. Free the two clips 15 and lift off the distributor cap 2. Carefully pull or lever off the rotor arm 4.

When maintenance is complete, replace both the rotor arm and the distributor cap. It is surprisingly easy to refit the cap and forget to replace the rotor arm and then find that the engine refuses to fire or start.

Lubrication:

The lubrication points are shown in **FIG 3 : 2**.
1 Pour a few drops of engine oil into the recess on top of the cam at 1. Do not remove the screw as there is a clearance around it for the passage of oil.
2 Put a single drop of oil onto the contact pivot at 2. **Ensure that no oil contaminates the contacts themselves.**
3 Lightly grease the cam at 3, spreading the grease all round the cam. Engine oil may be used if grease is not available.
4 Pour a few drops of oil through the hole in the contact plate through which the cam passes. **Take care not to allow any oil onto the contact points.**

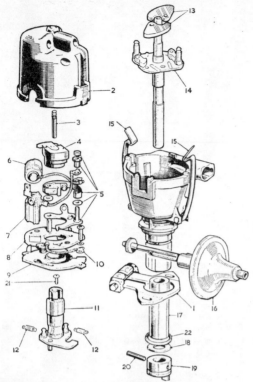

FIG 3:1   Distributor details

Key to Fig 3:1   1 Clamping plate   2 Moulded cap
3 Brush and spring   4 Rotor arm   5 Contacts (set)
6 Capacitor   7 Terminal and lead (low-tension)
8 Moving contact breaker plate   9 Contact breaker base plate
10 Earth lead   11 Cam   12 Automatic advance springs
13 Weight assembly   14 Shaft and action plate
15 Cap retaining clips   16 Vacuum unit   17 Bush
18 Thrust washer   19 Driving dog   20 Parallel pin
21 Cam screw   22 O-ring oil seal

Setting the contact points gap:

Before the gap is set, ensure that the points are clean and that they meet squarely. The method of adjustment is shown in **FIG 3:3**.

1 Turn the engine so that a lobe on the cam is directly under the follower on the moving contact.
2 Slacken the screw arrowed so that the fixed contact can be moved by turning the screwdriver inserted between the slots in the fixed contact and the contact breaker base plate. Do not overslacken the securing screw otherwise the fixed contact will float out of adjustment.
3 The correct gap is .014 to .015 inch (.35 to .40 mm) so insert a feeler gauge of the correct thickness between the contact points as shown.
4 Turn the screwdriver until a little drag is felt on the feeler gauge as it is moved slightly. Tighten the securing screw in this position.
5 Turn the engine over by hand and check that the setting is correct for the other three lobes of the cam.
It should be noted that the contact gap can also be set with the distributor removed from the engine.

Cleaning the contact points:

1 Remove the contact assembly 5 from the distributor. Undo the nut on top of the fixed contact threaded post and lift off the insulated bush followed by the wire terminals. The moving contact can then be lifted out. Collect the two insulated washers that lie between the contacts and remove the fixed contact after taking out its securing screw.
2 Clean the points using a fine file, fine emerycloth or a carborundum stone. The points must be cleaned so that they meet squarely and the surfaces are left matt grey. Do not attempt to obtain a polished finish on the points. Pitting may be removed by grinding the points on garage equipment but if the points are deeply pitted or excessively worn then they should be renewed. Use methylated spirits (denatured alcohol) to remove any oil or protectives from the contact points.
3 Refit the contact points in the reverse order of removal, making sure that the insulated washers are in position between the contacts. Check that the moving contact pivots freely on the pivot post. If the moving contact is sluggish clean the pivot with a strip of fine emerycloth and lubricate it with a single drop of oil.
4 Set the contact points gap as described earlier. Before replacing the distributor cap and rotor arm, wipe the inside of the cap and all over the rotor arm with a soft clean piece of cloth. Do not use abrasives on the contacts of the rotor arm or distributor cap.

On cars fitted with emission controlled engines the performance of the distributor should be regularly checked using an engine tester such as 'Sun' or 'Crypton'.

3:3 Ignition faults

If the engine runs unevenly and the carburetters are correctly adjusted set the engine to idle at a fast speed. Carefully pull back the insulating sleeves on the HT leads, **avoiding touching the metal clip,** and short out each sparking plug in turn, using an insulated handle screwdriver between the metal clip on the HT lead and the cylinder head. If shrouded sparking plug covers are fitted the same effect can be obtained by disconnecting each HT lead in turn. Shorting, or disconnecting, a sparking plug that is operating will make the uneven running more pronounced and may even stop the engine. Shorting a sparking plug that is not firing will make no difference.

Having located the faulty cylinder (or cylinders) disconnect the HT lead and carefully hold it so that the metal clip is about $\frac{3}{16}$ inch (5 mm) from the cylinder head. A strong regular spark shows that the fault may lie with the sparking plug. Stop the engine and either clean and test the sparking plug (see **Section 3:6**) or else replace it with a new one.

If the spark appears weak and irregular, first examine the HT lead and renew it if it appears defective (see **Section 3:7**). If this makes no improvement, clean and examine the distributor cap and rotor arm. Clean them both all over, paying particular attention to the crannies between the HT leads, and the contacts inside the distributor cap. Methylated spirits (denatured alcohol) may be used as a cleaning solvent. Examine the cap for cracks or tracking and renew it if it is defective. Tracking will show up as thin black lines between electrodes or from an electrode to metal part in contact with the cap.

Check the carbon brush (3 in **FIG 3:1**). The brush must move freely in the distributor cap and protrude sufficiently to contact the rotor arm 4, when the cap is fitted. If the brush is damaged the old one can be pulled out of the cap and a new one pushed into place.

It should be noted that if the contact points are dirty or incorrectly adjusted they can cause misfiring and rough running.

Testing the low-tension circuit:

Before carrying out any checks make sure that the contact points are clean and correctly set.

1 Remove the distributor cap so that the action of the points can be observed. Disconnect both ends of the cable connecting the CB terminal on the ignition coil to the low-tension terminal on the distributor and replace it with a low-wattage 12-volt test lamp. Turn the engine slowly over by hand with the ignition switched on. If the circuit is satisfactory then the lamp will light when the contacts close and go out as they open.

2 If the lamp does not light at all then repeat the test with the test lamp connected between the SW terminal on the coil and low-tension terminal. If the lamp now lights and goes out correctly then the ignition coil is defective and must be renewed. If in both cases the lamp lights and stays on continuously then there is a shortcircuit in the distributor itself. A shortcircuit may be caused by a defective capacitor but it is more likely to be caused by the internal leads having chafed through their insulation or incorrect assembly of the contact points.

3 If the lamp does not light at all in the previous two tests, switch on the ignition and operate the direction indicators, or any circuit controlled by the ignition switch. If this circuit operates then it shows that supply is reaching as far as the terminal on the fuse box and the fault lies between this terminal and the ignition coil.

4 If the ignition switch controlled circuit does not operate then the fault will have to be found by tracing back through the wiring, connecting a voltmeter or 12-volt test lamp between the terminals to be tested and a good earth. Check both the input and output sides of the ignition switch itself as the switch may be defective.

Capacitor (condenser):

Capacitor failure is most infrequent and if it does fail it is most unlikely to shortcircuit. The design of the capacitor is such that shortcircuits should be self-healing.

An open circuit failure of the capacitor is difficult to detect without special equipment but it may be suspected if the points are either burnt or badly 'blued' and starting is difficult.

The best test available without using special equipment is to fit a new capacitor in place of the suspect one.

3:4 Servicing the distributor:

Conventional type:

Removal:

1 Disconnect the HT leads from the sparking plugs, marking them for correct replacement, and the HT lead

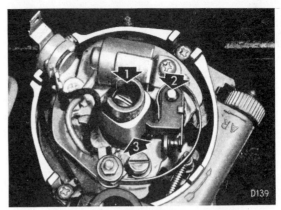

FIG 3:2 Distributor lubrication points

FIG 3:3 Method of adjusting distributor contact points

from the ignition coil. Instead of disconnecting the HT leads, the distributor cap may be removed from the distributor.

2 Disconnect the vacuum pipe from the vacuum unit and the lead from the low-tension terminal on the distributor.

3 Remove the two bolts securing the distributor clamping plate to the engine housing. Do not slacken the pinch bolt on the clamping plate otherwise the ignition timing will be lost. Withdraw the distributor from the engine.

Dismantling:

Refer to **FIG 3:1**.

1 With the distributor removed from the engine and the cap 2 and rotor arm removed proceed as follows. Slide out the terminal assembly 7 from its slot in the housing. Disconnect the spring of the vacuum unit 16 from its stud on the moving plate 8. Take out the two securing screws, noting that the earth lead 10 is secured to one of them, and lift out the complete contact breaker assembly.

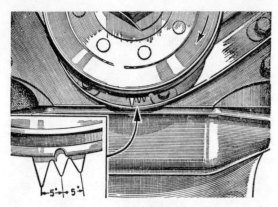

FIG 3:4 Engine timing marks—early cars. The inset shows the timing set at 5 deg. BTDC

2 The moving plate 8 can be separated from the base plate 9 after the contact points have been removed (see **Section 3:2**) and the capacitor removed by taking out its securing screw. Rotate the moving plate to disengage its stud from the base plate and then removing the C spring.

3 **Carefully note the relation of the slot in the cam 11 to the offset on the driving dog 19.** Disconnect the springs 12, taking great care not to bend or distort them. Take out the screw 21 and take out the cam 11 and weights 13.

4 Check the shaft 14 for end float and play in the bush 17. Drive out the pin 20 and remove the driving dog 19 and thrust washer 18. Clean any burrs of the end of the shaft with fine emerycloth and withdraw the shaft 14 from the casing. Note the nylon washer.

5 Remove the spring clip from the end of the vacuum unit threaded shaft and unscrew the micrometer adjusting nut to remove the vacuum unit 16.

End float:

If the end float checked in operation 4 exceeds $\frac{1}{32}$ inch (.8 mm) the nylon washer under the action plate and the thrust washer 18 must be renewed.

Bearing:

The wear on the bush 17 should be checked either using a new shaft 14 or a .490 inch (12.45 mm) diameter test bar.

1 Drive out the old bush, downwards from inside the body.

2 Soak the new bush in engine oil for 24 hours, or else soak it for 2 hours in oil at the temperature of boiling water and leave the oil to cool before taking out the bath.

3 Insert the smallest diameter of the bush into the bottom of the distributor body and press it in by hand until the larger diameter prevents further entry. Squeeze the bush fully into place between the padded jaws of a vice so that it is flush with the end of the body. **Do not bore or machine the bush.**

4 Drill a new drain hole through the bush using the shank drain hole as a guide. Remove all metal particles

and check that the inside of the bush is smooth at the drain hole.

5 Make sure that the shaft 14 is completely free from burrs, especially at the end and around the hole for the securing pin. Lubricate the shaft with engine oil and slide it into position in the bearing. **Check that the shaft rotates freely.** If it does not then remove it and clean the shaft with fine emerycloth until it does rotate freely. Use a test rig or lathe to spin the shaft in the body for 15 minutes. Relubricate the shaft and reassemble the distributor.

Reassembly:

The distributor is reassembled in the reverse order of dismantling but noting the following points:

1 Lubricate all bearing surfaces with clean engine oil.

2 Make sure that the slot in the cam bears the same relationship to the offset of the driving dog as it did before dismantling. If this precaution is not observed then the timing will be 180 degrees out.

3 Set the contacts gap before refitting the distributor.

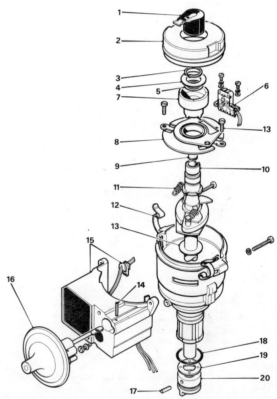

FIG 3:5 The electronic distributor, Lucas 45 DE4

Key to Fig 3:5   1 Rotor arm   2 Anti-flash shield
3 Circlip   4 Washer   5 'O' ring   6 Pick-up unit
7 Timing rotor   8 Base plate   9 Felt pad   10 Spindle
11 Return spring   12 Spring clip   13 Shim   14 Pin
15 Amplifier module   16 Vacuum advance unit   17 Driving
dog pin   18 'O' ring   19 Thrust washer   20 Driving dog

Replacement:

Turn the engine to TDC on No. 1 cylinder and check that the distributor drive spindle is correctly positioned as described in **Chapter 1, Section 1:9**. Fit a new sealing ring 22 and lower the distributor down the housing. Slowly rotate the rotor arm until the drive dogs engage with the drive spindle offset and the distributor slips fully into place. If the pinch bolt on the clamp plate has not been slackened then the rotor arm will point to the contact in the distributor cap for No. 1 cylinder. Secure the distributor in place with the two bolts.

The electronic distributor:

Latest models, from engine Nos. 18V 801E and 18V 802E, equipped with a catalytic converter and destined for certain areas with stringent emission control regulations, are fitted with an electronic distributor, Lucas 45DE4, shown in **FIG 3:5**. This distributor is contactless, having a timing rotor and pick-up unit in place of the conventional contact breaker. The advantage of this type of system is the elimination of the possibility of mechanical wear and malfunction of the contact breaker.

The only periodic attention required is routine maintenance detailed later and the checking of the pick-up air gap, shown in **FIG 3:6**, as follows:

1 Disconnect the battery. This is essential as the ignition system must be de-energized before checking the air gap.
2 Remove the distributor cap and pull off the rotor arm.
3 Refer to **FIG 3:5** and remove the anti-flash shield 2.
4 Refer to **FIG 3:6**. Insert a feeler gauge, .010 to .017 inch (.25 to .43 mm) thick, into the gap between the pick-up unit and the edge of the timing rotor as shown at A. The feeler gauge must be inserted between the part of the pick-up which stands proud and the timing rotor.
5 If the gap is incorrect, adjust by slackening the two screws which secure the pick-up unit, and moving the unit as necessary to correct. Hold the unit steady in the correct position and tighten the two screws.

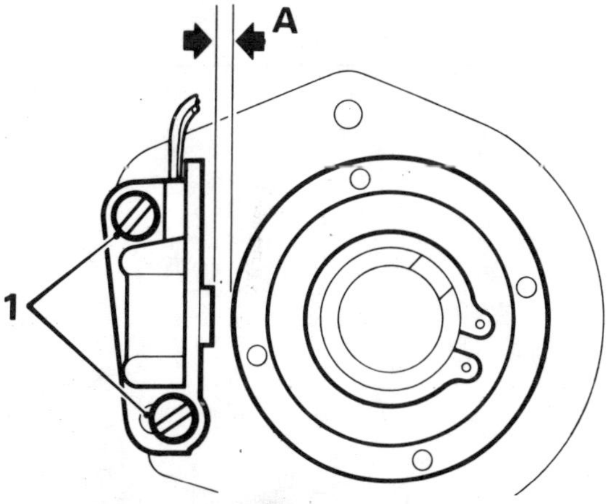

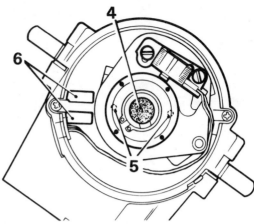

FIG 3:7 The lubrication points for the electronic distributor

Key to Fig 3:7   4 Felt pad   5 Pick-up plate centre
bearing holes   6 Apertures (for lubricating the centrifugal
mechanism)

6 Recheck the gap once the screws are tightened. The unit can move when the screws are being tightened.
7 Refit the anti-flash shield ensuring that the cutouts are aligned with the distributor cap retaining clips. Refit the distributor cap.

Routine maintenance of the distributor consists of cleaning and lubricating as follows:

Remove the distributor cap, rotor arm and anti-flash shield.

Add a few drops of oil to the felt pad in the top of the timing rotor carrier as shown at 4 in **FIG 3:7**. Lubricate the pick-up plate centre bearing with a drop of oil in each of the two holes 5 in the baseplate. Finally, apply a few drops of oil through the apertures 6 to lubricate the centrifugal timing control.

Clean the inside of the distributor cover, the rotor arm and the anti-flash shield with a clean lint-less cloth.

Check the carbon brush in the centre of the distributor cap to ensure that it is not worn and that it moves freely in its housing. Remove the carbon brush if worn.

Inspect the distributor cap and rotor arm for cracks and traces of tracking. Renew the cap or rotor if cracked or tracking.

Refit the anti-flash shield ensuring that the cut-outs are aligned with the distributor cap retaining clips.

Removing and refitting the electronic distributor:
1 Disconnect the battery and remove the distributor cap and leads.
2 Disconnect the low tension distributor leads and remove No. 1 spark plug.
3 Set the ignition static timing by turning the engine in the normal direction of rotation until the crankshaft pulley is at TDC (see **FIGS 3:4** and **3:10**) at the end of the compression stroke for No. 1 cylinder (see **Section 3:5**). The rotor arm should then be in the firing position for No. 1 spark plug, i.e. it will point to the metal segment in the distributor cap which connects to No. 1 spark plug.

FIG 3:6   The Pick-up air gap

Key to Fig 3:6   A = .010 to .017 inch (.25 to .43 mm)
1 Adjustment and fixing screws

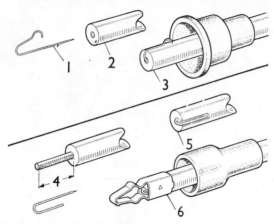

FIG 3:8 HT lead attachments to sparking plugs and ignition coil

Key to Fig 3:8   **Coil lead** 1 Fish-hook connector
2 Flush cable end   3 Assembly of fish-hook and lead cover
Plug leads   4 Insulation removed for $\frac{1}{2}$ inch (12.7 mm)
5 Inner cord folded onto cable, staple pushed into the centre of
the cord as far as possible.
6 Cord and staple must make a good contact with body of
connector.

4 Slacken the distributor clamp pinchbolt and remove
the distributor.

Refitting is the exact reversal of removal, ensuring
that the engine has not turned while the distributor was
removed. If the engine was turned and the timing lost,
repeat the procedure for setting the ignition static
timing, and then refit the distributor. On completion,
check the ignition timing using a stroboscopic timing
light as detailed in the next section.

Dismantling the electronic distributor:

1 Remove the distributor as detailed earlier.
2 Remove the rotor arm.
3 Pull off the felt pad (see **FIG 3:7**).
4 Refer to **FIG 3:6**. Remove the two screws 1, spring
washers and plain washers securing the pick-up unit.
5 Remove the three screws and washers securing the
amplifier module (**FIG 3:5**) to the distributor body.
Pull the amplifier module out a little to expose the
vacuum unit link. Detach the link from the pin on the
distributor moving plate.
6 Detach the pick-up wiring grommet from the distributor body and remove the amplifier module complete
with pick-up unit and wiring.
7 The vacuum unit 16 can be removed from the
amplifier module by driving out the small pin 14
securing the two together.
8 The timing rotor (**FIG 3:6**) can be removed by
removing the circlip shown securing it. Remove the
timing rotor and the rubber 'O' ring fitted under it.
9 The mechanical components, centrifugal mechanism,
driving dog and shaft are similar to those of the
conventional distributor and can be removed as
detailed at the beginning of this section. Servicing
the mechanical components is also described in the
same paragraphs and in **Section 3:8**. The amplifier

module and the vacuum unit are sealed and cannot be
repaired. New units should be fitted if the original ones
become faulty.

Reassembling is the reversal of removal, setting the
timing, on refitting, as detailed next. Adjust the air gap as
detailed earlier, before refitting the distributor.

3:5 Setting the ignition timing

1 Remove No. 1 (front) spark plug and turn the engine
in the normal clockwise (viewed from the front)
direction of rotation until No. 1 piston is at TDC on
the compression stroke. The compression stroke
can be identified by placing a thumb over the spark
plug hole as the engine is being turned. Pressure will
be felt under the thumb as compression increases.
Continue turning the engine, refer to **FIGS 3:4** and
3:10, and align the timing marks on the crankshaft
pulley and pointer. The best method for all cars is
to align the pulley notch with the TDC pointer mark
and then advance the timing by a few degrees as
necessary using the stroboscopic method detailed
later.
2 In the TDC position just described, the distributor
rotor arm should be pointing to the metal segment,
in the distributor cap, which connects to No. 1 spark
plug, and one of the cam lobes should be about to
open the contact points, i.e. if the engine is rotated a
little more, the points should open. If the rotor, and
hence the cam lobe, is not in the correct position,
slacken the distributor clamp pinchbolt and turn the
distributor as necessary to correct the setting.
3 Hold the distributor in this position, and tighten the
clamp pinchbolt to secure and refit the distributor cap
and spark plug. Carry out fine adjustments of the
timing using the stroboscopic method described next.

Stroboscopic timing:

This method must be used if the timing is to be
accurately set resulting in efficient engine operation, fuel
economy and conforming with emission control
regulations.

Obtain and connect a stroboscopic timing light in
accordance with the manufacturer's instructions.

Start the engine and direct the timing light flashes at
the appropriate timing marks. Earlier models have the

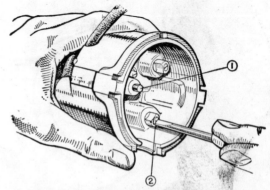

FIG 3:9 Attaching HT leads to distributor cap

Key to Fig 3:9 1 Carbon brush 2 HT lead securing screw

timing marks at the bottom as shown in **FIG 3:4**. Later models have timing marks at the top as shown in the upper portion of **FIG 3:10**. The lower marks are accessible from under the front of the car, while the upper marks can be viewed from inside the engine compartment. All marks should be cleaned and chalk or paint marked to make them clearly visible in the timing light flashes.

Refer to **Technical Data** and set the engine to idle at the appropriate speed for the stroboscopic timing check. Disconnect the pipe from the distributor vacuum advance unit and then direct the timing light flashes at the timing marks. The notch on the crankshaft pulley will appear stationary although the pulley is rotating. If the pulley notch is not opposite the appropriate pointer mark, slacken the distributor clamp pinchbolt and turn the distributor body slowly to align the marks. Turning the distributor clockwise will advance the timing, while turning it counter-clockwise will retard it. When the correct timing is obtained, tighten the distributor pinch-bolt and recheck with the timing light. For example, if the distributor is turned and the pulley notch appears aligned with the 15 deg. pointer mark, as shown in the upper portion of **FIG 3:10**, the timing is set at 15 deg. BTDC (Before Top Dead Centre) which is suitable for engines No. 18GK as detailed in **Technical Data**.

When the timing is correct, switch off the engine and remove the timing light and reconnect the vacuum advance pipe.

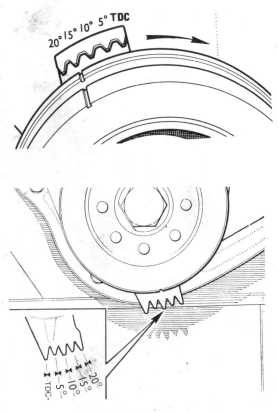

FIG 3:10   Timing marks

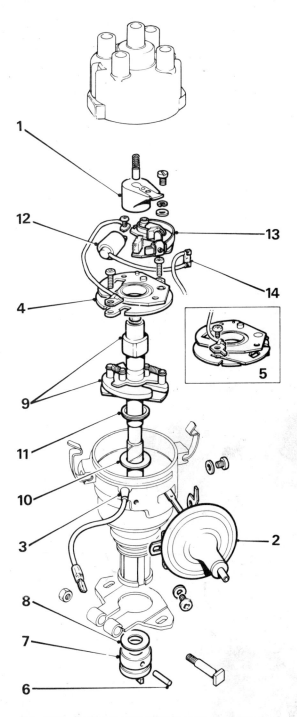

FIG 3:11   Exploded view showing the components of Lucas distributor type 45D4

Key to Fig 3:11   1 Rotor   2 Vacuum unit   3 Low tension lead   4 Base plate   5 Base plate, early models   6 Pin   7 Drive dog   8 Washer   9 Cam and weights assembly   10 Washer   11 Spacer   12 Capacitor   13 Contact set   14 LT connector

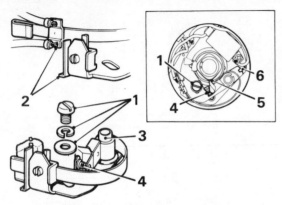

FIG 3:12   The one-piece contact breaker set

Key to Fig 3:12   1 Securing screw and washers
2 Terminal plate and spring   3 Pivot   4 Points   5 Heel on
cam lobe   6 Slot

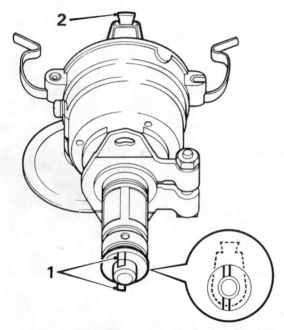

FIG 3:13   Showing the correct relation between the
drive dog 1 and the rotor arm 2

3:6 The sparking plugs

It is advisable that the sparking plugs are cleaned,
adjusted and tested at 6000 mile intervals and renewed at
12,000 mile intervals.

Remove the sparking plugs by loosening each one a
couple of turns and then using an airline or tyre pump to
blow away loose dust and dirt. The sparking plugs should
then, if possible, be fully unscrewed by hand. Store the
plugs in their correct order as the type of deposits will give
an accurate guide to the conditions in each cylinder.

Examine the firing ends. If the deposits are powdery
and range in colour from brown to greyish tan then

conditions are normal and satisfactory. If the deposits are
white or yellowish then this indicates long periods of
constant-speed driving or much low-speed city driving.
Provided that the electrodes are not badly worn, cleaning
and resetting the sparking plugs is all that is required.

Black wet deposits are caused by oil entering the
combustion chamber. Sparking plugs which run hotter
may help to alleviate the problem but the only cure is an
engine overhaul, or attending to the valve stems, valve
guides and valve seals.

Dry fluffy, black deposits are the results of poor combustion. They may be caused by running with too rich a
mixture, defective ignition or excessive idling.

Overheated plugs have a white blistered look about the
centre electrode and insulator. The electrode may also be
badly eroded. This may be caused by poor cooling,
incorrectly set ignition, incorrect grade of sparking plug
or running at sustained high speeds with heavy loads.

Check the external portion of the insulators, cleaning
them with fuel or methylated spirits (denatured alchohol).
Renew any plug that has a cracked insulator.

Have the sparking plugs cleaned on an abrasive blasting
machine and then pressure tested after attention to the
electrodes. A plug may be considered in good condition
if it sparks continuously at a pressure of 100 lb/sq in
(7 kg/sq cm) when the gap is .022 inch (.56 mm).
Before pressure testing, file the electrodes until they are
clean, bright and square and then set them to the gap
given. Before refitting the sparking plugs to the engine
their gaps must be set to .024 to .026 inch (.625 to .66 mm).

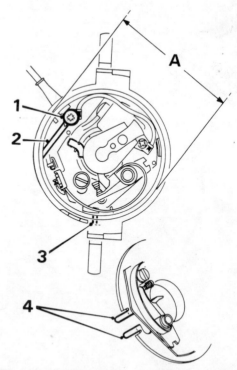

FIG 3:14   Refitting the base plate on early models

Key to Fig 3:14   1 Base plate   2 Slot   3 Screw hole
4 Prongs

When adjusting the gap never bend the centre electrode.

Before refitting the sparking plugs, clean their threads with a wire brush. If the threads are still tight use a well greased tap to clean out the threads in the cylinder head. Failing a tap, use an old sparking plug with a cross-cut down the threads. The sparking plug threads may be greased using nothing but graphite grease. Screw the plugs in by hand using a box spanner for the last few turns only. Tighten the plugs to a torque load of 27 to 30 lb ft (3.7 to 4.1 kgm).

3:7 HT leads

The HT leads are of the resistive type using a graphite impregnated core. **Only the correct type may be used as a replacement and the metal cored type of HT lead must not be used.**

Some check can be made on the cables as they should have a resistance of approximately 420 ohms per inch (2.5 cm), but they should be renewed if they are cracked or appear perished.

The attachments for the ignition coil and sparking plugs are shown in **FIG 3:8** and the key is self-explanatory. The method of attaching the leads to the distributor cap is shown in **FIG 3:9**. Slacken back the screws 2 and pull the old leads out of the cap. Thoroughly clean the cap with methylated spirits and pack the holes for the leads with silicone grease. Cut the new leads squarely off to length and press them back into the cap, securing them by screwing in the screws 2 so that their spikes penetrate into the leads. The leads are fitted in the firing order of 1−3−4−2 in an anticlockwise direction.

3:8 Lucas distributor type 45D4

This type of distributor is fitted to certain later cars, particularly those equipped to EEC requirements. The components are shown in the exploded view of **FIG 3:11** and the most noticeable points of difference from the earlier type are the one piece contact breaker set and the absence of the vernier timing adjustment.

Renewing and adjusting the contact breaker:

Refer to **FIG 3:12**. Remove the securing screw 1 and its washers and lift the contact set.

Press the spring 2 to release the terminal as shown.

Use petrol or methylated spirit to clean any protective coat off the new points and then attach the terminal plate to the end of the spring.

Place the contact set on the base plate and lightly secure the screw 1, ensuring that the spring is correctly positioned in its register. Adjust the points gap as follows:

Turn the engine until the heel of the moving point is on the peak of a cam as shown at 5 and measure the gap which should be between .014 and .016 inch (.35 to .40 mm).

To adjust the gap, insert a small screwdriver blade in the slot 6 and twist it as necessary against the pip or cut-out on the base plate. Tighten the securing screw and recheck the gap on the other lobes of the camshaft.

Servicing the distributor:

No difficulty should be experienced in dismantling the distributor for inspection if this is necessary, but there are a few points to be observed when reassembling.

If any of the moving parts in the centrifugal advance mechanism are badly worn, it will be necessary to renew the complete spindle assembly. Similarly, if the spindle bearing is worn, the complete distributor will have to be replaced.

Note the relative position of the offset drive dog, 1 in **FIG 3:13**, to the rotor arm 2.

Ensure that, on early models, the base plate is firmly pressed into the register in the body with the chamfered edge engaging the undercut. Measure across the body, as at A in **FIG 3:14**, at rightangles to the slot in the base plate. Note that the two prongs 4 must straddle the hole 3 for one of the retaining screws.

Tighten the securing screw and re-measure the distance A across the body. Unless this dimension has increased by at least .006 inch (.152 mm), the base plate must be renewed.

Complete assembly in the reverse order of dismantling and check the ignition static timing as described in **Section 3:5**. On 18V and 846 and 847F engines the specified timing with these distributors is 7 deg. BTDC.

3:9 Fault diagnosis

(a) Engine will not fire

1 Battery discharged, or dirty battery connections
2 Distributor points dirty, pitted or maladjusted
3 Distributor cap dirty, cracked or tracking
4 Carbon brush inside cap not touching rotor
5 Faulty cable or loose connections in low-tension circuit
6 Distributor rotor arm cracked, or left out when reassembling
7 Faulty coil
8 HT coil lead cracked or perished
9 Broken contact breaker spring
10 Contact points stuck open
11 Internal shortcircuit in distributor
12 Damp or water on HT leads and distributor cap

(b) Engine misfires

1 Check 2, 3, 5 and 7 in (a)
2 Weak contact breaker spring
3 HT lead cracked or perished
4 Sparking plug(s) loose
5 Sparking plug insulation cracked
6 Sparking plug gap incorrectly set
7 Ignition timing too far advanced

NOTES

CHAPTER 4

THE COOLING SYSTEM

4:1 Description

Excess heat is removed from the engine by the coolant circulating around the cylinder bores and through the cylinder head. The hot coolant then passes out through a thermostat valve and flows through the radiator where it is cooled by the passage of air on the outside of the radiator cooling fins. The natural thermo-syphon action of the water is assisted by a belt driven pump which draws the water from the bottom of the radiator and returns to the engine. A cooling fan is fitted to assist the passage of air over the radiator cooling fins.

A pressurized filler cap is fitted to the top header tank on the radiator on early cars, later cars have an expansion tank. The cap contains two concentric valves. One valve limits the pressure rise in the system to 7 lb/sq in. This was raised to 10 lb/sq in on later cars. This pressurization raises the boiling point of the coolant and helps to prevent boiling at localized hot spots in the engine. The other valve releases under vacuum and allows air back into the system as it cools. **The filler cap should not be removed when the engine is very hot or boiling.** Allow the engine to cool, protect the hand with rags and release the cap to its first stop when pressure will be released through the overflow pipe. The cap can then be fully removed.

The thermostat valve remains closed when the coolant is cold so that the coolant bypasses the radiator and a quicker warm up period is assured. As the coolant heats up, the valve gradually opens allowing the coolant to pass through the radiator.

4:2 Routine maintenance

There are no lubrication points in the system and the lubrication point screw shown on the water pump is no longer fitted.

Drain and flush the cooling system at regular intervals. It is suggested that this is done yearly. Antifreeze may be left in for the whole year as it contains corrosion inhibitors but it should be renewed every two years as the inhibitors loose their effect.

Draining:

Remove the filler cap on early engines and set the heater control to hot. Open the two drain taps. The radiator drain tap is shown as item 3 in **FIG 4:1**, and the cylinder block drain tap is fitted at the rear on the righthand side of the block. Use a short piece of wire to clear the taps if the flow is obstructed. Collect the coolant in a clean container for re-use if the antifreeze is not time-expired.

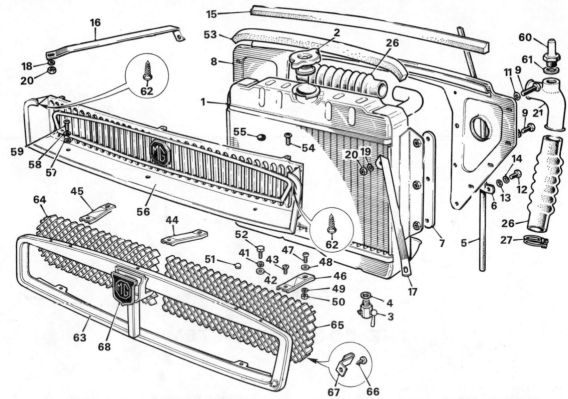

FIG 4:1 The radiator assembly and alternative grille assemblies for GHN5 and GHD5 cars

Key to Figs 4:1 and 4:2 1 Core assembly—radiator 2 Cap—filler 3 Tap—drain (early cars) 4 Washer for tap (early cars) 5 Tube—drain 6 Clip—drain tube 7 Packing 8 Diaphragm—radiator 9 Screw—long—radiator to diaphragm 10 Screw—short—radiator to diaphragm 11 Washer—spring—for screw 12 Screw—diaphragm to body 13 Washer—plain—for screw 14 Washer—spring—for screw 15 Rubber—radiator air seal 16 Tie—radiator—RH 17 Tie—radiator—LH 18 Washer—plain—radiator tie 19 Washer—spring—radiator tie 20 Nut—tie 21 Pipe—water pump connector 22 Plug—connector pipe 23 Washer—plug 24 Hose—connector 25 Clip—hose 26 Hose—top and bottom 27 Clip—hose 28 Case and grille assembly—radiator 29 Case assembly 30 Grille assembly 31 Bar—grille fixing—top 32 Bar—grille fixing—bottom 33 Slats—grille 34 Rivet—slat fixing 35 Bar and badge housing—centre 36 Badge 37 Fixing—blind badge 38 Screw—grille to case 39—Nut—spring 40 Fix—push on—badge housing to case 41 Washer—spring 42 Washer—plain 43 Screw—grille to steady bracket 44 Bracket—steady grille centre assembly 45 Bracket—steady grille side assembly—RH 46 Bracket—steady grille side assembly—LH 47 Screw—steady bracket to bonnet lock platform 48 Washer—plain 49 Washer—spring 50 Nut 51 Buffer—grille top rail 52 Screw—grille to radiator duct panel 53 Rubber—radiator air seal 54 Screw radiator grille to bonnet lock platform 55 Plug—sealing 56 Grille assembly 57 Washer 58 Washer—spring 59 Screw 60 Heater hose connection 61 Sealing washer 62 Self-tapping screw 63 Case assembly 64 Grille—RH 65 Grille—LH 66 Bracket—retaining grille to case 67 Screw 68 Motif

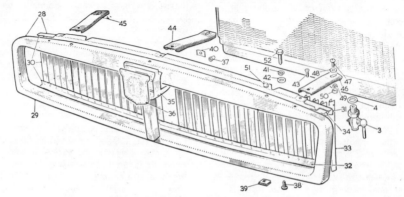

FIG 4:2 Earlier radiator grille details

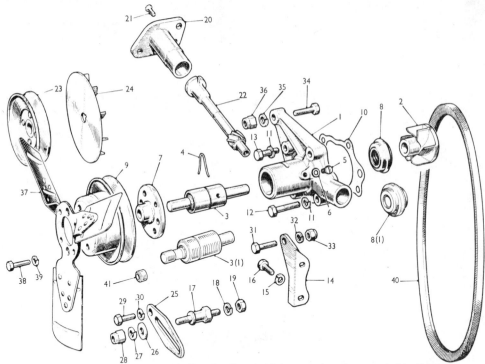

FIG 4:3 Water pump details. The distributor driving gear is not connected to the pump

Key to Fig 4:3   1 Pump assembly   2 Impeller   3 Bearing assembly (not fitted)   3 (1) Bearing assembly   4 Wire—
bearing locating   5 Screw—lubricating point (not fitted)   6 Washer—fibre—screw (not fitted)   7 Hub—pulley   8 Seal
8 (1) Pressure balanced seal (later pumps)   9 Pulley   10 Gasket   11 Washer   12 Bolt—long   13 Bolt—short
14 Alternator rear bracket   15 Washer   16 Bolt   17 Pillar   18 Washer   19 Nut   20 Housing   21 Screw   22 Spindle
—distributor driving   23 Alternator pulley   24 Alternator fan   25 Alternator adjusting link   26 Washer   27 Washer
28 Nut   29 Bolt   30 Washer   31 Bolt   32 Washer   33 Nut   34 Bolt   35 Washer   36 Nut   37 Fan
38 Screw   39 Washer   40 Fan belt   41 Distance piece

On later engines the cylinder block drain tap is replaced by a removable plug and sealing washer. Later cars have no provision for draining the radiator and the use of antifreeze all the year round is recommended. To drain the coolant from the radiator, slacken off the clip on the bottom hose and remove the hose from the radiator.

On cars with an expansion tank stand the car on level ground and remove the cap from the expansion tank and the filler plug from the outlet pipe, the clip from the bottom hose and the cylinder block drain plug.

Flushing:

A proprietary compound may be used, in which case follow the instructions on the tin. The system may also be flushed with clean water only.

Drain the cooling system and remove the drain taps so as to provide an unobstructed flow for the water. Insert a hosepipe into the filler neck on the radiator and run clean water through until it comes out clean from the drain holes. If an adaptor can be made, fit the hosepipe to the drain holes and flush through in a reverse direction. In bad cases the radiator will have to be removed, inverted and flushed through separately in a reverse direction. Refit the drain taps when flushing is completed.

Filling:

Make sure on early models that the drain taps are closed. Fill the system through the radiator filler with soft clean water. Refit the filler cap and check the water level when it is cool after a period of running. Some room for expansion must be left above the coolant, though excess coolant will be vented overboard through the overflow pipe.

On models with an expansion tank refit the bottom hose and cylinder block drain plug. Check that all hose connections are tight and open the heater valve. Top up the expansion tank with coolant to half full and refit the cap. Fill the system through the filler neck up to the bottom of the threads and refit the plug. Run the engine until the top hose is warm and switch off.

Top up the expansion tank to half full if necessary, and also to the bottom of the filler plug threads.

4:3 The radiator

The radiator details are shown in **FIG 4:1** and the earlier grille details are shown in **FIG 4:2**. The oil cooler, if fitted, is bolted to the front of the radiator.

Occasionally the accumulation of dirt and flies should be removed from the radiator fins by flushing through with water under pressure from the rear of the radiator. In bad cases the fins will have to be scrubbed with, or soaked in, very hot water and detergent.

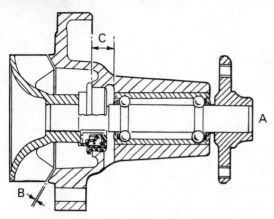

FIG 4:4 Sectional view of water pump

Key to Fig 4:4   **A** Hub face flush with spindle
B .020 to .030 inch (.51 to .76 mm) clearance   **C** .534 ±
.005 inch (13.56 ± .13 mm) between rear face of outer bearing
track and seal housing shoulder   **D** .042 to .062 inch
(1.1 to 1.6 mm) clearance on earlier pumps fitted with thrower

Removal:

If an oil cooler is fitted, disconnect the oil pipes from
both the cooler and from the engine.

1 Drain the cooling system. Disconnect the top and
  bottom hoses from the radiator. Where fitted disconnect the expansion tank hose from the radiator
  and the thermostatic switch wires connector.
2 Release the stays by undoing the diaphragm to
  radiator bolts that hold the stays. Remove the bolts that
  secure the diaphragm sides to the body and lift the
  assembly out.
3 Free the overflow pipe and remove the bolts that
  secure the radiator to the diaphragm.

Refit the radiator in the reverse order of removal. Fill
the system and check for leaks before starting the engine.

4:4 The fan belt

The fan belt tension should be such that there is 1 inch
(2.5 cm) total lateral play at the centre of the longest run
when the fan belt is moved by moderate hand pressure.
Excessive tension will damage the alternator bearings
while if the belt is slack the alternator and water pump
will slip.

Adjustment:

1 Slacken the nut on the alternator pivot bolt and
  slacken the nut on the slotted adjustment link.
2 Pull the alternator up and away from the cylinder block
  until the belt is at the correct tension. It is best to move
  the alternator by hand only, but if a lever is used it
  must be wooden and only used under the drive end
  bracket otherwise the alternator will be damaged.
3 With the alternator in position tighten all the nuts.

Removal:

On emission controlled engines fitted with an air pump,
the pump driving belt must be slackened off and removed
from the pump pulley before the fan belt can be removed.

Slacken the alternator mounting nuts and bolts and
press it down to slacken the fan belt as much as possible.
Ease the fan belt off the alternator driving pulley in the
direction of rotation (clockwise). If the belt is too tight to
be fully removed, turn the engine over by hand so that the
added leverage frees the belt from the remainder of the
pulley. Lift the belt off the crankshaft pulley and then lift
it over the individual fan blades.

Replace the belt(s) in the reverse order of removal and
set the correct tension. The pump driving belt should be
tensioned so that it has $\frac{1}{2}$ inch total play at the centre of
the longest run.

4:5 The thermostat

The thermostat is fitted under the elbow on the cylinder
head (see **FIG 1:2** in **Chapter 1**).

In very hot climates the thermostat may be removed
and left out. **If the thermostat is removed it is
essential to fit a thermostat blanking sleeve otherwise higher operating temperatures will be
reached.** Two grades of thermostat are supplied to cope
with different climatic conditions (see Technical Data).

Removal:

Drain the cooling system so that the level of the coolant
is below the thermostat. Disconnect the radiator top hose
from the elbow and remove the elbow and its gasket after
taking off the three securing nuts and washers. Withdraw
the thermostat from its housing.

Testing:

Suspend the thermostat in water and heat the water,
measuring the temperature with an accurate thermometer.
Keep the water well stirred so that the temperature is even
throughout. Note the temperature at which the valve
starts to open and if it varies more than 5° from the
temperature stamped on the flange reject the thermostat
and fit a new one. Similarly reject the thermostat if the
valve sticks in the open position.

Replacement:

Clean out any sludge or sediment from the housing and
replace the thermostat in the reverse order of removal.
Note that the thermostat is fitted first and the gasket placed
on top of the thermostat. Renew the gasket if it is damaged,
scrape away all traces of gasket or jointing compound and
fit the new gasket using a little grease or jointing compound to ensure a good seal.

4:6 The water pump

The details of the water pump are shown in **FIG 4:3**.
The lubrication screw 5 and its fibre washer 6 are no
longer fitted. A cross-section of the latest type pump is
shown in **FIG 4:4**. Some earlier pumps may have a
different type of seal and this is shown in **FIG 4:5**.

Removal:

1 Drain the cooling system and disconnect the water
  hoses to the pump.
2 Remove the fan belt (see **Section 4:4**), support the
  alternator and take out its mounting bolts. Lift the
  alternator out of the car after disconnecting its multi-
  socket connector.

3 Take out the securing bolts 38 and remove the washers 39, cooling fan 37 and pulley 9 from the water pump spindle.

4 Remove the bolts 12 and 13 with their washers 11 and withdraw the pump from the engine. If the old gasket 10 adheres to either the pump or crankcase, carefully scrape the parts clean.

Refit the pump in the reverse order of removal, using a new gasket 10 lightly smeared with grease or jointing compound. Refit the alternator and tension the belt(s). Fill the cooling system and check for leaks, both before and after starting the engine.

Dismantling:

Use an extractor to withdraw the pulley hub 7 from the shaft of the spindle 3(1). Remove the bearing locating wire 4 through the aperture in the body and tap the spindle and impeller rearwards to remove them from the body. Again use an extractor to remove the impeller from the spindle and then take off the old seal 8(1) or 8. **The spindle and bearings cannot be dismantled.**

Reassembly:

Brush the parts with clean water so as to remove any sediment. Clean any scale or rust off the spindle using fine emerycloth. If the interference fit between the spindle and the hub or impeller has been lost, renew parts as required. If the bearings are noisy or worn then renew the complete assembly 3(1). Renew the seal 8(1) if it is damaged or shows signs of having leaked. If the bore for the bearings is worn or pitted then the body 1 must be renewed though it is likely that if this occurs the whole pump will be worn and it will be advisable to fit a new (complete) unit.

Reassemble the pump in the reverse order of dismantling, ensuring that the dimensions shown in **FIG 4:4** are adhered to. Pumps fitted with a thrower (earlier type) must be assembled to the dimensions shown in **FIG 4:5**. On both types of pump the joint face on the seal should be lightly smeared with mineral based oil.

4:7 Frost precautions

The only adequate frost precaution is to add sufficient antifreeze to the cooling water as in very cold weather the radiator may freeze even though the engine is running. Draining the cooling system overnight is not sufficient as some water will remain in the heater.

Only ethylene glycol based antifreeze to specification BS.3151 or BS.3152 should be used and the degree of protection given is shown in the following table:

	25 per cent	30 per cent	35 per cent
Complete protection	10°F (—12°C)	3°F (—16°C)	—4°F (—20°C)
Safe limit*	0°F (—17°C)	—8°F (—22°C)	—18°F (—28°C)
Lower protection limit**	—14°F (—26°C)	—22°F (—30°C)	—28°F (—33°C)

*Coolant mushy, but engine may be driven after a short warm up period.

**No damage but engine must not be started until it has been thawed out.

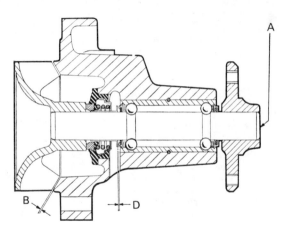

FIG 4:5 Sectional view of earlier type of water pump fitted with thrower and earlier type of seal

Key to Fig 4:5   **A** Hub face flush with spindle **B** .020 to .030 inch (.51 to .76 mm) clearance   **C** .534 ± .005 inch (13.56 ± .13 mm) between rear face of outer bearing track and seal housing shoulder   **D** .042 to .062 inch (1.1 to 1.6 mm) clearance on earlier pumps fitted with thrower

The percentage of antifreeze in the coolant may be checked using a hydrometer. The instrument will have a table correlating the specific gravity readings with the percentage of antifreeze.

For 25 per cent antifreeze solution; 2½ Imperial pints (3 US pints, 1.4 litres) of antifreeze are required in the engine.

Before adding antifreeze the cooling system should be flushed out. **Close the drain taps after flushing.** Pour in the correct quantity of antifreeze and then fill the system to the normal cold level with clean soft water. Run the engine until the thermostat has opened, indicated by the heating of the radiator header tank, so as to mix the antifreeze with the water.

If topping up is required, use a mixture of antifreeze and water. If water only is used for topping-up then the antifreeze in the system will become excessively diluted.

4:8 Fan motor

From car No. 41002 an electric motor drives the cooling fan blades under the control of a thermostatic switch mounted on the radiator.

Removal:

Remove the radiator fan guard from the bonnet lock platform and disconnect the fan motor wires at the multi-connector. Slacken the grub screw and remove the fan blades from the motor spindle.

Slacken the two screws clamping the fan motor bracket and withdraw the fan motor.

Refit in the reverse order ensuring that the motor is fitted to the mounting bracket so that the fan end of the motor protrudes 2 inch (50.8 mm) from the mounting bracket.

Servicing of the motor is dealt with in **Chapter 12**.

4:9 Fault diagnosis

(a) Internal water leakage

1 Cracked cylinder wall
2 Cracked cylinder head
3 Cracked tappet chest wall
4 Loose cylinder head nuts
5 Faulty cylinder head gasket

(b) Poor circulation

1 Radiator core blocked
2 Engine water passages restricted
3 Low water level
4 Loose fan belt
5 Defective thermostat
6 Perished or collapsed hoses

(c) Corrosion

1 Impurities in the water
2 Neglected draining and flushing

(d) Overheating

1 Check (b)
2 Sludge in crankcase
3 Incorrect ignition timing
4 Low oil level in engine sump
5 Tight engine
6 Choked exhaust system
7 Binding brakes
8 Slipping clutch
9 Incorrect valve timing
10 Mixture too weak

CHAPTER 5

THE CLUTCH

5:1 Description

The clutch hydraulic system is shown in **FIG 5:1** and a sectioned view of the clutch itself is shown in **FIG 5:2**.

The pressure plate 10 and diaphragm spring 9 parts rotate with the cover 1 which is securely bolted to the engine flywheel. The splines in the hub of the driven plate assembly 11 mate onto the splines on the gearbox input shaft so that this always revolves with the driven plate. The release bearing 6, which is graphite-faced, moves on the end of a lever pivotted in the bellhousing and attached at its other end to the pushrod of the hydraulic slave cylinder.

Normally the release bearing 6 exerts no pressure on the release plate 7 and the diaphragm spring 9 exerts a strong forward thrust on the pressure plate 10. This action firmly grips the driven plate 11 by its friction surfaces, between the rear face of the flywheel and the forward machined face of the pressure plate 10, so that the driven plate is forced to revolve with the engine and transmit drive to the gearbox.

When the clutch pedal is pressed, hydraulic pressure is generated in the master cylinder and this pressure is transmitted, by metal and flexible pipelines, to the slave cylinder. The slave cylinder piston moves, rotating the lever so that the release bearing 6 moves forwards, taking the release plate 7 with it. The release plate in turn presses on the inner ends of the diaphragm spring fingers so that it levers about the fulcrum rings and releases the pressure on the pressure plate 10 and driven plate 11. The driven plate and gearbox input shaft are then free to revolve, or come to a stop, without transmitting any drive.

When the clutch pedal is released normally, the pressure on the driven plate is gradually increased. At first it slips as drive is taken up but in a short time it is rotating at engine speed. Coil springs are fitted to the driven plate to ease the shock from sudden engagements.

No hard and fast rules can be laid down about the life of a clutch as some drivers will burn it out within a few thousand miles while very careful drivers may make it last practically the life of the car. On average however, the wear rate on the friction linings is .001 inch (.02 mm) per 1000 miles (1600 km).

5:2 Routine maintenance

A hydrostatic type of slave cylinder is fitted so no adjustments are required.

1 At regular intervals check the level of the fluid in the master cylinder reservoir. Wipe the top and cap clean before removing the cap so as to prevent dirt from falling into the reservoir. The level must never be

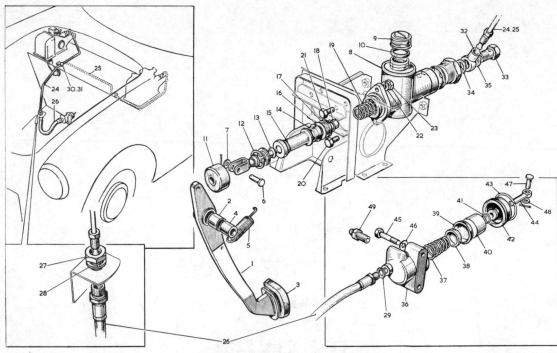

FIG 5:1 Hydraulic system details

Key to Fig 5:1   1 Clutch pedal   2 Bush   3 Pad   4 Distance tube   5 Spring—pedal pull-off   6 Clevis pin   7 Washer
8 Barrel and tank   9 Filler cap   10 Seal—cap   11 Dust cover   12 Circlip   13 Pushrod   14 Cup—secondary   15 Piston
16 Washer—piston   17 Cup—main   18 Retainer   19 Spring   20 Bolt   21 Bolt   22 Washer   23 Nut   24 Pipe—
master cylinder to hose   25 Pipe—master cylinder to hose   26 Hose   27 Locknut for hose   28 Washer—shakeproof
29 Seal   30 Clip—clutch pipe to bulkhead   31 Clip—clutch pipe to bulkhead   32 Banjo connection   33 Bolt for banjo
connection   34 Gasket   35 Gasket   36 Body   37 Spring   38 Filler—piston cup   39 Piston cup seal   40 Piston
41 Clip   42 Dust cover   43 Clip   44 Pushrod   45 Bolt   46 Washer   47 Clevis pin   48 Washer   49 Bleed screw

higher than $\frac{1}{4}$ inch (6.35 mm) below the bottom of the filler neck and it must never be allowed to drop below half full. If required, top up using Lockheed Disc Brake Fluid (Series 329). **Never use anything but the recommended fluid.** There should be very little loss of fluid and regular or excessive topping-up indicates a leak in the system which should have immediate attention.

2 It is strongly recommended that the complete hydraulic system be stripped every 40,000 miles (65,000 km) or 3 years and old seals and fluid discarded. The master cylinder and slave cylinder parts should be inspected at the same time and the system reassembled with new parts as required, all new seals and fresh hydraulic fluid.

5:3 Servicing the master cylinder

The master cylinder details are shown in **FIG 5:1**.

When the clutch pedal 1 is pressed the pushrod 13 forces the piston 15, together with its cup seals 14 and 17, down the bore of the cylinder so that the fluid in front of it is pressurized and acts on the slave cylinder through the metal pipe 24 or 25 and the flexible hose 26. When the pedal is released the spring 19 returns the piston back up the bore, and at the end of its stroke the piston uncovers

an interconnecting port between the cylinder and the reservoir. Fluid pressure is reduced to atmospheric pressure and any losses in the system can be replenished from the reservoir. This port is disconnected from the pressure chamber as soon as the piston moves down the bore but to prevent the reservoir fluid from leaking away behind the piston, the port connects with the annular portion of the piston 15 and is prevented from leaking out by the secondary cup seal 14.

Removal and replacement:

1 Take out the screws and remove the cover from over the master cylinders. Either syphon the fluid out of the reservoir or else pump it out through a tube attached to the opened bleed screw on the slave cylinder. If it is suspected that there is gum or dirt in the pipelines they should be flushed out by pumping at least a pint ($\frac{1}{2}$ litre) of methylated spirits (denatured alchohol) through the system.

2 Extract the splitpin and remove the clevis pin 6 and its washer 7 to free the clutch pedal 1 from the fork of the pushrod 13.

3 Disconnect the metal pipeline from the end of the master cylinder. Normally the method is to undo the union on the pipeline but sometimes these are very

stiff and either the corners of the union wear off or else the union tends to turn the pipe with it causing the pipe to fracture or twist. If this starts occuring remove the banjo bolt 33 instead.

4 Take out the two bolts 20 and 21 and lift the master cylinder assembly out of the car.

Replace the master cylinder in the reverse order of removal. The longer bolt 21 passes through the stiffener plate. Fill the reservoir and bleed the system as described in **Section 5:5**.

Dismantling:

1 Pull back the rubber dust cover 11 and lightly press in the pushrod 13 to relieve the pressure on the circlip 12. Use a long-nosed pair of pliers and remove the circlip from its groove in the cylinder. The pushrod 13 with its integral stop washer can now be removed.

2 Shake out the internal parts and use only the fingers to remove the secondary seal 14.

Examination:

1 Clean all the parts with methylated spirits (denatured alchohol) or hydraulic fluid. The seals may be washed in methylated spirits but they should be dipped in clean hydraulic fluid before they are dry. **No other solvents may be allowed to come in contact with the seals.**

2 The seals should always be renewed unless the old seals are in very good condition. Check the lips for scoring or wear, but do not turn the seals inside out.

3 Examine the bore of the cylinder and renew the master cylinder if the bore shows any defects. Likely defects are scoring, pitting or wear. A bore in good condition should appear smooth and highly-polished.

4 Make sure that the bypass ports are clear.

Reassembly:

All the internal parts, including seals, should be dipped in clean hydraulic fluid and then reassembled wet.

1 Use the fingers to stretch the secondary cup seal 14 over the piston so that the lips will face into the bore. Still using only the fingers fit it into position and work it round so that it is squarely seated.

2 Insert the spring 19, largest diameter leading, into the bore of the cylinder and fit the retainer 18 to the outer end of the spring.

3 Carefully fit the main cup seal 17 down the bore, taking great care not to bend back or damage its lips. Follow the seal by the washer 16 and the piston assembly. Again take great care when entering the secondary cup seal 14 into the bore.

4 Hold the piston in the bore and refit the pushrod assembly 13, securing it in place with the circlip 12.

5 Check that the piston and pushrod return freely under the action of the return spring. Pull the dust cover 11 back into place.

5:4 Servicing the slave cylinder

The slave cylinder details are shown in **FIG 5:1**.

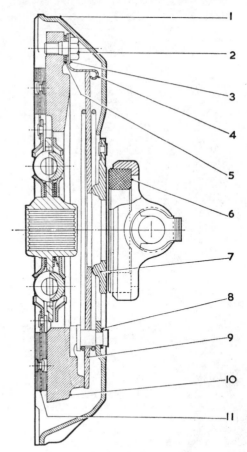

FIG 5:2   Sectioned views of clutch unit

Key to Fig 5:2   1 Cover   2 Strap bolt   3 Tabwasher
4 Clip   5 Strap—diaphragm cover   6 Release bearing
7 Release plate   8 Strap—release plate/cover   9 Diaphragm
spring   10 Pressure plate   11 Driven plate

Removal and replacement:

Whenever the slave cylinder is removed or replaced, great care must be taken not to twist or strain the flexible portion of the hose 26. The metal pipe union should be undone first, followed by the locknut 27 and washer 28 while holding the hose 26 with a spanner. The hose can then be unscrewed from the slave cylinder. If the hose is left attached to the bracket then the hose must be held with a spanner and the slave cylinder rotated about the hose.

1 Drain the hydraulic system by pumping out the fluid through the bleed screw 49 on the slave cylinder.

2 Extract the splitpin and remove the clevis pin 47 and washer securing the pushrod 44 to the clutch operating lever.

3 Take out the two bolts 45 and their washers 46 and disconnect the supply hose 26.

Replace the slave cylinder in the reverse order of removal. Fill and bleed the hydraulic system as described in **Section 5:5**.

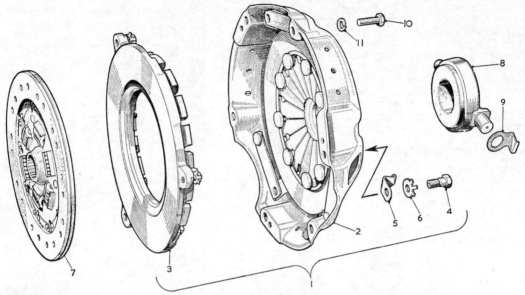

FIG 5:3   Clutch details

Key to Fig 5:3   1 Cover assembly   2 Cover with straps, diaphragm spring and release plate   3 Pressure plate   4 Bolt
5 Clip—pressure plate   6 Tabwasher   7 Driven plate assembly   8 Release bearing assembly   9 Bearing retainer   10 Bolt
11 Washer

Dismantling:

Free the large circlip 43 and remove the dust cover 42 and pushrod 44 assembly. Use gentle air pressure at the inlet to blow out the internal parts.

Check the bore of the cylinder and renew the complete assembly if the bore is pitted, worn or scored.

Reassembly:

Wash the parts in methylated spirits, dip them into clean hydraulic fluid and reassemble them wet. It is most advisable to fit a new seal 39.

Insert the spring 37, large end leading, down the bore and place the filler 38 on the outer end of the spring. Very carefully fit the seal 39 into the bore, taking great care not to bend back or damage the lips of the seal. Refit the piston 40, flat end leading, and keep it lightly pressed in while refitting the pushrod and dust cover. Secure the dust cover in place with the circlip 43.

If the dust cover 43 is split or damaged then it should be renewed. It is held to the pushrod by the small circlip 41.

5:5 Bleeding the hydraulic system

Bleeding is always required if the system has been dismantled or the fluid level in the reservoir has fallen so low that air has been drawn into the system.

Always use fresh hydraulic fluid and discard fluid that has been bled through the system, unless it is perfectly clean. If fluid is to be re-used then it must be kept in a clean container for at least 24 hours so as to allow the minute air bubbles to disperse.

Top up the reservoir and keep it fully topped up throughout the bleeding operation. Fluid will be drawn through the system throughout the operation and if the reservoir is not refilled then the level will fall so far that air is again drawn into the system.

1 Attach a length of rubber or plastic tube to the bleed screw 49 and put the free end of the tube into a little clean hydraulic fluid contained in a clean glass jar.

2 Open the bleed screw three-quarters of a turn and have an assistant pump the clutch pedal with full slow strokes.

3 At first air bubbles will be ejected with the fluid through the tube and the pumping should be carried on until the fluid comes out completely free from any air bubbles. Tighten the bleed screw either on a downstroke of the pedal or when it is held fully depressed.

4 In difficult cases, tighten the bleed screw at the end of each downstroke and open it again after slight pressure has been applied on the next downstroke.

5 Remove the bleed tube and check the system for leaks with the clutch pedal depressed. Top up the fluid level in the reservoir to the correct level.

5:6 Servicing the clutch

A sectioned view of the clutch is shown in **FIG 5:2** and the clutch components are shown in **FIG 5:3**. The clutch is removed and replaced as described in **Chapter 1, Section 1:10**. When the cover assembly is removed the driven plate assembly will be free so do not allow it to drop. When refitting the clutch the driven plate must be centralized with a mandrel. Special tool No. 18G.1027 is designed for this purpose but an old input shaft from the gearbox will do as well.

It is most advisable to fit an exchange unit if the clutch is defective.

Tolerances:

If the flywheel or the driven plate are not within limits there will be fierce chattering or drag on the clutch. Driven plate misalignment will cause rapid wear on its splines and in extreme cases it may even cause the hub to break loose giving complete clutch failure and expensive repairs.

Check the flywheel for runout with a DTI (Dial Test Indicator). The maximum runout should not exceed .003 inch (.07 mm) at any point on the operating face.

The driven plate must be aligned within .015 inch (.38 mm).

Driven plate condition:

The driven plate must be renewed if any of the following defects are present:

1 The friction linings are so worn that the rivet heads are flush, or nearly flush, with the faces of the linings.
2 Oil or grease has contaminated the linings so that their grain is no longer visible.
3 Loose rivets, weak or broken coil springs or the springs are loose in their mountings.
4 Wear or damage to the hub splines.

The friction linings of a driven plate in good efficient condition will be light coloured with a polished glaze through which the grain of the friction material will be clearly visible. Contrary to expectation a rough surface is not as efficient as the ideal polished surface as the rough one is made up of innumerable minute hills and only the crests of these hills form contact whereas on a smooth surface the whole area is in contact.

Oil on the clutch will impair its efficiency. Small amounts of oil are burnt to form darker coloured smears. Larger quantities of oil form a dark glazed deposit through which the grain of the friction material can no longer be seen. This will produce a 'fierce' clutch which will tend to stick on disengagement as well as spin excessively on engagement. Large quantities of oil are obvious from the black oil soaked appearance of the linings and the free oil present in the bellhousing. The source of any oil leaks must be traced and cured before a new driven plate is fitted.

Clutch cover components

Examine the working face of the pressure plate. The pressure plate must be renewed if it is scored, has hairline cracks or shows excessive burn marks. Rather than renewing just the pressure plate it is strongly advised that an exchange clutch unit be fitted.

Free the tabwashers 6 and unscrew each of the three bolts 4 a turn at a time until the diaphragm spring contacts the cover. Remove the bolts 4, tabwashers 6 and clips 5 and lift out the pressure plate 3, shown in **FIG 5 : 3**. **No further dismantling should be attempted.**

Refit the pressure plate in the reverse order of removal after thoroughly cleaning the parts and lightly lubricating pivot surfaces with white zinc-based grease.

Clutch release bearing:

This is only accessible after the gearbox has been separated from the engine. An exchange unit must be fitted if the carbon face on the old one is either scored or worn nearly down to the metal cup.

To remove the bearing 8, rotate the spring retainers 9 through 90 degrees and withdraw the bearing from the fork of the operating lever. Refit the new bearing and make sure that the spring retainers are correctly positioned.

5 : 7 Fault diagnosis

(a) Drag or spin

1 Oil or grease on the driven plate linings
2 Air in the clutch hydraulic system
3 Leaking master cylinder, slave cylinder or pipelines
4 Driven plate hub binding on input shaft splines
5 Distorted driven plate
6 Warped or damaged pressure plate
7 Broken drive plate linings

(b) Fierceness or snatch

1 Check 1 in (a)
2 Worn driven plate linings

(c) Slip

1 Check 1 in (a) and 2 in (b)
2 Weak diaphragm spring
3 Seized piston in clutch slave cylinder

(d) Judder

1 Check 1, 5, 6 and 7 in (a)
2 Pressure plate not parallel with flywheel face
3 Contact area on friction linings not evenly distributed
4 Bent input shaft in gearbox
5 Faulty engine or gearbox mountings
6 Worn suspension shackles
7 Weak rear springs
8 Loose propeller shaft bolts

(e) Rattle

1 Broken coil springs in driven plate
2 Worn release mechanism
3 Excessive backlash in transmission
4 Wear in transmission bearings
5 Release bearing loose on fork

(f) Tick or knock

1 Worn crankshaft spigot bearing
2 Badly worn splines in driven plate hub
3 Faulty starter motor drive
4 Loose flywheel

(g) Driven plate fracture

1 Misaligned driven plate
2 Drag or distortion due to hanging gearbox in plate hub

NOTES

CHAPTER 6

THE GEARBOX AND OVERDRIVE

6:1 Description

PART 1   THE GEARBOX

6:2 Removing the gearbox
6:3 Dismantling the gearbox
6:4 Reassembling the gearbox
6:5 Fault diagnosis

PART 2   THE OVERDRIVE

6:6 Operation
6:7 Servicing
6:8 Removing and replacing
6:9 Fault diagnosis

6:1 Description

The gearbox fitted to the models covered by this manual is a modified version of the gearbox fitted to earlier models. All four forward gears are fitted with synchromesh engagement (as opposed to the top three on earlier models), and the gear ratios have also been altered. The details of the earlier gearbox are shown in **FIG 6:1**, and this figure may be used for reference.

A Laycock LH type overdrive may be fitted as an optional extra. The overdrive is selected by an electrical switch which operates a solenoid valve to direct oil to the overdrive pistons.

A combined filler cap and dipstick is fitted to the top of the gearbox, accessible after removing the rubber plug on the gearbox cover, and a drain plug is fitted underneath the gearbox. If an overdrive is fitted this shares the same oil supply as the gearbox, and the two are filled and drained as a unit through the gearbox filler and drain plugs. As they share the same oil supply, **no friction-reducing additives may be added to the gearbox when an overdrive is fitted.** The dangers of lack of oil or a low oil level are fairly obvious but excessive oil can also be harmful, so keep the oil level between the two marks on the dipstick. Excessive oil may well leak out of the gearbox and contaminate the clutch.

PART 1   THE GEARBOX

6:2 Removing the gearbox

The gearbox cannot be taken out leaving the engine in place. Remove the complete power unit from the car, as described in **Chapter 1, Section 1:2.** Remove the starter motor by taking out the two securing bolts. Support the gearbox and remove the bolts securing the bellhousing to the engine. Withdraw the gearbox from the engine. **Great care must be taken during this operation not to allow the weight of the gearbox to hang by the input shaft in the clutch.** If this occurs the clutch may be damaged and later break up at high speed.

Refit the gearbox in the reverse order of removal, again taking great care not to allow the weight of the gearbox to hang on the clutch.

6:3 Dismantling the gearbox

For ease of reference the separate components have been placed under sub-headings. The removal of any

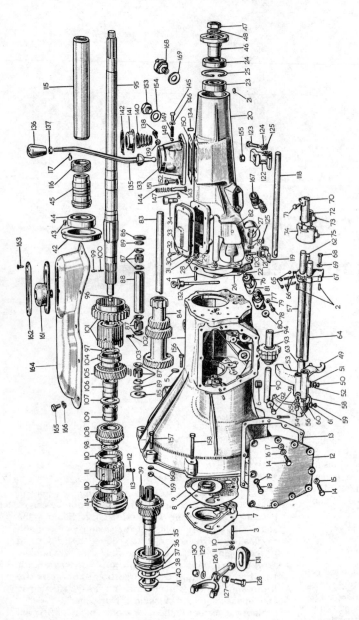

FIG 6:1 Early gearbox details

Key to Fig 6:1 1 Casing assembly 2 Dowel—locating block to gearbox 3 Stud—front cover 4 Stud—rear extension 5 Welch plug 6 Drain plug 7 Cover 8 Oil seal 9 Gasket 10 Washer 11 Nut 12 Cover—gearbox side 13 Gasket 14 Bolt 15 Washer 16 Washer—plain 17 Washer—fibre 18 Countersunk screw 19 Washer 20 Rear extension 21 Plug 22 Thrust button—speedometer 23 Bearing—rear extension 24 Oil seal 25 Circlip 26 Gasket 27 Bolt 28 Nut 29 Nut 30 Rear extension cover 31 Gasket 32 Bolt 33 Washer 34 Breather assembly 35 Input shaft 36 Bearing 37 Circlip 38 Shim—.002 inch (.051 mm) 39 Needle roller 40 Washer 41 Nut 42 Housing—rear bearing 43 Peg—rear bearing housing 44 Bearing 45 Distance piece 46 Flange 47 Nut 48 Washer 49 Fork—reverse 50 Bolt—reverse fork locating 51 Washer 52 Nut 53 Fork—first and second speed 54 Bolt—fork locating 55 Washer 56 Nut 57 Rod—first and second speed fork 58 Fork—third and fourth speed 59 Bolt—fork locating 60 Washer 61 Nut 62 Rod—third and fourth speed fork 63 Distance piece 64 Rod—reverse fork 65 Ball 66 Spring—locating ball 67 Block—sliding shaft locating—third and fourth gear 68 Washer 69 Washer 70 Selector—first and second gear 71 Bolt—selector locating 72 Selector 73 Block—selector locating 74 Selector—reverse gear 75 Bolt—selector locating 76 Pinion—speedometer 77 Bush 78 Bolt 79 Washer 80 Oil seal 81 Gasket 82 Arm assembly—interlocking 83 Countershaft 84 Gear unit—layshaft 85 Thrust washer 86 Thrust washer 87 Needle bearing 88 Distance tube 89 Circlip 90 Shaft—reverse 91 Bolt 92 Washer 93 Gear assembly—reverse 94 Bush 95 Output shaft 96 Restrictor—oil 97 Thrust washer 98 Thrust washer 99 Peg 100 Spring 101 First speed wheel and synchronizer 102 Ball 103 Spring 104 Baulk ring—second speed gear 105 Second speed gear 106 Bush 107 Ring—interlocking—second and third 108 Third speed gear 109 Bush 110 Baulk ring—third and fourth speed 111 Synchronizer—third and fourth speed 112 Spring 113 Ball 114 Sliding coupling—third and fourth speed 115 Distance piece 116 Gear—speedometer 117 Key 118 Remote control shaft (rear extension) 119 Selector 120 Bolt 121 Washer 122 Selector lever—rear 123 Bolt 124 Washer 125 Key—selector lever 126 Clutch withdrawal—lever 127 Bush 128 Bolt 129 Washer 130 Washer 131 Dust cover 132 Dipstick 133 Tower—remote control 134 Dowel 135 Gearlever 136 Knob 137 Pin 138 Pin 139 Washer 140 Spring 141 Cover 142 Circlip 143 Plunger—reverse selector 144 Spring 145 Bolt 146 Bolt 147 Locknut 148 Ball 149 Spring 150 Gearlever 151 Bolt 152 Washer 153 Plug 154 Cover—gearbox remote control 155 Joint washer 156 Bush 157 Bolt 158 Bolt 159 Grommet—gearlever 160 Washer 161 Bush 162 Retainer 163 Bolt 164 Cover 165 Bolt 166 Washer 167 Box 168 Reverse light switch (later cars) 169 Washer for switch (later cars) speedometer drive adaptor

component requires the removal of the other components preceding it in this section.

Rear extension:

1 Drain the gearbox by removing the drain plug underneath.
2 Hold the driving flange to stop it rotating, preferably using special spanner 18G.34A, and remove the nut and washer which secures it. Remove the driving flange.
3 Take off the remote control housing after removing its securing bolts. Withdraw the selector interlocking arm and plate assembly.
4 Take off the nuts securing the rear extension to the gearbox and remove the extension, taking care to collect the shims from gearbox output shaft. Use a rubber mallet to tap the extension rearwards if it is difficult to remove.
5 If there is a defect in the parts, drive out the old oil seal, then remove the circlip and press the bearing out of the rear extension.

Front cover:

It is not necessary to remove the rear extension for this operation.
1 Remove the clutch release bearing from the operating fork and take off the dust cover.
2 Take off the securing nuts and remove the front cover, collecting the input shaft shims from under the cover. Discard the old gasket.
3 If the oil seal is defective it should be driven out of the cover so that a new one can be fitted on reassembly. The clutch operating lever is secured to the front cover by a nut and bolt.

Selector rods and forks:

The front cover can be left in place for this operation.
1 Remove the side cover. Take out the detent plunger plugs and springs. Remove the selector fork bolts after slackening their locknuts. Withdraw the selector rods and lift out the selector forks as they come free.

Reverse idler gear:

The front cover can be left in place for this operation.
1 Remove the shaft retaining bolt, after freeing the lockwasher.
2 Remove the reverse idler shaft and lift out the gear.

Input shaft:

1 Drift out the countershaft allowing the countershaft gears to fall free.
2 Make sure that the countershaft gears are no longer in mesh with the input shaft gears and drift out the input assembly using a soft metal drift as shown in **FIG 6 : 2**.
3 If required, remove the needle roller bearing from the rear end of the shaft. Mount the shaft in the padded jaws of a vice, free the lockwasher, and use special spanner 18G.49 to remove the **lefthand threaded** nut. Press the bearing off the shaft.

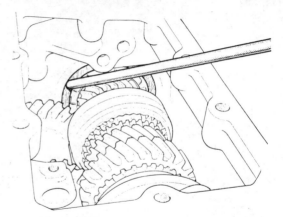

FIG 6 : 2   Drifting out the input shaft assembly

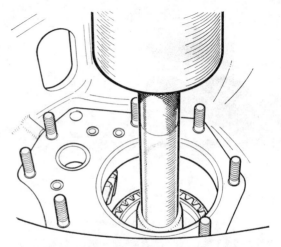

FIG 6 : 3   Pressing out the output shaft assembly using special tool No. 18G.1045

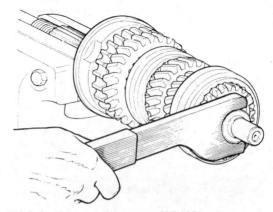

FIG 6 : 4   Using special spanner 18G.1024 to remove the locking nut from the output shaft

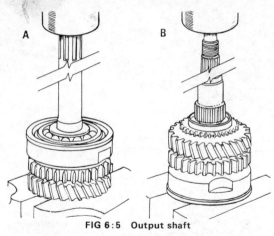

FIG 6:5   Output shaft

Key to Fig 6:5   **A** Pressing off the gears and bearing assembly   **B** Pressing back the gears and bearing assembly

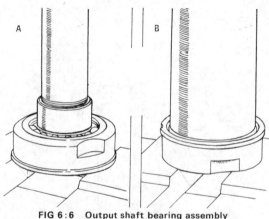

FIG 6:6   Output shaft bearing assembly

Key to Fig 6:6   **A** Pressing the bearing out of its housing   **B** Pressing the bearing back into its housing

Output shaft (standard):

With all the parts removed as described previously in this section, check that the countershaft gears are clear of the output gears.

1 Press the output shaft assembly clear out of the rear of the gearbox, using tool No. 18G.1045 as shown in **FIG 6:3**.

2 Withdraw the complete third and fourth-speed synchronizing assembly. Do not dismantle it unless it is defective. Remove the baulk rings, wrap the assembly in a piece of cloth and press out the hub from the sliding coupling. Store the parts separately.

3 Free the tabwasher and unscrew the nut, using special spanner 18G.1024 as shown in **FIG 6:4**. Withdraw the parts in the following order: shaft sleeve, third gear and interlocking thrust washer, second gear and thrust washer, first and second-speed synchronizing assembly complete, speedometer gear and removing its driving key, the shaft distance piece.

4 Press the first gear, reverse gear and the bearing complete with its housing from the shaft, as shown in

FIG 6:5. Press the bearing out of its housing as shown in **FIG 6:6**.

5 If required, dismantle the first/second-speed synchronizer assembly in the same manner as the third/fourth-speed assembly, but keep parts of the two units well separated as they are very similar in construction.

Output shaft (with overdrive):

This shaft is very similar to the shaft fitted to standard gearboxes and may be treated in practically the same manner. Special spanner 18G.391 should be used for unscrewing the output shaft nut.

Before removing the output shaft the overdrive and its adaptor plate must first be removed (see **Section 6:8**).

6:4 Reassembling the gearbox

Before reassembling any parts, clean them thoroughly using a suitable solvent and examine them for wear or damage. Check all splines and renew any parts that are worn or damaged. Similarly check all gears for worn, chipped or damaged teeth. It is advisable to fit new gaskets and seals, as even if they were satisfactory before they may well leak because they have been damaged or disturbed during dismantling.

Countershaft gear:

This will be free when the remainder of the gearbox has been dismantled. Check the needle roller bearings and renew them if required.

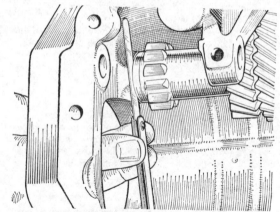

FIG 6:7   Checking the countershaft gear end float

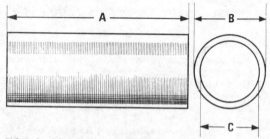

FIG 6:8   Dimensions of tool for refitting output shaft assembly

Key to Fig 6:8   **A** 19 inch (483 mm)   **B** 3 inch (76 mm)   **C** 2.75 inch (69 mm)

Hold the countershaft gear cluster assembly in place with the front thrust washer (larger washer) refitted. Slide the rear (smaller) thrust washer into place and insert the countershaft through the thrust washers and gear cluster. Use feeler gauges to measure the end float as shown in **FIG 6:7**. If the end float is outside the limits of .002 to .003 inch (.05 to .08 mm), a new rear thrust washer should be selectively fitted to restore the correct end float.

When the end float is correct, thread a long length of soft wire through the thrust washers and gear cluster so that the parts can be laid to clear the gears but still lifted up into position so that the countershaft can be refitted with the parts aligned. The thicknesses of the various rear thrust washers available are given in Technical Data.

Output shaft:

This is reassembled and refitted in the reverse order of removal. The assembly is pressed back into the gearbox using a tool made up to the dimensions shown in **FIG 6:8**, by the method shown in **FIG 6:9**. **The synchronizing assemblies may be fitted either way round but they may not be interchanged.**

Before refitting the shaft check that the end float of the first, second and third gears is .005 to .008 inch (.13 to .20 mm) and renew thrust washers as required to bring the end floats within limits.

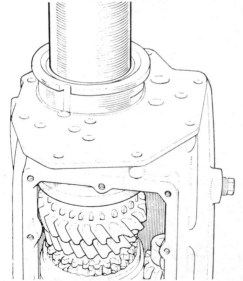

FIG 6:9   Pressing the output shaft assembly back into place using the made up tool

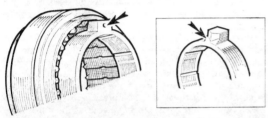

FIG 6:10   Identification of first/second speed synchronizer baulk rings

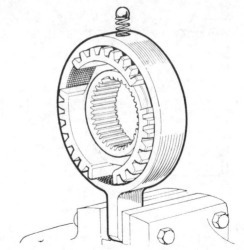

FIG 6:11   Using special tool 18G.1026 to reassemble the synchromesh assemblies

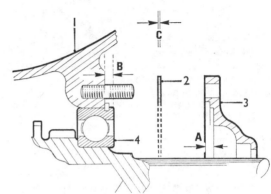

FIG 6:12   Front cover setting up

Key to Fig 6:12   1 Gearbox main casing   2 Gasket for front cover   3 Front cover   4 Bearing   **A** Depth of front cover to bearing register   **B** Input shaft bearing protrusion   **C** Compressed thickness of joint washer

Synchronizing assemblies:

Do not intermix the parts of the units. The baulk rings of the first/second-speed assembly are identified by the small drilled hole or the fillets on the lugs shown in **FIG 6:10**.

Either refit all the springs and balls, retaining them with grease and compress them into place with a large hoseclip, or else use tool No. 18G.1026 to fit the balls and springs to the hub, as shown in **FIG 6:11**, rotating the hub to retain the springs and balls as they are fitted. The springs should have been checked to the dimensions given in Technical Data. Align the cut-outs in coupling sleeve with those of the hub and press the hub assembly directly from the hoseclip, or special tool, so that the balls and springs are not lost. Fit the baulk rings to the hub and refit the complete assembly.

The remainder of the parts are fitted in the reverse order of removal, noting that the following must be carried out if certain new parts have been fitted.

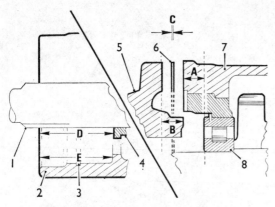

FIG 6:13   Rear extension setting up

Key to Fig 6:13   1 Output shaft   2 Rear extension
3 Rear bearing circlip groove   4 Distance tube   5 Rear
extension   6 Gasket for rear extension   7 Gearbox main
casing   8 Bearing   A Depth between bearing face and
gearbox main casing face   B Depth between rear
extension face and bearing flange   C Thickness of joint
washer   D Depth from rear extension face to distance
tube   E Depth from rear extension face to bearing register

Front cover:

If a new front cover, or any input shaft parts have been
renewed then the clearance between the front cover and
gearbox must be reset.

1 Measure the dimension A shown in **FIG 6:12** and to
this add .012 inch (.31 mm) for the compressed
thickness of the gasket 2 (dimension C).
2 Measure the protrusion B of the input shaft bearing.
3 Fit a new oil seal to the front cover using tool No.
18G.134 with adaptor No. 18G.134Q.
4 Refit the front cover to the gearbox, using sufficient
shims between them to ensure that there is a clearance
of .000 to .001 inch (.000 to .025 mm) between the
bearing and the front cover. This means that the
dimension B measured in 2 plus the total thickness of
shims will be .000 to .001 inch greater than A and C
combined as measured in 1.

Shims are available in thicknesses of .002 inch
(.05 mm) and .004 inch (.10 mm).

Rear extension:

If a new rear extension, or any new output shaft parts
have been fitted then the clearance between the rear
extension and the gearbox must be reset.

Calculate the shimming required between the rear
extension and the output shaft front bearings as follows:

1 Measure the depth A shown in **FIG 6:13** and to this
add C, the thickness of the gasket.
2 Measure the dimension B on the rear extension.
3 Refit the rear extension using shims to ensure that the
clearance between the rear extension and the front
output shaft bearing is .000 to .001 inch. This means
that the dimension B measured in 2 plus the thickness
of shims is .000 to .001 inch less than the dimension A
plus C measured in 1. Shims are available in .002 and
.004 inch thicknesses.
4 Fit and secure the rear extension in place.

Calculate the shimming required between the distance
tube and the rear bearing as follows:

1 Measure the depth D shown in **FIG 6:13**. Similarly
measure the depth E.
2 Fit shims so that the new depth D is .000 to .001 inch
less than the dimension E. Shims are available in the
following thicknesses; .002 inch (.05 mm), .005 inch
(.13 mm), and .010 inch (.25 mm).
3 Press the bearing back into the rear extension using tool
No. 18G.186. Three thicknesses of circlip are available
(see Technical Data) and the thickest one that can be
fitted should be used.
4 Press a new oil seal into place using special tool No.
18G.134 and adaptor No. 18G.134BK. Refit the drive
flange in the reverse order of removal.

6:5 Fault diagnosis

(a) Jumping out of gear

1 Broken or weak spring behind selector rod locating ball
2 Worn locating groove in selector shaft
3 Fork to selector rod securing screw loose

(b) Noisy gearbox

1 Insufficient oil
2 Excessive end float in countershaft gear
3 Worn or damaged bearings
4 Worn or damaged gear teeth

(c) Difficulty in engaging gear

1 Defective clutch release mechanism
2 Worn baulk rings

(d) Oil leaks

1 Excessive oil level
2 Damaged joint faces and gaskets
3 Worn or damaged oil seals
4 Defective front cover

PART 2   THE OVERDRIVE

The overdrive details are shown in **FIG 6:14**.

6:6 Operation

A schematic layout of the overdrive in the direct drive
position is shown in **FIG 6:15** and a similar circuit with
the overdrive engaged is shown in **FIG 6:16**.

The oil pump, driven by a cam from the gearbox output
shaft, produces an oil pressure which in the direct drive
condition is returned directly to the sump through the
low pressure relief valve 8. The conical clutch is held
firmly in contact with the annulus by the pressure of the
springs so that the epicyclic gearing revolves as a solid
unit giving direct drive.

When power is selected to the solenoid 7 the ball is
held down and oil can no longer pass to the low pressure
relief valve. Instead the oil passes to operate the pistons
in the overdrive and pull the conical clutch away from the
annulus and into contact with the brake ring fixed to the
body of the overdrive. If the oil pressure is too high then
it will be relieved by the relief valve 9. If the relief valve
fails to limit the pressure then the ball in the solenoid
valve will be lifted off its seating, acting as a safety valve.

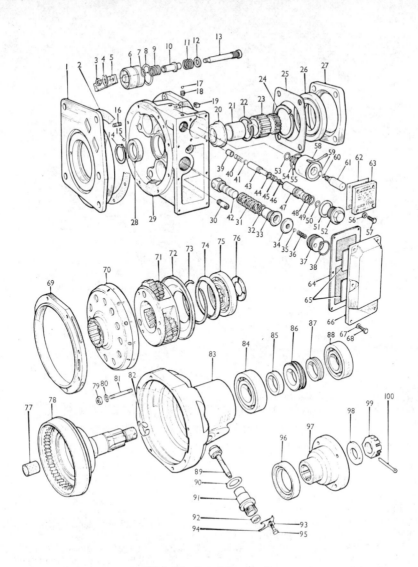

FIG 6:14 Overdrive details

Key to Fig 6:14   1 Adaptor plate   2 Gasket   3 Nut   4 Tabwasher   5 Bridge-piece   6 Operating piston   7 Circlip
8 O-ring   9 Spring   10 Thrust rod   11 Spring   12 Washer   13 Thrust housing pin   14 Circlip   15 Key   16 Stud
17 Steel ball   18 Plug   19 Grommet   20 Sun wheel thrust bush   21 Sun wheel bush   22 Circlip   23 Sun wheel
24 Circlip   25 Retainer plate   26 Thrust ballrace   27 Thrust ring   28 Pump cam   29 Main casing   30 Pump suction
tube   31 Spring   32 O-ring   33 Pump body   34 Non-return valve seat   35 Valve ball   36 Valve spring   37 Pump
plug   38 O-ring   39 Low pressure valve plug   40 Valve spring   41 Valve ball   42 Pump plunger   43 Low pressure
valve body   44 Washer   45 Relief valve spring   46 Valve plunger   47 Valve body   48 Filter   49 O-ring   50 O-ring
51 Washer   52 Plug   53 O-ring   54 Solenoid valve body   55 O-ring   56 Washer   57 Screw   58 Solenoid coil
59 Valve ball   60 O-ring   61 Solenoid plunger   62 Gasket   63 Solenoid cover   64 Sump filter and gasket   65 Filter
magnets   66 Sump   67 Washer   68 Screw   69 Brake ring   70 Clutch sliding member   71 Planet carrier assembly
72 Oil catcher   73 Circlip   74 Oil thrower   75 Unidirectional clutch   76 Thrust washer   77 Bush   78 Annulus   79 Nut
80 Washer   81 Stud   82 Spring ring   83 Rear casing   84 Annulus front bearing   85 Spacer   86 Speedometer drive
gear   87 Selective spacer   88 Annulus rear bearing   89 Speedometer driven gear   90 Sealing washer   91 Speedometer
bearing   92 Oil seal   93 Retaining clip   94 Washer   95 Bolt   96 Oil seal   97 Drive flange   98 Washer   99 Nut
100 Splitpin

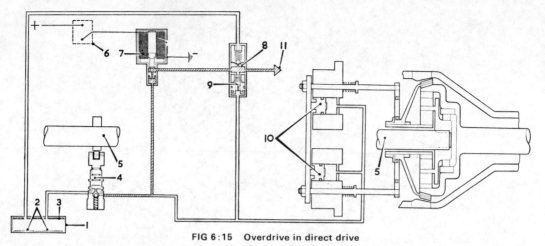

FIG 6:15   Overdrive in direct drive

Key to Fig 6:15   1 Sump   2 Magnet filters   3 Gauze filter   4 Pump   5 Third motion shaft (gearbox)   6 Control switch   7 Solenoid operating valve   8 Low pressure valve   9 Relief valve   10 Operating pistons   11 Oil return to sump

The planet carrier is splined to the input shaft so that when the conical clutch is prevented from rotating, by pressing onto the brake ring, then the planet gears drive the annulus, and output shaft which is splined to it, at a higher speed than the input shaft. A unidirectional clutch is fitted between the input shaft and the annulus.

If the unit sticks in the engaged position then the car must not be driven in reverse or serious damage will result to the overdrive. On new or reconditioned units the conical clutch may stick to the brake ring. If this occurs raise the car onto a ramp or stands and give the brake ring several smart blows with a hammer.

6:7 Servicing

It is not advisable for the average owner to attempt to dismantle or repair the internals of the overdrive as too many tools are required. Certain servicing operations may still be carried out and certain defects repaired. If faults still persist after these operations have been carried out, the car should be taken to a suitably equipped service station for further investigation and repairs.

Most of the operations in this section require the draining of the gearbox and overdrive oil (through the gearbox drain plugs) and strict cleanliness should be observed whenever parts are removed or replaced. Refill the unit after servicing.

Filters:

1 Remove the sump 66 and thoroughly clean both the filter gauze 64 and the filter magnets 65. Some particles may be expected in the sump, but if there is an excess of any sort of particles then the unit should be given further examination.

2 The relief valve filter 48 can be cleaned after the plug 52 has been removed and the filter withdrawn from the overdrive.

3 Replace the parts in the reverse order of removal, renewing seals and gaskets as required. Fill the gearbox and overdrive to the correct level shown on the gearbox dipstick.

Relief valves:

1 Remove the plug 52 and withdraw the parts from the overdrive.

2 The low pressure valve, parts 39 to 43, must be replaced as an assembly if the low pressure valve is defective.

3 Check the relief valve plunger 46 and its seating for damage or wear, and renew parts as required. Renew spring 45 if it is weak or appears damaged.

4 Refit the parts in the reverse order of dismantling, using new O-rings if the old ones are damaged.

Solenoid valve:

1 Remove the name plate 63 and its gasket 64. Carefully pull on the electrical lead to withdraw the solenoid valve assembly from the overdrive.

2 Dismantle the solenoid parts and renew the ball 59 and its seat if they are pitted and worn. The ball may be reseated by lightly tapping it onto its seat with a copper drift.

3 Refit the parts in the reverse order of removal, using new O-rings 53, 55 and 60 if the old ones are perished or damaged. In all cases a new gasket 62 should be fitted.

Pump and non-return valve:

1 Remove the sump 66 and filter assembly 64. Unscrew the plug 37 using a well-fitting peg spanner or special tool No. 18G.1118.

2 Remove the internal parts 31 to 36 and the plunger 42. Use a suitable drift to drive out the non-return valve seat 34 from the pump body 33, taking care not to damage the bore of the pump.

3 Check the parts for wear, scoring and pitting. Renew parts as required. The seat for the ball can be partially remade by lightly tapping the ball 35 onto its seat in 34.

4 Refit the non-return valve seat 34 to the pump body 33. Insert the plunger 42 back into the body of the overdrive, making sure that the flat face is towards the rear. Hold the plunger in position with special tool No. 18G.1117, as shown in **FIG 6:17**. Refit the remainder of the parts in the reverse order of removal.

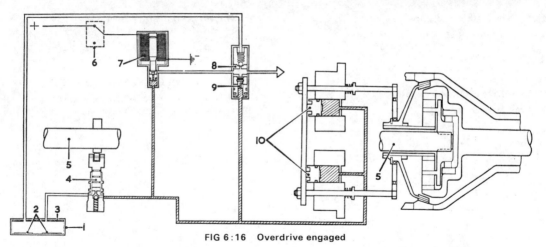

FIG 6:16 Overdrive engaged

Key to Fig 6:16   1 Sump   2 Magnet filters   3 Gauze filter   4 Pump   5 Third motion shaft (gearbox)   6 Control switch   7 Solenoid operating valve   8 Low pressure valve   9 Relief valve   10 Operating pistons

Hydraulic pressure:

1 Check that the oil in the gearbox and overdrive is at the correct level, and top up if required.

2 **Jack up the rear of the car and place it securely on stands so that the rear wheels are safely clear of the ground. Chock the front wheels to prevent the car from rolling in either direction.**

3 Remove the relief valve plug 52 and fit the adaptor 18G.251 E and pressure gauge 18G.251 in place of the plug, using the seal 51.

4 Start the engine and select top gear. Run the engine so that the speedometer reads 30 mile/hr (48 kilometre/hr). There should be no pressure reading on the gauge with the overdrive in direct. Select overdrive and the pressure gauge reading should then be 400 to 420 lb/sq in (28 to 29.5 kg/sq cm).

6:8 Removing and replacing

Overdrive:

1 Remove the engine and gearbox assembly from the car. Drain the oil from the gearbox and overdrive (through gearbox drain plug).

2 Take out the six securing bolts and remove the remote control assembly from the gearbox.

3 Remove the eight nuts securing the overdrive to the adaptor and withdraw the overdrive from the adaptor. The unit is refitted in the reverse order of removal. The splines in the planet carrier must be aligned with the splines in the unidirectional clutch, preferably using special tool No. 18G.185. Undue force must not be used in the operation, in case the splines have become misaligned.

Overdrive adaptor:

1 With the overdrive removed from the gearbox, slide off the overdrive operating cam from the gearbox output shaft and remove the cam locking ball from its pocket in the shaft.

2 Remove the pump cam circlip, preferably using special tool No. 18G.1004.

3 Withdraw the selector interlocking arm and plate assembly.

4 Take off the eight nuts and withdraw the adaptor from the gearbox.

The overdrive adaptor is refitted in the reverse order of removal.

6:9 Fault diagnosis

Only faults that can be dealt with by the owner are given in this section. If the fault cannot be cured by carrying out operations given in this chapter then the car should be taken to a suitable garage.

(a) All faults

1 Check that there is sufficient oil in the unit
2 Check through the electrical system

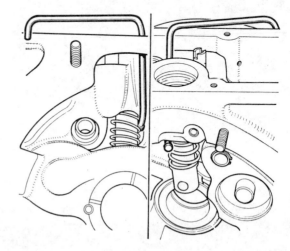

FIG 6:17 Using special tool **18G.1117** to retain the pump components

(b) Low hydraulic pressure

1 Pump non-return valve not seating correctly
2 Solenoid ball valve not seating correctly
3 Pump filter choked

(c) Overdrive does not engage

1 Check (a) and (b)

(d) Overdrive does not disengage

1 Check (a)
2 Sticking conical clutch
   Do not drive the car in reverse

(e) Overdrive slips when engaged

1 Check 1 in (a) also check 1 and 2 in (b)
2 Partially blocked sump or relief valve filter

CHAPTER 7

AUTOMATIC TRANSMISSION

7:1 Description

An automatic transmission unit may be fitted in place of the standard manually operated synchromesh gearbox. The automatic transmission system may be considered as two parts; a torque converter taking the place of the standard clutch, and an epicyclic gearbox. The epicyclic gearbox operates using oil pressure from an internal pump and contains controls which select the required gear ratio.

The combination of the two assemblies eliminates the need for the clutch pedal though a manual selector is still fitted to exercise a degree of control over the unit. The two units do eliminate the need for conventional gear-changing as the selector can be set to the desired position and the car can then be driven using only the brake and throttle controls.

Torque converter:

The torque converter provides a smooth transfer of power, using a fluid medium, combined with an infinitely variable torque multiplication between the ratios of 2.2:1 and 1:1. The unit is sealed and its position is shown in **FIG 7:1**.

The torque converter consists of three parts; an impeller connected to the engine, a turbine connected to the gearbox input shaft and a stator rotating between these two.

When the impeller is rotated by the engine, energy is transmitted to the fluid within the unit, and the energy is directed as a fluid flow towards the turbine. When the turbine is stationary the fluid is redirected back to the impeller via the stator. A rotary flow of fluid is set up in the unit and at the correct speed with the turbine stationary the driving effect of the fluid on the turbine gives a torque multiplication of up to 2.2:1.

As the turbine starts moving less energy is fed back to the impeller via the stator and the torque multiplication drops as the turbine speed increases, until the ratio is 1:1 when the turbine and impeller are moving at approximately the same speed.

Epicyclic gearbox:

The unit consists of an epicyclic gear train and the various ratios are selected by hydraulic pressure acting on an internal clutch and individual brake bands. The actual selection is carried out by a complex valve system which uses both the position of the throttle, through the down-shift cable assembly (26 in **FIG 7:1**), and a pressure proportional to the output speed, from the governor assembly 85, shown in **FIG 7:2**, as datum points. A manually operated selector mechanism (shown in **FIG 7:3**) overrides the valve assembly as required and also selects the direction of drive.

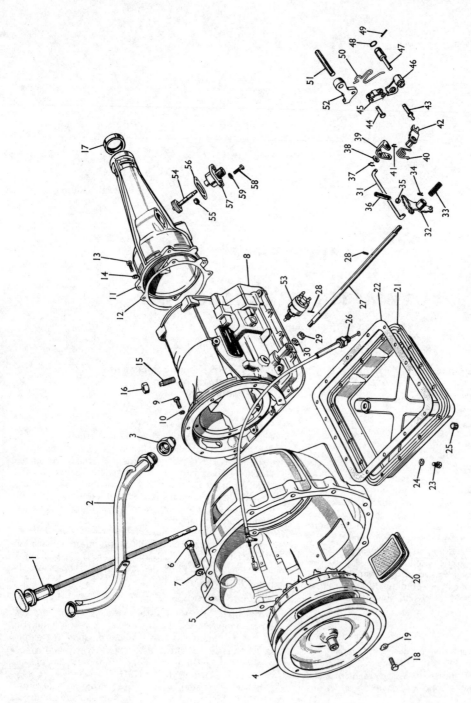

FIG 7:1 Automatic transmission external components

Key to Fig 7:1 1 Dipstick 2 Oil filler tube and gearbox breather 3 Adaptor for filler tube 4 Converter assembly 5 Converter housing 6 Bolt for housing 7 Spring washer for bolt 8 Case assembly 9 Bolt for case 10 Spring washer for bolt 11 Rear extension housing 12 Gasket for extension housing 13 Bolt for extension housing 14 Spring washer for bolt 15 Rear brake band adjusting screw 16 Locknut for adjusting screw 17 Rear oil seal 18 Bolt for converter 19 Lockwasher for bolt 20 Stoneguard 21 Oil pan assembly 22 Gasket for oil pan 23 Bolt for oil pan 24 Washer for bolt 25 Drain plug 26 Down-shift cable assembly 27 Manual control shaft 28 Roll-pin 29 Collar 30 Oil seal 31 Manual linkage rod 32 Manual detent lever 33 Toggle lever 34 Clip 35 Ball 36 Spring 37 Clip 38 Washer 39 Torsion lever 40 Spring 41 Clip 42 Toggle arm assembly 43 Toggle pin 44 Toggle linkpin 45 Toggle link 46 Toggle lever 47 Toggle lever 48 O-ring for pin 49 Slotted pin 50 Parking brake release spring 51 Parking brake anchor pin 52 Parking brake pawl 53 Inhibitor switch 54 Speedometer pinion 55 Oil seal for pinion 56 Gasket for pinion bush 57 Speedometer pinion bush 58 Bolt for pinion bush 59 Washer for bolt

86

Oil pressure to lubricate and operate the gearbox is produced by an oil pump mounted internally and driven by the input shaft of the gearbox. The oil pump parts are shown as items 37 in **FIG 7:2**.

An inhibitor switch 53 (see **FIG 7:1**) is fitted to the gearbox to prevent the engine from starting in any but the P and N positions. This is to prevent the car from moving away immediately the engine is started, which could be the cause of an accident in a confined space. The switch also controls the operation of the reverse light and ensures that this only functions when R is selected.

The details of the valve selector mechanism are not shown. An automatic transmission unit is a very complex piece of equipment requiring not only many special tools but a great deal of skill as well to service and dismantle it. **If the unit has to be dismantled or faults cannot be cured by operations given in this chapter the owner should take the car to a firm specializing in automatic transmissions.** Not all garages are equipped to deal with them.

7:2 Operation

The owner will be familiar with the various selections of the manual selector but he may still be unsure of other points.

Towing:

The car cannot be tow-started. However, provided that the unit is in a satisfactory condition and contains the correct amount of oil, the car may be towed for a distance of up to 40 miles (64 km) at a speed not exceeding 30 mile/hr (48 km/hr). If the unit is damaged or the car has to be towed further than the distance given then either the propeller shaft should be disconnected or the rear wheels raised clear off the ground.

Rocking:

If the car is stuck in mud or snowy conditions it will often be found helpful to rock the car between reverse and forward gear so that the car works its way out. Do not use excessive throttle as not only may it be harmful but it may cause wheelspin which will only dig the car in deeper.

Parking:

The P position is for parking and an internal pawl locks the gearbox to prevent the car from rolling. **The P position alone should not be relied on to hold the car and the handbrake should also always be applied.**

7:3 Routine maintenance

Cleanliness is always essential in any operations involving the automatic transmission.

The outside of the unit and especially the stone guard under the torque converter should always be kept clean and free from mud or stones. The unit gives off large amounts of heat compared to a conventional gearbox and if external cleanliness is neglected then the unit may overheat because of the added insulation, especially in climates where high ambient temperatures are common.

At regular intervals the level of the fluid in the unit should be checked. **Wipe the top of the dipstick and filler clean before removing the dipstick.** When the transmission is cold the reading on the dipstick will be $\frac{5}{16}$ inch (8 mm) low, though the unit should be checked warm and running. Stand the car on level ground, start the engine and allow it to idle for two minutes with the selector at P and the handbrake applied. Withdraw the dipstick, wipe it clean on a piece of non-fluffy clean cloth, reinsert it fully and then immediately withdraw it again. Note the quantity of oil in the unit. The difference between the MAX and MIN marks on the dipstick equals 1 Imperial pint (1.2 US pints, .57 litres). **Do not use old or contaminated fluid. Use the correct grade of automatic transmission fluid. Never use engine oil.** If the unit has been drained but not dismantled, anything up to 5 Imperial pints (6 US pints, 2.8 litres) may remain in the torque converter.

7:4 Adjustments

The correct procedures given must be adhered to and if the special tools required are not available then the car must be taken to a properly equipped service station for the adjustments to be carried out.

Draining:

The unit is drained through the drain plug 25 underneath the sump 21 of the unit. If the sump is removed an oil strainer will be found secured by four screws to the unit. Clean the filter thoroughly with clean fuel and renew it if the wire gauze is damaged. The sump and filter should also be examined for particles. A few particles are normal but if a lot of friction material or metallic particles are found then the cause must be investigated.

When refilling the unit anything up to 5 pints of fluid may be left in the torque converter. Do not use the old fluid if it is at all contaminated or dirty.

Inhibitor switch:

Chock the wheels before carrying out any adjustments on the inhibitor switch as the car may inadvertently be started in gear.

The starter switch should always function if terminals 1 and 3 are shorted together and the reverse light should stay on all the time that terminals 2 and 4 are shorted together.

1 Slacken the locknut securing the inhibitor switch, preferably with special tool No. 18G.679.
2 Connect a battery and test lamp between the terminals 1 and 3 (starter) and another test lamp battery across the terminals 2 and 4 (reverse light).
3 Unscrew the switch from the casing, select D, L1 or L2. Screw the switch back in until the test lamp for the reverse light illuminates. Carefully mark the position of the switch relative to the casing.
4 Carry on screwing the switch in until the test lamp for the starter illuminates. Mark this position on the casing and switch.
5 Unscrew the switch to the position midway between the positions marked in 3 and 4. Lock the switch in position by tightening the locknut. Remove the test lamps and reconnect the original wiring.
6 Check that the switch now operates correctly. If the reverse light comes on in any other position than R or the engine starts, other than in P or N, then the switch is defective and must be renewed.

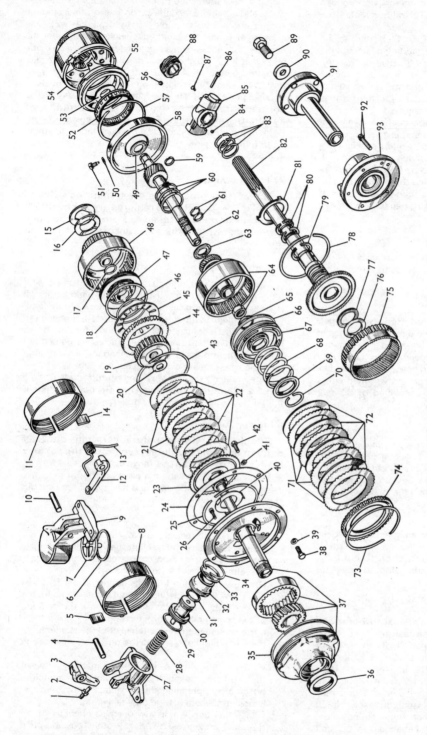

FIG 7:2   Automatic transmission internal components

Key to Fig 7:2   1 Front servo adjuster   2 Locknut for adjuster   3 Front servo lever   4 Pivot pin for lever   5 Strut for front servo   6 O-ring for rear servo piston   7 Rear servo piston   8 Front brake band   9 Rear servo body   10 Pivot pin for rear servo lever   11 Rear servo lever   12 Rear brake band   13 Rear servo spring   14 Strut for rear servo   15 Front clutch thrust washer   16 Front clutch thrust washer   17 O-ring   18 Front clutch sealing ring   19 Front clutch hub   20 Thrust washer   21 Front clutch plates—inner   22 Front clutch plates—outer   23 Input shaft assembly   24 Gasket for converter support   25 Circlip   26 Screw   27 Front servo body   28 Spring   29 Piston seal   30 Front servo piston   31 Piston seal   32 Front servo sleeve   33 Oil sealing ring   34 Circlip   35 O-ring   36 Front oil seal   37 Pump assembly   38 Bolt for pump   39 Washer for bolt   40 Input shaft thrust washer   41 Washer for bolt   42 Bolt for pump   43 Front clutch snap ring   44 Distance piece for front clutch   45 Spring for front clutch   46 Bearing ring for spring   47 Piston for front clutch   48 Front clutch housing   49 Needle thrust bearing   50 Lockwasher for bolt   51 Centre support bolt   52 One-way clutch assembly   53 Needle thrust bearing plate   54 Planet gear and rear drum assembly   55 One-way clutch outer race   56 Speedometer gear drive ball   57 Snap ring   58 Centre support   59 Output shaft oil sealing ring   60 Sealing rings—rear clutch   61 Oil sealing rings—outer   62 Forward sun gear   63 Needle thrust bearing   64 Front drum assembly   65 Rear clutch plates—outer   66 Rear clutch piston seal—inner   67 Rear clutch piston   68 Spring for rear clutch   69 Seat for spring   70 Snap ring   71 Needle thrust bearing   72 Rear clutch plates—inner   73 Snap ring   74 Pressure plate for rear clutch   75 Ring gear   76 Needle thrust bearing plate   77 Needle thrust bearing   78 Snap ring   79 Oil sealing ring   80 Oil sealing rings   81 Driven shaft   82 Driven shaft thrust washer   83 Oil sealing rings   84 Governor drive ball   85 Snap ring   86 Screw for governor valve   87 Screw for governor cover   88 Speedometer drive gear   89 Bolt for drive flange   90 Washer for bolt   91 Drive flange   92 Screw   93 Rear adaptor plate

88

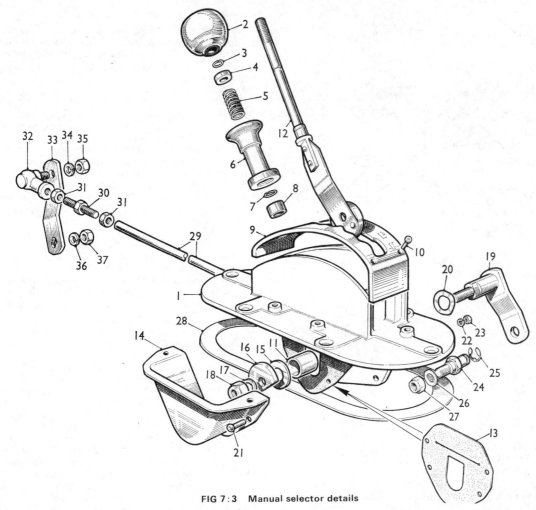

FIG 7:3   Manual selector details

Key to Fig 7:3   1 Housing   2 Lever knob   3 Spring ring   4 Washer   5 Spring   6 Stop pillar   7 Spring ring
8 Roller   9 Quadrant plate   10 Screw   11 Bearing   12 Selector lever   13 Seal   14 Cover   15 Washer (nylon)
16 Washer   17 Spring washer   18 Nut   19 Fulcrum pin assembly   20 Waved washer   21 Screw   22 Spring washer
23 Nut   24 Lever trunnion   25 'C' washer   26 Plain washer   27 Nut   28 Housing seal   29 Selector rod   30 Rod
adjuster   31 Locknut   32 Ball joint   33 Manual lever   34 Spring washer   35 Nut   36 Spring washer   37 Nut

Front brake band:

1 Drain the gearbox and remove the sump. Refer to **FIGS 7:2** and **7:4**. Slacken the locknut 2, move the front servo lever 3 outwards and place the spacer of tool No. 18G.678 between the servo adjusting screw 1 and the servo piston 30. Use the torque screwdriver 18G.681 to tighten the adjusting screw 1 to a torque of 10 lb in (.115 kgm).

2 Remove the special tools and tighten the locknut 2 to a torque load of 15 to 20 lb ft (2.07 to 2.77 kgm). Refit the sump, preferably using a new gasket 22, and refill the gearbox.

Rear brake band:

Refer to **FIG 7:5**. Slacken the locknut 2 and tighten the adjusting screw 1 to a torque of 10 lb ft (1.4 kgm). Slacken back the adjusting screw 1 one complete turn

and tighten the locknut 2 to a torque of 25 to 30 lb ft (3.46 to 4.15 kgm).

Manual selector:

Refer to **FIG 7:3**.

1 Remove the nut and washer 36 and 37 and free the lever 33 from the gearbox selector shaft.

2 Set the manual selector to the N position and also turn the gearbox shaft to the N position. The N position for the gearbox shaft is easily found by turning the shaft back (anticlockwise) as far as it will go and then turn it forwards by two clicks.

3 Slacken the locknuts 31 and rotate the adjuster 30 in the required direction until the lever 33 fits easily onto the flats of the gearbox selector shaft.

4 Tighten the locknuts 31 and replace the washer 36 and nut 37.

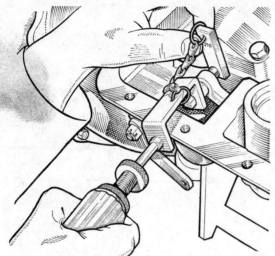

FIG 7:4 Adjusting the front brake band, using special tools No. 18G.678 and No. 18G.681

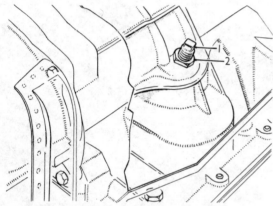

FIG 7:5 Rear brake band adjustment point

Key to Fig 7:5   1 Adjusting screw   2 Locknut

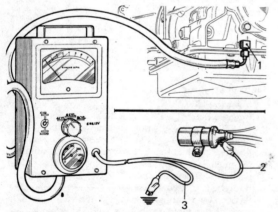

FIG 7:6 Attachments of service tool No. 18G.677.Z

Key to Fig 7:6   1 Pressure test connection   2 Red lead to coil connection   3 Black lead to earth

Downshift valve cable:

For all pressure checks service tool No. 18G.677Z should be used and connected to the car as shown in **FIG 7:6**. The tachometer fitted in the car may be used instead and a 0 to 200 lb/sq in pressure gauge connected to the gearbox.

1 The cable is shown as item 26 in **FIG 7:1**. Check that the carburetters are at their normal idling positions and that the crimped stop on the inner cable just contacts the abutment on the outer cable. Connect up the test equipment.

2 Start the engine and run it until it reaches its normal operating temperature. At idling speed the pressure gauge should read 55 to 65 lb/sq in.

3 Engage D, making sure that the handbrake is fully on and that the wheels are choked. Increase the engine speed to 1000 rev/min and check the pressure gauge reading which should be 90 to 100 lb/sq in.

4 If the pressure reading is low then adjust the cable so as to increase the effective length of the outer cable. Similarly if the pressure is high the effective length of the outer cable should be decreased.

5 Recheck the pressure reading after adjustment and when it is satisfactory, stop the engine, remove the test equipment and replace the blanking plug.

7:5 The governor assembly

If this is defective then the power unit must be removed from the car.

1 Hold the driving flange, preferably with special tool No. 18G.34A, and remove the nut and washer. Withdraw the driving flange. Take out the four bolts 13 and washers 14 then withdraw the rear housing 11.

2 The governor parts fitted to the output shaft are shown in **FIG 7:7**. Remove the circlips and speedometer drive gear as well as the speedometer drive ball 5. The governor 2 can then be slid off and its ball 1 removed.

3 The governor assembly parts are shown in **FIG 7:8**. Take off the coverplate 1 and free the counterweight 9 by taking out the screws 8. The rest of the parts can then be dismantled after removing the retainer 6.

4 Wash all the parts in clean fuel and examine them for scoring or any other damage. Renew parts as required. Make sure that the oilways are all clear.

5 Reassemble the parts in the reverse order of dismantling. Make sure that the oilways in the body 7 and counterweight 9 are aligned. Tighten the body to counterweight screws 8 to a torque of 4 to 5 lb ft and the cover screws 2 to a torque of 20 to 48 lb in (.23 to .552 kgm). **If these torque loads are not adhered to then the governor assembly may leak in service.**

6 Refit the governor to the gearbox, followed by the speedometer drive and circlips. Replace the rear housing 11 and refit the power unit to the car.

7:6 Stall speed test

This test provides a quick and accurate guide to the condition of the automatic transmission. The test, as the name implies, is carried out with the car stationary and the turbine stalled. All the power from the engine goes to setting up the flow of fluid in the torque converter and as the energy must be dispersed it is converted to heat. If the test is too prolonged then the unit will very rapidly overheat and damage may be caused. **For this reason a stall test should not last longer than 10 seconds and if the test has to be repeated, sufficient time must be given between tests to allow the unit to cool down.**

The engine condition will also partially affect the results of the test and if the engine is in poor condition the maximum rev/min will not be reached.

Carry out the test as follows:

1 Remove the blank plug and connect service tool 18G.677Z to the gearbox as shown in **FIG 7:6**.
2 Start the engine and run it until both the engine and automatic transmission are at their normal working temperatures. Check the fluid level in the automatic transmission.
3 Apply the handbrake and the footbrake. If there is any doubt the road wheels should also be chocked. Select L1 or R and press down the throttle pedal through the kick-down position. Leave the throttle open for a maximum of 10 seconds and note the maximum engine speed.
4 The correct speed should lie between 1800 to 2100 rev/min. Allow the transmission to cool down for a short period at idle speed, so as to spread the hot oil evenly. With the engine switched off remove the test equipment.

Other possible engine speeds and their causes are given below.

Under 1250 rev/min:

The stator of the torque converter is fitted with a one-way clutch and if this slips the torque multiplication effect cannot occur as the stator slips in the opposite direction to the turbine rotation (when it is moving). This causes a low maximum speed of the engine and the clutch slipping will probably be further confirmed by the car having poor acceleration from standstill and difficulty in driving away on steep hills.

1500 to 1800 rev/min:

A 300 rev/min drop from the normal stall speed is usually caused by the engine being in poor condition and not developing its full power.

1800 to 2100 rev/min:

This is the normal satisfactory stall speed.

If, however, the stall speed is normal but the maximum speeds in all gears, particularly top, are low and the automatic transmission also tends to overheat quickly and severely then it is likely that the one-way clutch on the stator has seized. This is not a common fault but one that should be borne in mind all the same.

Over 2700 rev/min:

This is caused by the gearbox slipping. If the fault is apparent in both L and R selections then it is most likely caused by low oil pressure or oil starvation. If the fault is only apparent at one selection then it is most likely caused by a brake band or clutch slipping.

7:7 Road test

This section will enable the owner to test the automatic transmission and diagnose faults, even though he may not be able to effect a cure himself. It is advisable to take

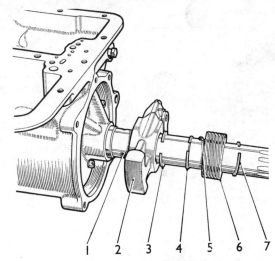

FIG 7:7 Governor fitted to output shaft

Key to Fig 7:7 1 Governor drive ball   2 Governor assembly   3 Governor circlip   4 Circlip   5 Speedometer drive ball   6 Speedometer drive gear   7 Circlip

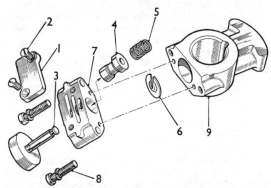

FIG 7:8 Governor components

Key to Fig 7:8 1 Coverplate   2 Screws for coverplate   3 Valve   4 Valve weight   5 Valve spring   6 Valve retainer   7 Valve body   8 Screws for valve body   9 Counterweight

an observer armed with note pad and pencils as it is difficult for the driver to make notes, check the speeds and drive safely.

Before driving away:

1 Start the engine and when the transmission has reached its normal working temperature check the fluid level.
2 Switch off the engine and attempt to start in all selector positions, also have the reverse light checked to see when it illuminates. The engine should only start in P and N selections, and the reverse light only operate in R selection. If there is a fault, check and adjust the inhibitor switch as described in **Section 7:4**.
3 Apply the handbrake and check that the car attempts to move in all the forward selections and that it attempts to move back in R.

Driving:

The upshifts and downshifts speeds for the various selections are given in the following table:

Driving conditions	Upshifts				Downshifts					
	1–2		2–3		3–2		3–1		2–1	
	mile/hr	kilo/hr	mile/hr	kilo/hr	mile/hr	kilo/hr	mile/hr	kilo/hr	mile/hr	kilo/hr
D selected:										
Minimum throttle	8–12	13–19	13–17	21–27						
Full throttle	22–29	35–46	41–48	65–78						
Forced throttle (kick-down)	30–37	48–60	57–62	91–100	50–57	80–91	20–26	32–41	20–26	32–41
L2 selected:										
Minimum throttle										
Full throttle									2–5	3–8
Forced throttle (kick-down)									20–26	32–41
L1 selected										
Minimum throttle									10–15	16–24

1 Select D and drive away from standing using the minimum throttle opening required. The change speeds should occur at the speeds given in the table, though they may be so smooth as to be unnoticeable. Stop the car.

2 Repeat the test 1 but this time using full throttle acceleration. **Do not press the throttle pedal through to the kick-down position.** The gear-changes should be definite and occur within the speed limits given in the table.

3 At 35 mile/hr (56 kilo/hr) steady speed press the throttle pedal down to the full throttle position, **not through the detent**, and check that the car accelerates away without changing down to second.

4 Drive at a steady 45 mile/hr (72 kilo/hr) and press the throttle pedal right through the detent position. The transmission should downshift to second gear and accelerate away.

5 Repeat the full kick-down of the throttle while driving at 15 mile/hr (24 kilo/hr) in third gear. The transmission should downshift to first gear. Stop the car.

6 Check the upshift speeds while accelerating away with the throttle pedal pressed through the detent.

7 Drive at a steady 40 mile/hr (64 kilo/hr), release the throttle and move the selector from D to L2. Check the downshifts and confirm that there is engine braking. Stop the car.

8 Leaving L2 selected, accelerate away using full throttle to a speed of 45 mile/hr (72 kilo/hr). Check the 1 to 2 upshift speed and also check for clutch slip or clutch squawk.

9 At a steady 25 mile/hr (40 kilo/hr) with L2 selected, release the throttle and select L1. Check the 2 to 1 downshift speed and confirm that there is engine braking. Stop the car.

10 Leaving L1 selected, use full throttle to accelerate up to 35 mile/hr (56 kilo/hr) and check that there is no upshift and that the clutch neither slips or squawks. Stop the car.

11 Select R and reverse using as much throttle as possible. There should be no clutch slip or squawk.

12 Find a suitable hill and stop the car facing downhill. Select P and release the brakes. Check that the car does not roll. **Apply the brakes before moving the** selector out of P. Turn the car around and repeat the test with the car facing uphill.

13 Park the car on a suitable level piece of ground and recheck the fluid level. If the fluid level has dropped, check the unit for fluid leaks. Some of the possible faults encountered in a road test, and their causes, are given in **Section 7:10**.

If the unit is known to be defective, or a fault is found, then the full road test should not be carried out because of the danger of causing further damage.

7:8 Removal and replacement

The automatic transmission cannot be removed from the engine while the power unit is still fitted to the car. Remove the power unit from the car as described in **Chapter 1, Section 1:2**.

1 Drain the fluid from the gearbox. **Discard the fluid if it is old, dirty or contaminated.**

2 Disconnect the throttle valve cable from the car-buretter linkage.

3 It is advisable to wash down the outside of the transmission to remove road dirt before separating the parts.

4 Remove the six sets of bolts and washers 9 and 10 shown in **FIG 7:1**, and withdraw the gearbox assembly from the converter housing 5.

Replace the gearbox in the reverse order of removal. Set both the manual selector and the throttle valve cable after the power unit has been refitted. Fill the automatic transmission with 5 Imperial pints (6 US pints, 2.8 litres) less than the system requires from dry. If the torque converter has been removed then practically all the required fluid should be poured straight into the unit. Run the engine and bring the fluid level up to at least the MIN mark on the dipstick as soon as possible. The unit should only be fully topped-up to the MAX mark when the fluid is at its normal operating temperature.

7:9 Torque converter

The symptoms that a defective torque converter is likely to produce have already been dealt with in **Section 7:7**. The unit is sealed and a defective torque converter must be renewed.

Removal:

1 Remove the power unit from the car and take off the gearbox, as described in **Section 7:9**.

2 Take out the bolts 6 and washers 7 and remove the converter housing 5 from the engine.

3 Note that the torque converter may still contain fluid. Free the tabwashers 19 and remove the four bolts 18 securing the torque converter 4 to the engine drive plate and remove the converter.

The unit is replaced in the reverse order of removal. Use new tabwashers 19. Care should be taken to centralize all the parts.

7:10 Fault diagnosis

This section does not cover all faults, only the more common ones that can be cured by the owner. If the fault persists after the adjustments or repairs recommended have been carried out then the car should be taken to a specialist firm dealing with automatic transmissions.

(a) Transmission overheats

1 Stoneguard on converter housing blocked
2 Unit covered with dirt
3 Stator one-way clutch locked in engaged condition (rare fault)
4 Rear brake band incorrectly adjusted
5 Front brake band incorrectly adjusted

(b) Noisy operation

1 Incorrect fluid level
2 Incorrectly adjusted manual control rod
3 Incorrectly adjusted throttle valve cable
4 Defective oil pump (screech or whine increasing with engine speed)

(c) Incorrect shift speeds

1 Check 2 and 3 in (b)
2 Governor valve sticking or incorrectly assembled

(d) No drive

1 Check 1, 2 and 3 in (b), 4 in (b) will also produce this defect but it is beyond the scope of the owner to check.

(e) Poor acceleration

1 Check 3, 4 and 5 in (a)
2 Stator one-way clutch slipping

(f) Jumps in engagement

1 Check 4 and 5 in (a) and also check 2 and 3 in (b)
2 Incorrect engine idling speed

(g) Car does not hold in P position

1 Check 2 in (b)

(h) Incorrect stall speed

1 Check 3, 4 and 5 in (a); also check (b) and (c). Check 2 in (e)

(i) Reverse slips or chatters

1 Check 4 in (a) and 2 in (b)

NOTES

CHAPTER 8

PROPELLER SHAFT, REAR AXLE AND REAR SUSPENSION

8:1 The propeller shaft

The details of the propeller shaft are shown in **FIG 8:1**. The propeller shaft transmits the drive from the output shaft of the gearbox to the differential in the rear axle. As the rear suspension moves there will be angular differences between the rear axle and the gearbox so a universal joint is fitted at either end of the propeller shaft to allow for these angular differences. The distance between the rear axle and gearbox will also vary slightly and the propeller shaft is fitted with a splined sliding joint to allow for these differences.

Routine maintenance is confined to greasing the three grease nipples on the shaft at regular intervals. Some shafts are fitted with sealed universal joints which are not fitted with grease nipples and there will be only one grease nipple on these propeller shafts.

When lubricating the propeller shaft, take the opportunity to examine the shaft for wear. A 'clonk' from the transmission on taking up drive, especially if the direction of travel is reversed, can be caused by a worn propeller shaft. Rotate the shaft backwards and forwards smartly by hand. Excessive play can be caused by either worn universal joints or a worn sliding joint. Lift the shaft upwards. Excessive movement indicates worn thrust faces.

Removal and replacement:

1 Securely and safely raise one rear road wheel from contact with the ground. Mark across the flanges of the rear universal joint and differential driving flange and similarly mark across the flanges of the front universal joint and gearbox driving flange, to ensure that the propeller shaft will be replaced in the original position.

2 Remove the nuts 15 and bolts 14 securing the front end of the shaft to the gearbox. The shaft can be rotated to a convenient working position and then locked in place by engaging a gear. Lower the front end of the propeller shaft and disconnect the rear end by removing the nuts bolts and washers 14, 15 and 16. The propeller shaft can now be removed from the car.

The propeller shaft is replaced in the reverse order of removal, making sure that it is refitted in its original position and that the mating faces of all four flanges are perfectly clean.

Universal joints:

If the joint is worn, all the parts supplied in a service kit should be renewed. **Do not renew individual components.**

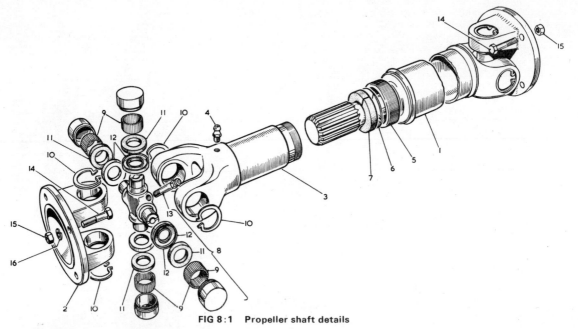

FIG 8:1   Propeller shaft details

Key to Fig 8:1   1 Shaft assembly   2 Flange yoke   3 Sleeve assembly—yoke   4 Grease nipple   5 Dust cap   6 Washer
—steel   7 Washer—cork   8 Journal assembly   9 Needle bearing assembly   10 Circlip   11 Gasket   12 Retainer
13 Grease nipple   14 Bolt   15 Nut   16 Spring washer

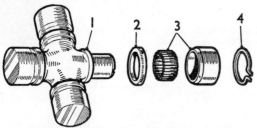

FIG 8:2   Sealed type universal joint details

Key to Fig 8:2   1 Journal spider   2 Rubber seal
3 Needle rollers and bearing   4 Circlip

FIG 8:3   Removing a bearing cup from the shaft

The parts of a sealed universal joint are shown in **FIG 8:2**. These joints may be treated very similarly to the other type but the seal 2 fits onto the bearing cup 3 and the reservoir holes in the spider 1 and the bearing cups must be well packed with fresh grease on reassembly.

1 Remove all four circlips 10, using circlip pliers or a pair of long-nosed pliers. Rust, dirt and enamel may have to be cleaned out of the bores and if the circlips are still stiff to remove, the bearing cups should be lightly tapped inwards to relieve the pressure on the circlip.

2 Hold the shaft as shown in **FIG 8:3** and by hammering as shown the bearing cup should start to emerge. Carry on tapping until sufficient of the cup has emerged to allow it to be withdrawn, using either the fingers or a pair of grips. Turn the shaft over and remove the opposite bearing in a similar manner. If the bearings will not move under this treatment support the arms of the flange yoke 2 on two blocks of wood or lead, and tap the bearings out in a similar manner to the one shown in **FIG 8:4**. As a last resort the bearings will have to be driven out using a small-diameter drift but the seals will be damaged by this method.

3 Manoeuvre the shaft off the spider and lay the exposed spider trunnions onto two blocks of lead or wood, as shown in **FIG 8:4**. Remove both the remaining bearings by this method.

4 Check the bearing holes in the flange yoke and the shaft. The bearing cups must be a light drive fit through them. After long service and inadequate lubrication the bearing holes may wear oval. The flange yokes 2 can be renewed but if the bearing holes in the shaft are worn then a new propeller shaft assembly must be fitted. **Do not attempt to cut off and then weld**

new parts to the propeller shaft otherwise both the alignment and balance will be lost.

5 If the seals on the spider are damaged, then remove them and fit new seals using a well-fitting tubular drift. A thin coat of shellac or jointing compound should be applied to the base of the retainers 12 to secure them in position.

6 Smear the inside of the bearing cups with grease and refit all the needle rollers. The right number of rollers exactly fills the cup. On sealed units pack both the spider reservoir holes and the bearings with grease, leaving no air pockets.

7 Refit the spider to the flange yoke 2 so that the grease nipple hole faces away from the flange yoke. Fit the bearing cup assemblies into place, either by driving them in using a soft-nosed drift or else by using a mandrel as shown in **FIG 8:5**. The mandrel or drift must be $\frac{1}{32}$ inch (.8 mm) smaller in diameter than the bearing cup. Refit the assembly to the propeller shaft and similarly refit the remaining two bearing assemblies. **Great care must be taken when refitting the bearing cups not to displace or snap a needle roller.** If the bearing cup stops moving check for the cause immediately and do not use excessive force as a needle roller may be displaced.

8 Secure the bearings in place with the circlips 10. Wipe away surplus grease and check that the bearings move freely. If the bearings are stiff, tap lightly on the arms to relieve the pressure on the bearings.

Sliding joint:

A single universal joint does not transmit a perfect drive when there is angular displacement and there are angular variations throughout the cycle. Two universal joints correctly assembled will cancel out the angular variations between them, and for this reason it is vital that the shaft is reassembled so that the universal joints are in the correct plane. If the joints are fitted out of phase then the angular variations will add to each other, causing vibration.

1 There should be two arrows stamped and aligned on the shaft 1 and sleeve assembly 3. If these arrows are not present, indelibly mark the parts so that they will be reassembled in the correct angular relationship with the arms parallel to each other.

2 Unscrew the metal dust cap 5 and separate the two halves of the shaft.

3 Clean off all dirt and old grease. Examine both sets of splines for wear or indentation and renew the complete shaft assembly if the splines are defective. Renew the cork washer 7 if it is damaged or stays compressed.

4 Align the arrows and slide the sleeve assembly 3 into place after packing it with grease. Secure the parts by tightening the dust cap 5 hand tight only. Wipe off surplus grease.

8:2 The rear axle

The rear axle is of the semi-floating type fitted with hypoid bevel gears. The standard axle is made to take disc-type wheels but by fitting a different set of axle shafts and hubs wire wheels can be fitted. The hub and axle shaft assemblies can be removed with the axle still fitted to the car. The details of the rear axle are shown in **FIG 8:6**.

FIG 8:4   Tapping bearing cup from the yoke

FIG 8:5   Refitting a bearing cup

The rear axle is different from the three-quarter-floating type of rear axle fitted to earlier models not covered by this manual.

Lubrication:

The combined filler and level plug is shown as item 34 and the drain plug is item 35. At regular intervals the filler plug 34 should be removed and the oil level topped up to the bottom of the hole. Use an oil gun to fill the unit and leave the filler plug out until any surplus oil has drained out. **Overfilling can cause oil to leak past the oil seals and contaminate the brakes.** When checking the level also check that the breather is clear as a blocked breather can cause an internal pressure rise which will force oil past the oil seals.

Only hypoid oil must be used and though several brands are recommended their additives may not all be compatible, so it is advisable to top up with the same brand of oil as is already in the unit. If the make is not known it is best to drain out all the oil and refill afresh with one brand.

Draining:

It is best to perform this operation when the oil is hot after a long run as it will flow more easily. Remove the drain and filler plugs and leave to drain for as long as possible as, even when hot, the oil is very viscid. **Do not**

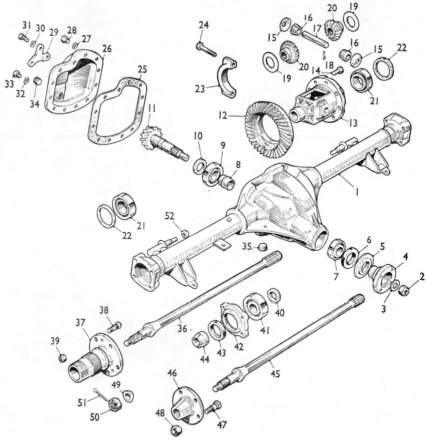

FIG 8:6 Semi-floating rear axle details

Key to Fig 8:6   1 Case assembly   2 Nut   3 Plain washer   4 Universal joint flange   5 Dust cover   6 Oil seal   7 Outer pinion bearing   8 Bearing spacer   9 Inner pinion bearing   10 Pinion thrust washer   11 Pinion   12 Crown wheel   13 Differential cage   14 Bolt   15 Thrust washer   16 Differential pinions   17 Pinion pin   18 Roll-pin   19 Thrust washer   20 Differential wheels   21 Differential bearing   22 Distance collars   23 Bearing cap   24 Bolt   25 Joint washer   26 Axle case cover   27 Spring washer   28 Setscrews   29 Compensating lever bracket   30 Spring washer   33 Setscrew   34 Filler and level plug   35 Drain plug   36 Axle shaft (Wire wheels only)   37 Driving flange (Wire wheels only)   38 Stud (Wire wheels only)   39 Nut (Wire wheels only)   40 Bearing spacer   41 Bearing   42 Bearing hub cap   43 Oil seal   44 Oil seal collar   45 Axle shaft (Disc wheels only)   46 Driving flange (Disc wheels only)   47 Wheel stud (Disc wheels only)   48 Wheel nut (Disc wheels only)   49 Axle shaft collar   50 Axle shaft nut   51 Splitpin

flush through the unit with any solvents. Solvents will attack the oil seals or some solvent will remain to dilute the fresh oil.

Differential:

If the unit is defective or causes any trouble then the car should be taken to a suitable garage. The gears must be set and meshed using special equipment and the bearings must be preloaded to the correct figures. The differential cannot be removed from the axle casing without using a special tool (18G.131C) which spreads the aperture by just the right amount to allow the differential assembly to come free.

If the differential is defective the garage may well recommend fitting an exchange unit, and though this is expensive it will probably be cheaper than the fitting of new parts and all the ensuing work.

Pinion oil seal:

If this leaks it can be renewed without taking the axle out of the car.

1 Carefully mark and disconnect the rear end of the propeller shaft (see **Section 8:1**).
2 Prevent the flange 4 from rotating, preferably with special tool No. 18G.34A and remove the nut 2 and washer 3. Either use an extractor or tap the flange forwards with a hide-faced hammer to remove it from the pinion 11.
3 Remove the dust seal 5 and prise out the old oil seal 6.
4 Press a new oil seal into place so that its lips face inwards. Lubricate the seal and replace the parts in the reverse order of dismantling, taking care not to damage the oil seal and tightening the nut 2 to a torque of 135 to 145 lb ft (19 to 20 kgm).

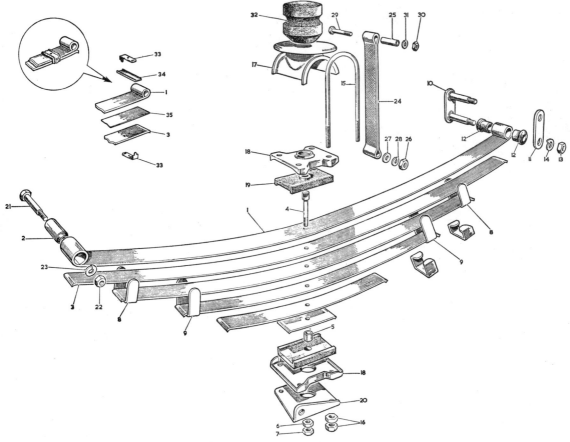

FIG 8:7   Rear suspension details

Key to Fig 8:7   1 Main leaf assembly   2 Bush (silentbloc)   3 Second leaf   4 Bolt   5 Distance piece   6 Nut
7 Locknut   8 Clip—third leaf   9 Clip—fourth leaf   10 Plate—shackle and pins   11 Plate—shackle   12 Bush—rubber
13 Nut   14 Washer   15 U-bolt   16 Nut   17 Pedestal   18 Plate—spring locating   19 Pad—spring seating
20 Righthand damper bracket   21 Bolt   22 Nut   23 Washer   24 Rebound strap   25 Distance tube   26 Nut
27 Washer—plain   28 Washer—spring   29 Bolt   30 Nut   31 Washer—spring   32 Bump rubber   33 Clip—second leaf
34 Pad—second leaf clip   35 Interleaf spring

Hub and axle shaft:

1 Jack up the rear of the car and place it on blocks under the springs as near to the axle as possible. Drain out the oil.

2 Remove the road wheel. Release the handbrake and if need be slacken the rear brake adjuster right off. Remove the brake drum.

3 Extract the splitpin 51 and remove the nut 50 and axle shaft collar 49. Remove the hub 46 or 37. On wire wheel hubs 37 use either extractor 18G.363 (12 TPI) or extractor 18G.1032 (8 TPI), depending on the number of threads to the inch on the hub. Standard hubs may be removed using either extractor No. 18G.304 or No. 18G.304Z which operates on hydraulic principles.

4 Drain the brake hydraulic system, disconnect the brake flexible hose and disconnect the handbrake (see **Chapter 11**). Remove the brake backplate.

5 Take out the bolts and remove the oil seal housing 42, oil seal 43 and oil seal collar 44. Attach adaptor 18G.284D between the axle shaft and the impulse extractor 18G.284. Slide the moving weight of the special tool smartly outwards along the slide so that it impacts on the handle and draws out the axle shaft. Press the bearing 41 from the shaft.

Thoroughly wash all the parts in clean fuel and examine them for wear. Renew any worn or damaged parts, paying particular attention to the oil seal 43. If the splines on the hub 37 are worn then the hub should be renewed. **The hubs 37 are handed and must be replaced on the correct side of the car.** The hubs on the lefthand side of the car have righthanded threads (unscrew anticlockwise) and the hubs on the righthand side of the car have lefthanded threads (unscrew clockwise).

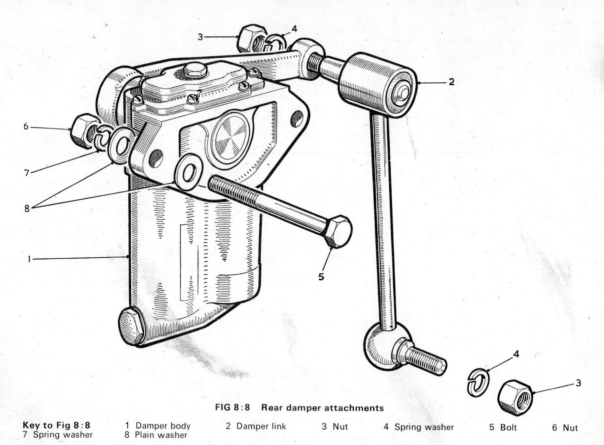

FIG 8:8   Rear damper attachments

Refit the parts in the reverse order of removal. Drive the axle shaft into position, preferably using special tool No. 18G.1067. Refit the oil seal 43 so that its lips face into the axle. After the parts have been refitted and replaced the brake system must be adjusted and bled as described in **Chapter 11**.

8:3 Rear suspension

The details of the rear suspension are shown in **FIG 8:7**. The dampers are not shown and will be dealt with separately in the next section.

Spring removal:

1 Jack up the rear of the car and place it securely onto stands or blocks. Remove the appropriate rear road wheel. Support the axle with a jack.
2 Disconnect the damper link from the axle by removing the nut securing it to the damper bracket 20.
3 Free the rebound strap 24 from the spindle on the axle by removing the nut 26 (item 52 in **FIG 8:6**) and the washers 27 and 28. If the rebound strap is defective it can be removed from the car by taking out the bolt 29 and nut 30.
4 Remove the nuts 13, washers 14 and outer shackle plate 11. Make sure that the axle is just supported without applying excess pressure to the spring and evenly drift out the shackle plate 10.

5 Undo the nut 22, remove the washer 23 and carefully drift out the bolt 21.
6 Remove the four sets of nuts 16 from the U-bolts 15 and collect the damper bracket 20, spring locating plate 18 and lower pad 19 as they come free. Tap out the U-bolts 15 and remove the spring from the car, collecting the upper spring locating plate 18, pad 19 and pedestal 17.

Dismantling the spring-

1 Press out the bush 2 from the front eye of the main leaf, and if not already done remove the rubber bushes 12 from the rear eye.
2 Straighten the ears on all the clips 8, 9 and 33.
3 Clamp the spring in a vice, with the top and bottom leaves flat against the jaws of the vice, so that the bolt 4 and nuts 6 and 7 are clear of the jaws. Remove the nuts 6 and 7 and carefully tap out the bolt 4.
4 Support the spring and slowly slacken off the vice until the tension is relieved and the leaves can be lifted out of the vice.

Reassembling the spring:

Use a wire brush to clean off all dirt and rust from the leaves. Examine each leaf in turn. The most likely place for cracks or fractures is around the centre bolt hole. Renew any defective leaves, being careful to quote the car number when ordering, and cover the surfaces of the leaves with Shell Ensis 260 fluid.

Discard the old clips and their rivets and fit new ones on reassembly. Renew the interleaf strips 35 if they are worn or damaged.

1 Press a new Silentbloc bush 2 into the front eye of the top leaf, making sure that the bush is fitted with equal gap on either side of it.
2 Rivet new clips to the third and fourth leaves.
3 Make up a mandrel of the same diameter as the bolt 4 with a long tapered nose. Fit the leaves to the mandrel in the correct order and with the interleaf strips in place. The longest half of each leaf faces towards the rear of the car.
4 Compress the spring between the jaws of a vice, keeping the leaf sides aligned, and remove the mandrel when the spring is clamped. Replace the mandrel with the centre bolt 4 and distance piece 5. Secure the assembly with the nut 6 and locknut 7.
5 Tap the leaves until they are in full alignment, replace the clip 33 and use a hammer to tap down the ears on all the clips. Make sure that the clips clamp the spring as tightly as possible, as loose clips can be a source of rattles.

Spring replacement:

1 Fit the spring into position and secure it at the front by pressing through the bolt 21. Renew the rubber bushes 12 if required. Lift the rear of the spring up into place and secure it by refitting the shackle plate and pins 10.
2 Refit the parts 17, 18, 19 and 20, securing them by passing through the U-bolts 15 and fitting the nuts 16. Tighten the nuts 16. The axle can be raised or lowered on the jack to give room for refitting the parts.
3 Refit the road wheels and lower the car back onto the ground. The shackle plate 11, washers 14 and nuts 15 can now be refitted and fully tightened at the rear of the spring, while the washer 23 and nut 22 can be replaced and tightened on the front of the spring. These nuts are tightened after the suspension has been loaded to ensure that the bushes are in their working positions.
4 Reconnect the rebound strap and damper link.

8:4 The dampers

All the dampers, including those fitted to the front suspension, are of the Armstrong double-acting type. **Though these are not of sealed construction they cannot be dismantled or adjusted and a defective damper must be renewed.** Before renewing a damper check that the defect is not temporary due to a low fluid level. A rear damper is shown in **FIG 8:8**.

Maintenance

Regularly check the outside of the damper for fluid leaks. A rough test on the damper condition can be given by bouncing each corner of the car up and down. There should be uniform movement and if the resistance is erratic or the car moves freely then the damper should be removed for further examination.

Before checking the fluid level, wipe the top of the damper clean otherwise dirt will fall into the unit when the filler plug is removed. The filler plug is always the one at the top of the unit and the rear damper fillers are

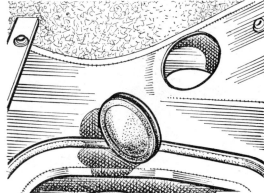

FIG 8:9 Rubber grommet removed from the rear floor panel to give access to the rear damper filler plug

accessible after removing the rubber grommet shown in **FIG 8:9**. Remove the filler plug and top up to the bottom of the filler plug hole. **Do not overfill the unit as it requires an air space above the fluid for its correct operation.** The correct fluid to use is Armstrong Super (Thin) Shock Absorber Fluid No. 624. Provided that the car is not going to be used in low temperature climates then any mineral oil to specification SAE.20W can be used.

Removal:

Refer to **FIG 8:8**. Securely jack up the rear of the car and remove the road wheel. Take off the nut 3 and washer 4 securing the damper link 2 to the bracket on the suspension. Remove the nuts 6, washers 7 and 8, and bolts 5 to free the damper from the car. **Always try to keep the damper vertical when it is free from the car,** otherwise the air above the fluid may work its way into the assembly and cause erratic operation of the damper.

Refit the damper in the reverse order of removal. If the damper has lain on its side or been in storage for some time, the air should be bled out of the working parts. Mount the damper vertically in the padded jaws of a vice and operate its arm through several short strokes about the midpoint. Gradually increase the length of the stroke until several full strokes are given. Check the fluid level before refitting the damper.

Testing:

The dampers may be roughly checked as described under maintenance. If the damper appears defective, remove it and mount it vertically in the padded jaws of a vice. Bleed the damper and check the fluid level as just previously described.

Move the arm through the full range of its movement. There should be a moderate and constant resistance to motion in both directions. If the resistance is still erratic or the lever moves freely, again check the fluid level, as it may have been so low that air is still in the operating mechanism. If the fluid level is still correct then the damper is defective and must be renewed. Excessive resistance to movement indicates an internal defect and renewal is again the only cure.

Check the outside of the unit for leaks. **The operating lever must not be removed.** Leaks around the top can

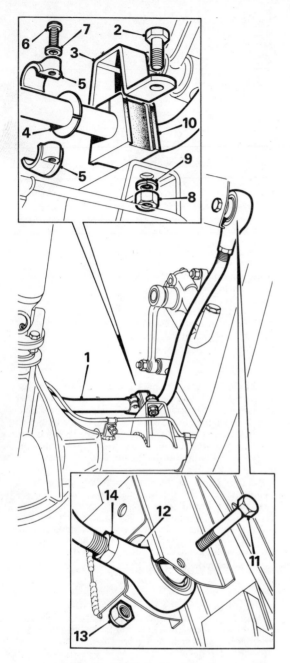

FIG 8:10 Anti-roll bar fitted to later models

be cured by removing the top cover and fitting a new gasket. Leaks around the bottom valve plug may possibly be cured by gently tightening the plug.

8:5 Removing and replacing the rear axle

1 Jack up the rear of the car and place it securely on chassis stands or blocks so that the rear wheels are clear of the ground.
2 Mark the flanges and disconnect the rear end of the propeller shaft from the rear axle.
3 Disconnect the damper link and rebound strap from the rear axle.
4 Disconnect the handbrake cables from the rear brakes and remove the self-locking nut and washer securing the handbrake balance lever to the pivot on the axle casing. Secure the handbrake cables out of the way. Drain the brake hydraulic system and disconnect the flexible hose connecting the chassis pipe system to the pipes on the rear axle. For further details see **Chapter 11**.
5 Release the exhaust pipe from the manifold connections and its securing clips. Lower and remove the exhaust pipe assembly.
6 Either support the axle with jacks or else use a trolley jack under the differential unit. Remove the nuts securing the road spring to the car. Drive out the bolt from the front spring eye and then remove the plates and shackle pins from the rear spring attachment. Lower the axle supports until the road wheels are on the ground and then wheel out the complete assembly from under the car.
7 The road wheels and springs can now be removed.

The rear axle is refitted in the reverse order of removal. Once the assembly has been refitted the brakes must be bled and adjusted (see **Chapter 11**).

8:6 Anti-roll bar

From car No. 410002 an anti-roll bar has been fitted (see **FIG 8:10**).

Removing:

Remove the battery. Raise and support the body just forward of the spring front shackle. Disconnect the anti-roll bar from the body brackets. Remove the bearing straps 3, bearing rubbers 10 and anti-roll bar. If a new anti-roll bar is being fitted remove the locators 5. Renew any worn parts.

Refit in the reverse order fitting the locators 5 so that their inner faces are $9\frac{5}{16}$ inch (237 mm) from the centre line of the car.

8:7 Fault diagnosis

(a) Noisy axle

1 Insufficient or incorrect lubricant
2 Worn bearings
3 Worn gears
4 Damaged or broken off gear teeth
5 Contact of crownwheel and pinion not correctly adjusted

Key to Fig 8:10   1 Anti-roll bar assembly   2 Screw
3 Bearing strap   4 Plastic washer   5 Locator   6 Screw
7 Spring washer   8 Nut   9 Spring washer   10 Bearing
rubber   11 Bolt   12 End fitting   13 Nut   14 Locknut

(b) Excessive backlash

1 Worn gear, bearings or bearing housings
2 Worn axle shaft splines
3 Worn universal joints
4 Loose or broken wheel studs. Worn wire wheel hub splines

(c) Oil leakage

1 Defective oil seal in hub
2 Defective pinion shaft seal
3 Defective seals on universal joint spiders
4 Blocked breather
5 Overfilled rear axle

(d) Vibration

1 Propeller shaft out of balance
2 Worn universal joints
3 Propeller shaft incorrectly assembled (universal joints out of phase)

(e) Rattles

1 Rubber bushes in damper links worn out
2 Dampers loose
3 U-bolts loose
4 Loose spring clips
5 Worn bushes in spring eyes and shackles
6 Broken spring leaves

(f) Settling

1 Weak or broken spring leaves
2 Badly worn shackle pins and bushes
3 Loose spring anchorages

(g) Axle knock

1 Badly worn splines on axle shaft or in differential gear
2 Badly worn splines on wire wheel hubs
3 Worn universal joints

NOTES

CHAPTER 9

FRONT SUSPENSION AND HUBS

9:1 Description

The front wheels are independently mounted onto a separate subframe that can be removed from the car. This subframe also supports the brackets for the steering rack unit, dealt with in the next chapter. Unequal length wishbones are used to mount the front wheels, the upper shorter wishbone being the arm for the front damper. The load is taken by a coil spring fitted between each lower wishbone and a spigot on the subframe. The subframe assembly removed from the car is shown in **FIG 9:1**.

A vertical swivel pin is fitted between the outer ends of the lower wishbone and damper arm so that the suspension is free to move in the vertical plane. A swivel axle assembly is free to rotate about the swivel pin to provide the front wheel steering. This swivel carries the stub axle about which the front wheel hub rotates on two opposed taper bearings. The swivel also supports the brake caliper and the dust shield for the disc brake. The disc for the brake is bolted to the front hub.

An anti-roll bar interconnects the lower wishbones so as to prevent body roll on fast cornering and also improve road holding.

The hubs shown in **FIG 9:1** are the type fitted for wire wheels. This type of hub is handed and must be fitted to the correct side of the car. The details of the front suspension are shown in **FIG 9:2** and the standard hub for disc wheels is shown as item 64 in that figure.

9:2 Routine maintenance

1 At regular intervals grease the upper and lower bearings on the swivel axle assembly. The two grease nipples on each suspension are shown as items 52 in **FIG 9:2**. Wipe the nipples clean, pump through fresh grease and wipe away any exuded grease. It is best to grease these with the front of the car jacked up and the weight taken off the suspension units.

2 At the same time as the swivel lubricators are greased the bottom swivel pin on each suspension should also be greased. The grease nipple for the righthand side is shown as item 61 in **FIG 9:2** and the grease nipple for the lefthand side is similarly situated.

3 At longer intervals the front hub bearings should be greased. Grease may be packed around the outside of the outer taper bearing, but it is better to remove the hub, clean out the old grease and refit the hub so that both bearings are packed with fresh grease.

9:3 Front hubs and discs

Securely jack up the front of the car so that both front wheels are lifted clear off the ground. Grasp the tyre with the hands at the twelve o'clock and six o'clock positions and try to rock the top of the tyre in and out. There should be practically no play at all. If there is play it will be caused by either worn vertical swivel pin (kingpin) bushes, worn

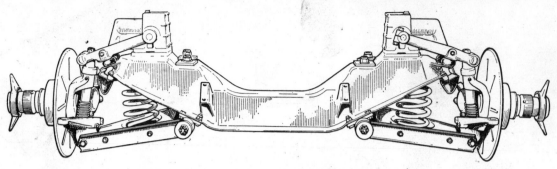

FIG 9:1 Front suspension assembly removed from the car

or badly adjusted wheel bearings, or badly worn suspension bushes. Worn suspension bushes can often be checked by the small relative movements between the parts of the suspension.

Repeat the rocking test but grasping the tyre at the three o'clock and nine o'clock positions. Do not confuse movement due to steering with play. If the play has now gone then the earlier play was most likely due to worn swivel pin bushes. If the play is still present then it is probably caused by worn or badly adjusted hub bearings.

Spin the road wheel. It should rotate freely and smoothly without making any grinding noises. The disc brake will make some noise so take care not to confuse this with the noise from a defective bearing. Noise from the bearings means that the bearings have either run dry or are worn out.

Tightening the hub nut may cure excessive play but it is far safer to remove the hub and check the bearings visually. A defective bearing is liable to seize and lock the wheel causing possible loss of control.

Removal:

The hubs 67 for wire wheels are handed and must be refitted to the correct side of the car.

A sectioned view of the standard hub is shown in **FIG 9:3**.

1 Securely jack up the front of the car with the handbrake applied. Remove the appropriate road wheel.
2 Remove the two bolts securing the brake caliper to the swivel axle 49. Slide the caliper off the disc and support it safely out of the way so that the flexible hose is not strained or kinked.
3 Remove the grease container, 76 with disc wheels and 77 with wire wheels. Extract the splitpin and remove the nut 75 and D-washer 74. On wire wheel hubs there is an access hole through the splines in the hub for the splitpin.
4 Withdraw the hub assembly from the stub axle, taking care not to drop the inner race of the outer bearing or shim 72 as they come free. If the hub is difficult to remove special tool No. 18G.363 can be used for wire wheel hubs and special tool No. 18G.304 with adaptors 18G.304B or 18G.304J can be used for disc wheel hubs.
5 Remove the inner race of the outer bearing and shims 72. Remove the oil seal 69 and its collar 68 as well as the inner race of the inner bearing from the inside of the hub. Take out the spacer 71 but leave the outer races of

the bearings in the hub unless they are defective. If the outer races are defective they can be drifted out.

Use newspaper and old rags to remove most of the old grease. The remainder of the grease should be washed off in clean paraffin (kerosene) or fuel. Wash the bearings separately in clean fuel and dry them with non-fluffy rags or an airline. Examine the bearings and renew them, complete with outer races, if they show any signs of wear, corrosion or other damage. Renew the oil seal 69 if this is damaged or worn.

Replacement:

1 Pack both the inner bearing races with grease and refit the parts to the hub. The outer tracks should also be lightly smeared with grease and the space between the oil seal and bearing filled with grease. **Do not fill the space between the bearings in the hub or the grease retainer cap 77 with grease.**
2 Refit the hub assembly to the stub axle, omitting the shims 72. Replace the D-washer 74 and nut 75. Spin the hub and tighten the nut 75 until the bearings start to bind. This is to ensure that the outer races of the bearings are pulled fully into position. Remove the nut, washer and inner race of the outer bearing.
3 Fit sufficient shims 72 to give the correct end float of .002 to .004 inch (.05 to .10 mm). Replace the bearing race, washer, nut and torque load the nut before fitting a new splitpin.
4 Replace the brake caliper, refit the road wheel and lower the car back to the ground.

Adjustment:

1 Spin the hub and tighten the nut 75 until the bearings just bind when no shims 72 are fitted.
2 Remove the nut, washer and inner race. Fit sufficient shims to ensure that the end float of the hub is excessive and replace the remainder of the parts. Tighten the nut while spinning the hub.
3 Mount a DTI (Dial Test Indicator) onto the brake caliper, or axle swivel, and measure the amount of end float there is on the hub. Remove the amount of shims required to reduce the end float to the correct limits of .002 to .004 inch (.05 to .10 mm) and again replace the parts.
4 Tighten the nut 75 to a torque load of 40 to 70 lb ft (5.3 to 9.6 kgm) and fit a new splitpin to lock the nut. The limits for torque loading the nut are sufficiently wide to ensure that a slot on the nut 75 and the splitpin

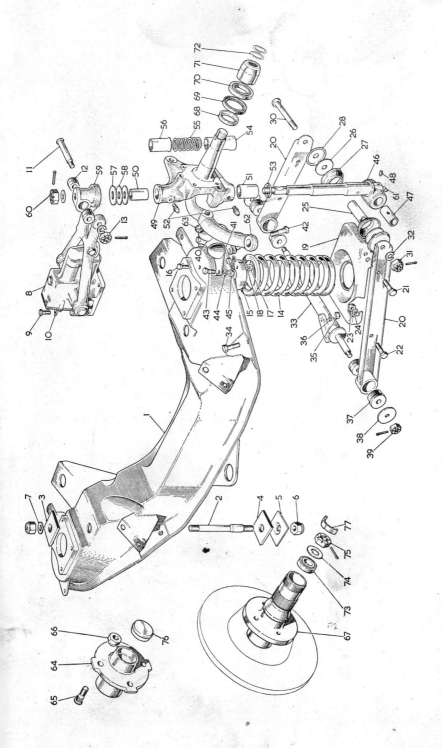

FIG 9:2   Front suspension details

Key to Fig 9:2   1 Subframe   2 Stud   3 Upper mounting pad (rubber)   4 Lower mounting pad (rubber)   5 Clamp plate   6 Nut   7 Washer   8 Damper
9 Bolt   10 Washer—spring   11 Fulcrum pin   12 Bearing—link   13 Nut   14 Coil spring   15 Spigot   16 Bolt   17 Nut   18 Washer   19 Spring pan assembly
20 Wishbone assembly—bottom   21 Bolt   22 Bolt   23 Nut   24 Washer   25 Distance tube   26 Thrust washer   27 Seal   28 Support   29 Nut   30 Bolt
31 Nut   32 Washer   33 Wishbone pivot   34 Bolt   35 Nut   36 Washer   37 Bush   38 Washer   39 Nut   40 Rebound buffer   50 Bush
41 Distance piece   42 Bolt   43 Bolt   44 Washer   45 Nut   46 Swivel pin   47 Bush   48 Grubscrew   49 Swivel axle assembly   50 Bush
51 Bush   52 Grease nipple   53 Ring (cork)   54 Dust excluder tube   55 Spring—dust excluder   56 Dust excluder tube   57 Thrust washer   58 Floating
thrust washer   59 Trunnion*   60 Nut   61 Grease nipple   62 Steering lever   63 Bolt   64 Hub assembly   65 Wheel stud   66 Nut—wheel stud   67 Hub
assembly   68 Collar   69 Oil seal   70 Bearing for hub—inner   71 Spacer   72 Shim   73 Bearing for hub—outer   74 Washer   75 Nut   76 Cup—
grease retaining   77 Cup—grease retaining

*The illustration shows the trunnion the wrong way round. The fulcrum pin 11 when fitted should be on the outboard side of the swivel pin 46

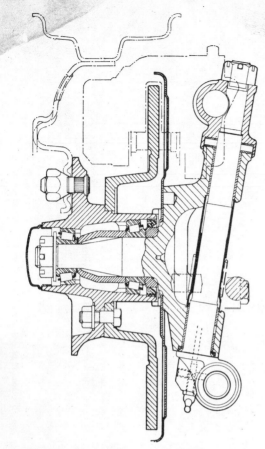

FIG 9:3 Sectioned view of swivel axle and hub assembly

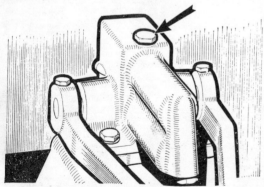

FIG 9:4 Front damper filler point

hole in the stub axle can be aligned. Refit the grease retainer.

9:4 The road springs

To remove a spring, special tool No. 18G.693 must be used to take the pressure of the spring. The tool must also be used in refitting the spring. The tool fits onto the lower wishbones and by turning the handle the pressure of the spring 14 on the spring pan 19 is relieved. When the spring pressure has been taken, disconnect the anti-roll bar link and remove the four sets of nuts 23, washers 24 and bolts 21 and 22 so as to free the spring pan 19 from the wishbones 20. Carefully unscrew the spring compressor and remove the spring pan and spring when the pressure has been released.

Refit the spring in the reverse order of removal, but inspect the spring before refitting it. It should correspond dimensionally to the details given in Technical Data and be free from any hairline cracks or other defects. Renew a defective spring or one that is shorter than the free length given. Be sure, when ordering, to quote the car type and number.

9:5 The dampers

The dampers form the top wishbone of the suspension unit. They are of the same type, Armstrong double-acting, as are fitted to the rear suspension and apart from 'Removal' and **FIG 8:8** of the section they are maintained and tested in exactly the same manner as the rear dampers (see **Chapter 8, Section 8:4**).

The filler point for the front damper is shown in **FIG 9:4** and it is most easily accessible after removing the road wheel. Clean the top of the damper and top up to the bottom of the filler hole using Armstrong Super (Thin) Shock Absorber Fluid No. 624, or any mineral-based SAE.20W oil. Note that only the recommended Armstrong Fluid is suitable for cold climates.

Removal:

1 Raise the front of the car and place it securely onto chassis stands. Remove the road wheel and use a jack under the lower wishbones to take the weight of the suspension.

2 Remove the splitpin, take off the nut and washer 13 and carefully remove the pivot bolt 11, shown in **FIG 9:2**. Either support the swivel axle and hub assembly, or else use a piece of wire from the body to hold them upright and prevent the brake flexible hose from being strained.

3 Remove the four bolts 9 and washers 10 securing the damper 8 to the subframe 1 and lift the damper free from the car. **Keep the damper vertical at all times to ensure that air does not move into the operating mechanism.**

Refit the damper in the reverse order of removal, after testing and filling it. **Do not remove the damper arms from the damper** as they are accurately set in relation to the internal parts and if incorrectly reassembled will prevent the damper from operating through its full stroke, with consequent damage when the suspension moves up and down.

9:6 The anti-roll bar

The details and attachments of the anti-roll bar are shown in **FIG 9:5**. It should be noted that the attachments on GT models vary slightly from those fitted to standard models.

No routine maintenance is required on the anti-roll bar but it is advisable to check the condition of the rubber bearings 5 and the Silentbloc bushes 2 at periodic intervals as these can wear or distort without being noticed until they are so worn that the anti-roll bar rattles.

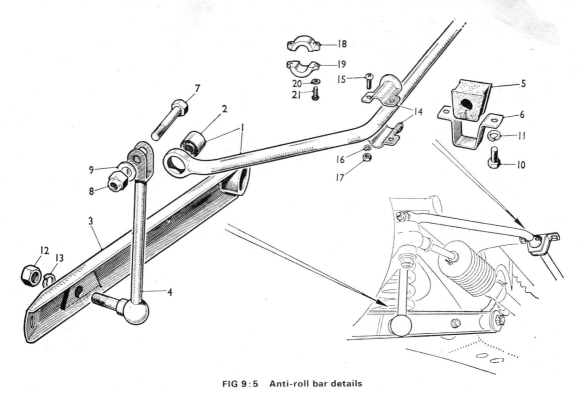

FIG 9:5 Anti-roll bar details

No parts need to be removed from the suspension
when working on the anti-roll bar but there will be more
access room if the front of the car is securely raised on
ramps or stands. There is torsion in the anti-roll bar when
the two suspensions are not at the same height, so ensure
that both suspensions are at equal height before freeing
any attachments. To ensure symmetry the stops 14,
deleted from car No. 410002, or 18 and 19, are fitted so
that their inner faces are $11\frac{1}{16}$ inch (28.1 cm) from the
centre line of the anti-roll bar. From car No. 410002 the
locators 18 and 19 are fitted on the inboard side of the
bushes 5 and their inboard faces should be $9\frac{5}{16}$ inch
(237 mm) from the centre of the roll bar.

9:7 Ball joints

Ball joints are fitted to the steering where two arms
have to swivel about one another while pressure is
accurately transmitted from one arm to the other without
any excess play. One arm is fitted with a very accurately
machined taper and into this taper is seated the taper of a
ball-headed pin. The head of the pin rotates in a socket
attached to the other arm allowing movement without
free play. Two mating tapers are pulled tightly together by
a nut working on the bottom threaded portion of the
ball-headed pin.

The ball joints are so designed that the only method of
separating the two arms is to remove the nut and free
the mating tapers, and after a short period of use the two

tapers become very tightly locked. The apparently
obvious method of freeing the tapers is to hammer on the
threaded end of the pin and drive the tapers apart. **This
method must not be used as even if a spare nut is
fitted to the threads damage will still be caused to
the ball joint.**

Extractors are made for separating ball joints (special
tool No. 18G.1063) but these may not be readily available.
In this case firmly pull or lever the two arms apart, leaving
the ball joint securing nut on the last few threads if there
is any danger of the arms flying apart and hitting pro-
jections or other parts. Lay a block of metal on one side
of the tapered eye and hammer on the side of the tapered
eye opposite to the metal block. This will jar but not
distort the tapered eye and the tapers will quickly part.

9:8 The swivel axles
Removal and dismantling:

1 Securely jack up the front of the car and remove the
   wheel hub and brake caliper as described in **Section
   9:3**.
2 Remove the bolts 63 and free the steering arm 62 from
   the swivel axle 49. If care is taken the ball joint from the
   tie rod need not be disconnected and the steering arm
   can be tied out of the way. Remove the securing bolts
   and take off the disc brake dust shield.
3 Remove the coil spring 14 and the spring pan 19 as
   described in **Section 9:4**.

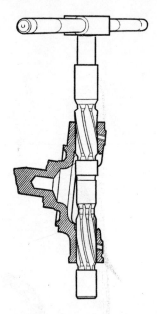

FIG 9:6 Line-reaming the swivel axle bushes using reamer 18G.597

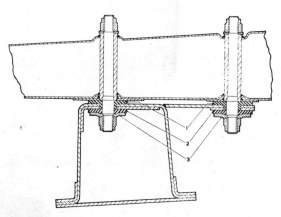

FIG 9:7 Sectioned view of subframe attachments to body sidemember

Key to Fig 9:7 1 Upper mounting pad   2 Lower mounting pad   3 Clamp plate

4 Extract the splitpin, remove the nut 13 and carefully drive out the bolt 11. Free the damper arm from the top trunnion 59. If the arm is tight, slacken the clamp bolt and nut at the centre of the damper arms.

5 Extract the splitpin, remove the nut 31 and washer 32 and carefully drive out the bolt 30 to free the swivel pin 46 from the lower wishbones, collecting the seals and washers 26, 27 and 28. Extract the splitpin and remove the nut 60 to free the trunnion 59 from the swivel pin 46. Remove the dust excluder tubes 54 and 56 with their spring 55.

6 The wishbones 20 can be removed from the suspension after extracting the splitpins and undoing the nuts 39.

Renewing the bushes:

When the parts have been dismantled all the pivot bolts and bushes should be examined. Renew the pivot bolts if they are worn. Similarly renew all rubber bushes and seals if they are worn, damaged or even suspect.

If the old lower swivel bush 47 is worn it should be pressed or drifted out. Thoroughly clean out the bore in the swivel pin 46 and make sure that the grease ways are clear. Squarely press in the new bush so that the slit is towards the outside face of the boss and the grease channels are aligned. Ream the new bush to a diameter of .7495 to .7505 inch (19.02 to 19.05 mm) leaving the best possible surface finish.

Wear on the bushes 50 and 51 is most noticeable when the road wheel is fitted and rocked by the method described in the first paragraph of **Section 9:3**. Special tool No. 18G.596 is designed for removing and replacing the bushes but if this is not obtainable the old bushes can be carefully drifted out and new ones pressed into place. Press out the old bushes from the bottom of the axle and press in the new bushes similarly from the bottom of the axle. Press the upper bush 50 in with the open end of its oil groove upwards and the hole in the bush aligned with the groove in the axle, and press it in until the top is flush with the top of the swivel axle. Refit the lower bush 51 in a similar manner and press it in until its bottom edge is flush with the counterbore on the underside of the swivel axle.

When new bushes 50 and 51 have been fitted they must be line reamed to size. The bore for the upper bush 50 must be .7815 to .7820 inch (19.83 to 19.86 mm) and the bore for the bottom bush 51 .9075 to .9080 inch (23.03 to 23.06 mm). In both cases the surface finish must be the best possible. **The bushes must be line-reamed and must not be reamed separately.** If the bushes are reamed separately they will not be truly concentric and the steering will be stiff. Reamer No. 18G.597 should be used to ream the bushes as shown in **FIG 9:6**.

Reassembly:

The parts are replaced in the reverse order of removal, noting the following points:

1 The nuts 13, 31 and 39 should be left slightly slack until just before replacing the coil spring 14. Raise the suspension to its normal working position and support it there while the nuts are fully tightened and split-pinned. This ensures that all the bushes are working about their normal static position and are not stressed when the car is stationary.

2 Selectively fit thrust washers 58 so that there is a maximum of .002 inch (.05 mm) end float on the trunnion 59 when it is fitted and locked to the swivel pin 46 by the bolt 11. Thrust washers are available in the following sizes:

    .052 to .057 (1.32 to 1.44 mm)
    .058 to .063 inch (1.47 to 1.60 mm)
    .064 to .069 inch (1.62 to 1.75 mm)

When the end float has been established, check that the swivel pin rotates freely in the trunnion.

3 Check that end float on the swivel pin lower fulcrum assembly is .008 to .013 inch (.20 to .32 mm). If the limits are exceeded new thrust washers 26 or a new distance tube 25 will have to be fitted.

4 Check the full and free movement of the suspension throughout its range before refitting the coil spring. Raise and lower the suspension as far as possible with a jack to check the freedom of movement after the coil spring has been refitted. Make sure that the swivel axle also rotates freely through its range of movement.

9:9 Removing and replacing the front suspension unit

1 Jack up the front of the car and place it securely onto chassis stands or blocks. Do not support the car under the front suspension subframe or suspension wishbones. Remove the front road wheels.
2 Remove the steering rack unit (see **Chapter 10**).
3 Disconnect the anti-roll bar links from the spring pans (see **Section 9:6**).
4 Drain the hydraulic fluid from the brake system. Disconnect the metal brake pipes from the clips on the subframe and disconnect the flexible hoses (see **Chapter 11**).
5 Support the subframe with a trolley jack under its centre point. Remove the nuts and washers 6 and 7 from the tops of the support studs 2. Lower the assembly on the trolley jack and draw it out on the jack from underneath the car.
6 Remove the nuts 6, clamp plates 5, rubber mounting pads 4 and studs 2 from underneath the unit. Lift off the rubber mounting pads 3 from on top of the unit.

If the assembly requires dismantling then the various parts can be removed in exactly the same manner as if the assembly was still fitted to the car.

Replace the assembly in the reverse order of removal, renewing the rubber pads 3 and 4 if they are worn, perished or defective in any way. A sectioned view of the subframe mounting to the body sidemember is shown in **FIG 9:7**.

9:10 Suspension geometry

The safe and correct handling characteristics of the car as well as tyre life are dependent on the correct suspension geometry. Badly worn suspension bushes can alter the steering geometry but normally it does not alter unless there is accident damage to the suspension. Specialized equipment is necessary to check the geometry and angles so the task should be entrusted to a suitably equipped garage.

The terms 'Camber' and 'Castor' are explained in the Glossary of Terms at the end of this manual. KPI (Steering axis inclination) is the angle an imaginary line drawn through the centre line of the swivel pin makes with the vertical when viewed from the front of the car.

9:11 Fault diagnosis

(a) Wheel wobble

1 Worn hub bearings
2 Broken or weak front springs
3 Uneven tyre wear
4 Worn suspension linkage
5 Loose wheel attachments

(b) Bottoming of suspension

1 Check 2 in (a)
2 Rebound rubbers worn or missing
3 Dampers not working

(c) Heavy steering

1 Neglected swivel pin lubrication
2 Incorrect suspension geometry
3 Incorrectly reamed swivel pin bushes

(d) Excessive tyre wear

1 Check 4 in (a); 3 in (b) and 2 in (c)

(e) Rattles

1 Check 2 in (a)
2 Pivot lubrication neglected, rubber bushes worn
3 Damper mountings loose
4 Anti-roll bar mountings loose or bearings worn
5 Defective packing pieces between subframe and body

(f) Excessive 'rolling'

1 Check 2 in (a) and 3 in (b)
2 Anti-roll bar broken, mountings loose or bearings badly worn

NOTES

CHAPTER 10

THE STEERING SYSTEM

10:1 Description

Rack-and-pinion type steering is fitted as standard to all models. This type of unit gives more precise control and lighter control forces than most other designs of steering box. The pinion is directly attached to the steering column and so rotates with the steering wheel. As the pinion rotates it drives a toothed rack which moves from side to side in the housing. The outer ends of the rack are connected to the steering arms on the swivel axles by tie rods. Ball joints are fitted at either end of the tie rods to allow for the suspension movement. This type of design avoids the need for drag links or idler boxes and the moving parts are kept to a minimum.

The steering column on all models is fitted with a universal joint so that the rake of the steering wheel is set to a comfortable angle and the height of the steering wheel is in relation to the body line of the car. All steering columns are also fitted with multi-operation switches for the various electrical circuits (see **Chapter 12**). On some models a combined ignition and steering lock switch is also fitted to the steering column.

Originally fitted to cars for the USA, a different type of steering column may be used on later cars. This is an energy absorbing type which collapses in a controlled manner under heavy impact. This is a safety precaution to prevent the driver being impaled on the column in the event of a head-on crash.

10:2 Routine maintenance

Only the earliest cars were fitted with a grease nipple on the steering unit housing and the outer ball joints are of the sealed-for-life type with no grease nipples fitted. If lubrication of the steering unit is required only Extreme Pressure SAE.90 oil may be used.

At regular intervals the front of the car should be raised on stands or ramps and all the rubber sealing bellows inspected. If these are damaged or torn then dirt will enter the components causing rapid wear. At the same time check the steering for full and free movement with the front wheels off the ground.

10:3 Track (front wheel alignment)

The track should be checked after the steering rack unit has been removed and replaced. It should also be checked after the car has been run heavily into the kerb or any solid obstruction to the front wheels. The front tyres wearing unevenly and leaving a feathered edge to one side of the tread is an indication that the track is out.

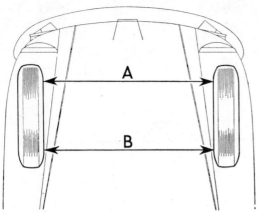

FIG 10:1 Checking the front wheel alignment

The track can be quickly checked by a garage using special equipment and gauges, but if care is taken it can also be checked and adjusted by the owner without any particular special equipment except accurate measuring equipment.

Drive the car onto a suitable level piece of ground, preferably a good concrete floor. Turn the front wheels into the straight-ahead position and push the car forwards for a few yards to settle the bearings and suspension units. Leave the car unladen. Measure, as accurately as possible, the distance between the inside of the wheel rims at the front of the wheels and at wheel centre height, shown as dimension A in FIG 10:1. Mark the position with chalk, push the car forwards so that the wheels turn exactly half a revolution and again measure the distance between the same points on the wheel rims, giving the dimension B. The dimension B must also be measured at wheel centre height and if the car is pushed too far, so that the chalked marks on the rim are above wheel centre height, then the car must be pushed forward further until the wheels turn a full revolution to bring the marks to the correct position. **Do not push the car backwards if the correct position is overshot.**

The difference between the two dimensions A and B represents the front wheel alignment. A should be less than B by $\frac{1}{16}$ to $\frac{3}{32}$ inch (1.6 to 2.4 mm) for the correct alignment. As the difference in the dimensions is the vital figure, a solid trammel of reasonable fixed length can be used. One pointer of the trammel is held against one wheel rim and, instead of measuring the total length, the gaps between the other pointer and wheel rim are measured. The difference between the gaps then gives the actual tracking.

Adjustment:

Refer to **FIG 10:2**, which shows the details of the steering system for all models covered by this Section.

1 Slacken the locknuts 36 and smaller outer bellows clips 29 on both the tie rods 22.
2 Use a wrench or Stilson to rotate both the tie rods 22, in the required direction and by equal amounts, to

adjust the front wheel alignment. **Both the tie rods are fitted with righthand threads.** If the tie rods are not equally adjusted then the steering wheel will not be in the straight-ahead position when the front wheels are.
3 Hold the tie rods and tighten the locknuts. Recheck the front wheel alignment as described earlier. Only if a very small adjustment is required may one track rod only be adjusted.
4 As a precaution, measure the amount of threads visible behind each locknut and check that they are the same on each tie rod. If they are different and the steering wheel is straight-ahead at the same time as the front wheels, then there is either damage to a suspension or the rack unit is not central.
5 Make sure that both outer ball joints are in the same plane and tighten the clips securing the bellows.

PART I THE STANDARD STEERING SYSTEM

The details are shown in FIG 10:2.

10:4 Removing and replacing the steering unit

1 Jack up the front of the car and place it securely onto stands or blocks. Remove the front road wheels.
2 Remove the nuts 35. **The washers 34 are no longer fitted and no washers must be fitted on reassembly.** Disconnect the ball joints 30 from the steering arms on the suspension (see **Chapter 9, Section 9:7**).
3 On righthand drive models turn the steering to the full left lock and on lefthand drive models turn the steering to the full right lock. Remove the nut and pinch bolt which secure the steering column universal joint 40 to the splines on the pinion 13.
4 Remove the nuts, bolts and washers 37, 38 and 39 securing the assembly to the suspension subframe and withdraw the unit downwards.

The steering unit is replaced in the reverse order of removal, noting the following points:

1 The front wheels and the steering wheel must be all in the straight-ahead position when the universal joint is reconnected.
2 The steering column and pinion centre lines must intersect at the centre point of the universal joint spider. Shims may be fitted between the steering rack housing and the suspension subframe to achieve this. Refit the steering unit, leaving its attachment nuts and bolts slack. If there are gaps between the housing and the subframe when the universal joint is reconnected then these gaps must be filled with shims.

10:5 Servicing the steering unit

Dismantling:

1 Mount the unit in the padded jaws of a vice. Take out the bolts 20 and remove the pinion end cover 18 and its gasket 19. Remove the end cover with a suitable container held underneath it to catch the oil as it drains out of the unit.
2 Remove the setscrews 11 and take off the cover 10 and shims 8 and gasket 9. Withdraw the damper pad 5, spring 7 and damper pad 6. The pinion 13, complete with bearing 15, washer 17 and nut 16, can then be

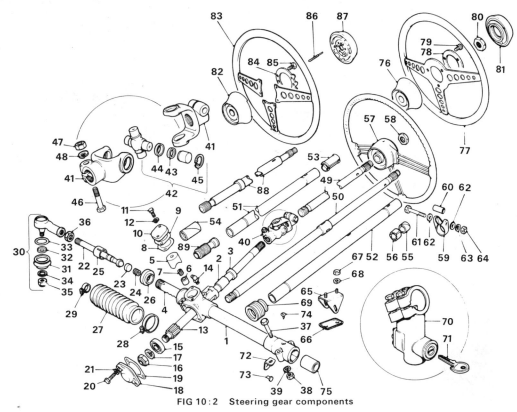

FIG 10 : 2   Steering gear components

Key to Fig 10 : 2   1 Housing assembly   2 Pinion bush   3 Oil seal   4 Rack   5 Rack support yoke   6 Damper pad
7 Damper pad spring   8 Coverplate shim   9 Coverplate joint   10 Yoke coverplate   11 Coverplate bolt   12 Spring washer
13 Pinion   14 Pinion shaft lubricator   15 Pinion ballbearing   16 Pinion bearing nut   17 Spring washer   18 End cover
19 End cover joint   20 End cover bolt   21 Spring washer   22 Tie rod   23 Ball seat   24 Ball seat thrust spring
25 Ball housing   26 Ball housing locknut   27 Rack seal   28 Inner seal clip   29 Outer seal clip   30 Ball socket assembly
31 Boot   32 Boot retainer   33 Garter spring   34 Boot   35 Ballpin nut   36 Locknut   37 Track to bracket bolt
38 Nut   39 Spring washer   40 Steering column universal joint   41 Yoke   42 Journal assembly   43 Journal joint
44 Joint retainer   45 Circlip   46 Universal joint bolt   47 Nut   48 Spring washer   49 Inner column assembly
50 Inner column assembly (righthand drive)   51 Column outer tube   52 Column outer tube (righthand drive)
53 Upper column bearing   54 Lower column bearing   55 Felt bush (when steering lock is fitted)   56 Retaining clip (when
steering lock is fitted)   57 Steering wheel   58 Steering wheel nut   59 Steering column clamp   60 Distance piece   61 Clamp bolt
62 Plain washer   63 Spring washer   64 Nut   65 Steering column lower bracket   66 Bracket blanking plate
67 Bracket to body nut   68 Spring washer   69 Column to bulkhead draught excluder   70 Steering and ignition lock assembly
71 Key   72 Crossmember shim bracket   73 Rivet   74 Bush retaining screw   75 Rack housing bush
GHN5/GHD5 car only   76 Wheel hub   77 Steering wheel   78 Lock ring   79 Screw   80 Nut   81 Motif and housing
82 Wheel hub   83 Steering wheel   84 Lock ring   85 Bolt   86 Horn push contact   87 Horn push   88 Steering column*
89 Sealing tube*
* From car No. 258001

withdrawn from the housing. If required, remove the
nut 16 and press the bearing 15 from the pinion 13.

3 Slacken the locknuts 36 and remove the outer ball
joints 30. Both the ball joints are fitted with righthand
threads. Remove the locknuts 36 from the tie rods 22.
Slacken all four clips 28 and 29 and slide the bellows
27 off along the tie rods.

4 Prise out the tabs on the locknuts 26 from their
recesses. Unscrew the housings 25, after slackening
the locknuts 26, and free the tie rods 22, ball seats 23
and springs 24 from the ends of the rack 4.

5 Unscrew the locknuts 26 and discard them. Remove
the rack 4 from the pinion end of the housing to
prevent the rack teeth from damaging the bush 75.

6 The bush 75 can be left in place unless it is worn or
damaged. Remove the screw 74 and use a long drift
to drive the bush out of the housing.

Inspection:

1 Wash all the parts in clean paraffin (kerosene) or fuel.
These are the most easily obtainable solvents but
provided all seals and rubber parts are removed and
cleaned separately in fuel any grease removing solvent
may be used on the metal parts. It is advisable to wash
the outside parts first, discard the dirty solvent, and
then wash completely in clean solvent.

2 Check the rubber bellows 27 and 31 for splits or
damage and renew them if they are defective or have
weak spots chafed on them. **If the bellows 21 have
been split for some time then it is best to renew
the ball joint assembly as dirt will have entered
it and caused wear.** The ball joint assemblies 30
cannot be dismantled and therefore must be renewed
if at all defective.

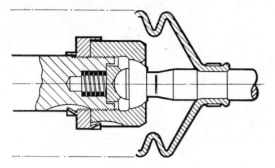

FIG 10:3 Sectioned view of inner ball joint assembly

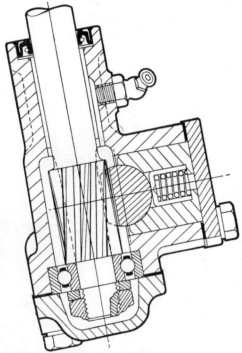

FIG 10:4 Sectioned view of rack and pinion housing

3 Check the teeth on the rack 4 and pinion 13. There must be no wear, pitting or roughness and the parts will have to be renewed if the teeth are defective.

4 Renew the tie rods 22, housings 25 and ball seats 23 if any of these parts show wear or pitting.

Reassembly:

1 If the bush 75 has been removed press a new bush in until it is flush with the end of the housing. The type of bush to be used is of sintered iron with a steel outer shell and injected with rubber. The earlier lead/bronze type of bush is not to be used. Drill to a depth of .24 inch (6.3 mm) through the retaining screw hole using a $\frac{7}{64}$ inch (2.78 mm) drill so as to provide a hole in the bush for the retaining screw 74. Use jointing compound under the head of the screw.

2 Refit the rack 4 from the pinion housing end. Screw on new locknuts 26 and replace the springs 24, ball seats 23, tie rods 22 and ball housings 25 lubricating liberally with SAE.90 oil. Tighten the housings to the rack until all end play in the tie rods is taken up. Adjust the housings 25 until the tie rods articulate when a torque load of 32 to 52 lb inch (.359 to .594 kgm) is applied. Tighten the locknuts 26 to a torque load of 33 to 37 lb ft (4.60 to 5.63 kgm) and lock them by drifting their lips into the recesses in the rack and housings. A sectioned view of the inner ball joint assembly is shown in **FIG 10:3**.

3 Refit the pinion and its end cover in the reverse order of removal, using a little jointing compound on the gasket. If the nut 16 has been removed from the pinion it should be peened into the slot in the pinion after reassembly. Replace the damper pad 6, yoke 5 and cover 10, omitting the spring 7 and shims 8. Tighten the setscrews 11 until it is just possible to rotate the pinion by moving the rack. Use feeler gauges to measure the gap between the cover and the housing. Make up a shim pack 8 equal in thickness to the dimension measured plus .0005 to .003 inch (.013 to .076 mm) to allow for the correct end float. Remove the cover and parts. Replace them, fitting the spring 7 and shim pack 8, using a little jointing compound on the gasket 9. A sectioned view of the assembly is shown in **FIG 10:4**.

4 Replace the remainder of the parts in the reverse order of removal. Before tightening the clips on the last bellows 27, stand the unit on end and pour $\frac{1}{3}$ Imperial pint (.4 US pint, .2 litre) of Extreme Pressure SAE.90 oil into it. Make sure that the tie rods are of equal length by measuring and equalizing the number of threads visible behind the locknuts 36.

10:6 The steering wheel

The types of steering wheel fitted are shown in **FIG 10:2**. Remove the horn push or central motif, which is normally secured by three grub screws through the hub of the wheel. Remove the nut and carefully mark across the splines and wheel hub. Use a suitable puller to remove the steering wheel.

The steering wheel is replaced in the reverse order of removal, carefully aligning the marks made across the hub and splines. If the marks have been omitted, set the front wheels to the straight-ahead position and refit the steering wheel with the bottom set of spokes vertical. Use a little Loctite on the nut and tighten it to a torque load of 41 to 43 ft lb (5.7 to 5.9 kgm).

10:7 The steering column

Removal:

1 Turn the steering to a suitable position for access and remove the nut and pinch bolt securing the universal joint 40 to the inner column 49 or 50. On cars with the column shown at 88 (see **FIG 10:2**) and sealing tube 89 turn the steering to the straightahead position and mark the inner column and universal joint to ensure correct alignment on reassembly, and then remove the pinchbolt.

2 Disconnect all the leads for the steering column switches at their snap connectors or multi-connectors

under the facia. Unscrew the covers and remove the switches, carefully drawing out the electrical leads.

3 Take out the clamping bolts, washers and nuts from the two clamps that support the column and withdraw the complete column assembly from the car.

Bushes:

With the steering column assembly removed from the car, pull out the inner column from the outer column. Pull out the polythene bush and prise out the felt bush.

The bushes are replaced in the reverse order of removal. Soak the felt bushes in colloidal graphite or graphite oil before replacing them. **Never use ordinary oil on the felt bushes otherwise they will drag.**

If the bushes have been removed or are being checked because of steering tightness then the inner column should be checked for truth. A bent inner column will cause stiffness in the steering.

Universal joint:

The universal joint can be removed after taking out both sets of nuts and pinch bolts securing it, slackening the column clamp bolts and partially withdrawing the column.

The universal joint is serviced in exactly the same manner as the sealed universal joints fitted to the propeller shaft (see **Chapter 8, Section 8:1**).

Replacement:

The steering column is replaced in the reverse order of removal. The centre lines of both the inner column and the steering unit pinion must intersect at the centre of the universal joint spider, otherwise the steering may be stiff. Sufficient adjustment is available in the steering column clamps to allow the steering column to be moved into the optimum position.

On cars with the column 88 (see **FIG 10:2**) set the rack and column in the straightahead position and ensure the marks made on removal align. Fit the sealing tube 89 with the gaitered end towards the toe-board.

10:8 The steering column lock

This is not a standard fixture on all models and is only fitted for special markets where a thief-proofing device is mandatory. The slotted sleeve 56 is fitted to the inner column and the outer column has a slot cut in it for the passage of the lock tongue.

The lock is secured in place by special waisted bolts. When the bolts reach their correct torque loading they break off at the waist and the head falls off so that they cannot be undone with a spanner. Remove the steering column and use an 'Easy-out' on the bolts to remove the lock.

Two types of lock are used and their external differences may be seen in **FIG 10:5,** which also shows the location on the steering column. Both types have four positions marked 0, I II and III, but type A uses a single entry key and has 270 deg. of movement, whereas type B has a double entry key and only 120 deg. of key movement.

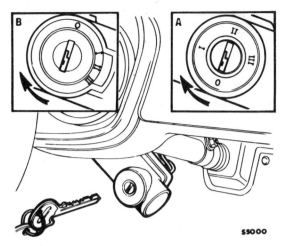

FIG 10:5 Showing location of the two types of steering lock

Operation:

The function of the four switch positions is as follows:

0 In this position only can the key be inserted or removed.

I Steering unlocked, ignition off. Electrical accessories available. Use this position when towing the car.

II Ignition switched on.

III Movement to this position is spring loaded and operates the starter. Release as soon as the engine fires.

Locking the steering:
Type A

Turn the key to the 0 position and withdraw the key. The steering lock is set during the withdrawal of the key and rotation of the steering wheel engages it.

Type B

With the key in position I press it inwards and at the same time turn it anticlockwise to position 0 and withdraw.

Under no circumstances should the key be moved from I position towards 0 when the car is in motion.

Do not interfere with the switch. Serious consequences may result from any alterations which could allow the engine to be started with the lock engaged.

PART II ENERGY ABSORBING STEERING COLUMN

The attachments are shown in **FIG 10:6**. The steering unit is removed, serviced and replaced in the same manner as the unit on the standard system (see **Sections 10:4** and **10:5**).

10:9 The steering column
Removal:

1 Disconnect the battery. Remove the carburetter air cleaners.

2 Remove the lower panel from under the lefthand side of the facia and disconnect all the steering column switch wires from their snap connectors. If there is any

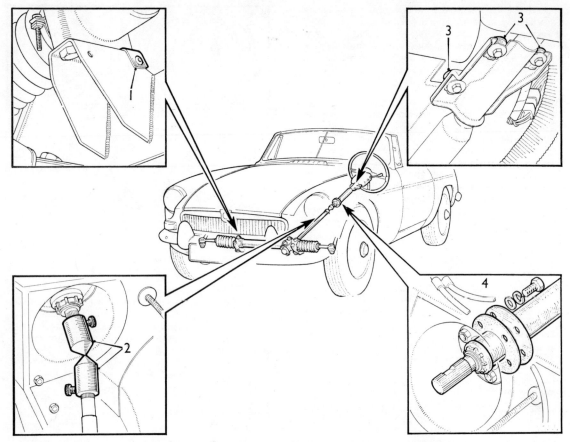

FIG 10 : 6   Energy absorbing steering column attachments

Key to Fig 10 : 6   1 Rack shims   2 Alignment gauge, 18G.1140   3 Packing washers fitted between column top fixing brackets   4 Toe-plate fixings

doubt about the correct colours or connections then the wires should be labelled.

3 Remove the three sets of bolts and washers securing the column to the toe board, shown in inset 4.

4 Remove the bolts from the upper clamp, while holding the clamp plate in place. **Note very accurately the exact positions and quantities of the packing washers 3 and then remove the plate and packing washers.** These packing washers control the alignment of the steering column and if their positions are lost the steering column will have to be aligned as described in **Section 10 : 10.**

5 Rotate the steering wheel to a convenient position and remove the nut and pinch bolt securing the universal joint to the inner column. Withdraw the steering column assembly, complete with switches, from the car.

Dismantling:

1 Remove the central motif, unscrew the securing nut and withdraw the steering wheel using a suitable extractor.

2 Take out the screws holding the switch cowls and remove the cowls. The stalk-operated switches are secured in place by two screws each and the ignition switch is held in place by four screws. Remove the screws and detach the switches complete with their electrical leads.

3 The steering column should not be dismantled any further and if it is defective or has suffered impact damage an exchange unit must be fitted.

Reassembling and refitting:

The steering column assembly is reassembled in the reverse order of dismantling and is replaced in the reverse order of removal. If a new steering column is fitted or the positions of the packing washers 3 are uncertain, then the column and steering unit must be aligned as described in the next section.

10 : 10 Aligning the steering column

This must be carried out if a new steering unit or steering column assembly are fitted. It must also be carried out if the quantity and position of

the shims 1 and packing washers 3 are uncertain.

1 Remove the universal joint and slide the column into position. Fit one cone of the special tool 18G.1140 to the inner column so that the retaining screw tightens onto the flat machined surface across the splines. Fit the other cone to the pinion shaft, making sure that the retaining screw tightens into the radial groove machined in the splines. The fitted position of the tool is shown at 2.

2 Fit one packing washer only in the positions 3 and secure the clamp plate in place by tightening the bolts finger tight only. Check that the column is free to move under pressure.

3 Secure the column to the toe board with the bolts only finger tight.

4 Adjust the gauges until their points are on the same plane but not overlapping: The parts are in alignment when the gauge points meet exactly. Horizontal adjustment is by moving the steering column into line.

5 If the vertical alignment is out the shims 1 under the steering unit will have to be adjusted. Remove the nuts and bolts securing the unit and free the old shims by carefully drilling out the securing rivets. Add shims until the vertical alignment is correct. Secure the steering unit back in place with the nuts and bolts and check that the alignment is still correct before riveting the new shims into place.

6 Remove the steering unit assembly and take off the gauges. Refit the universal joint to the inner column and set the steering wheel in the straight-ahead position. Refit the steering unit in the straight-ahead position, and fully tighten its securing bolts. Reconnect the universal joint while refitting the unit.

7 Tighten the three toe board securing bolts and tighten the upper two clamp plate bolts to a torque load of 12 to 17 lb ft (1.66 to 2.35 kgm), leaving the third bolt slack. Fit the amount of packing washers 3 required to fill the gap between the clamp plate and the body bracket and then tighten the third bolt to the same torque load as the other two bolts.

8 Refit the pinch bolts and nuts to the universal joint and tighten them to a torque load of 20 to 22 lb ft (2.8 to 3.04 kgm).

10:11 Fault diagnosis

This section covers both the standard systems and those fitted with Energy Absorbing Columns.

(a) Wheel wobble

1 Unbalanced wheels and tyres
2 Slack steering connections
3 Incorrect steering geometry
4 Excessive play in the steering gear
5 Broken or weak front springs
6 Worn hub bearings

(b) Wander

1 Check 2, 3 and 4 in (a)
2 Front suspension and rear axle mounting points out of line
3 Uneven tyre pressures
4 Uneven tyre wear
5 Weak dampers or springs

(c) Heavy steering

1 Check 3 in (a)
2 Very low tyre pressures
3 Neglected lubrication
4 Wheels out of track
5 Steering rack unit maladjusted
6 Steering column bent or misaligned
7 Steering column bushes tight
8 Steering column universal joint defective
9 Steering rack unit misaligned
10 Defective ball joints

(d) Lost motion

1 Check 8 in (c)
2 Loose steering wheel or worn splines
3 Worn rack and pinion teeth
4 Worn ball joints
5 Worn suspension system and swivel axle bushes

NOTES

CHAPTER 11

THE BRAKING SYSTEM

11:1 Description

Disc brakes are fitted to the front wheels while the rear wheels are fitted with drum brakes. All four brakes are hydraulically operated using the foot brake pedal, but the handbrake lever operates only the two rear drum brakes using a mechanical linkage.

The front disc brakes are of the fixed caliper and rotating disc type. Wear is automatically taken up and no adjustments are required. The brakes are actuated by hydraulic pressure from the master cylinder operating on the caliper pistons. The pistons press the friction pads, equally and simultaneously, into contact with the rotating brake disc.

The rear brakes are of the internally expanding shoe type fitted with one trailing and one leading shoe. Under the action of the hydraulic pressure from the master cylinder the pistons are pressed out from the single wheel cylinder and the shoes pivot into contact with the brake drum about the adjuster. When the pressure is released the brake shoes are returned to the off position by the action of return springs. Wear on the linings is taken up by using the single adjuster per brake.

The handbrake is operated from a lever mounted on the righthand side of the transmission tunnel, through cables and a compensator mechanism fitted to the rear axle. A balanced lever is fitted in each rear brake to ensure that both brake shoes are applied with equal pressure. Normally, adjusting the rear brakes also adjusts the handbrake but provision is made for further adjustment to allow for any stretch in the operating cables.

The master cylinder generates hydraulic pressure when the brake pedal is pressed, and this pressure is led to the brakes through a system of metal pipelines and flexible hoses. The standard master cylinder is of very similar construction to the master cylinder fitted to the clutch system. For the USA and certain other areas it is a legal requirement that in the event of failure of one part of the braking system some braking will still be available using the foot pedal. To achieve this the front half of the system is hydraulically isolated from the rear half and a tandem master cylinder is fitted in place of the standard master cylinder. A pressure failure switch is fitted in between the front and rear brake lines so that a failure in one half of the system will allow the pressure differential to move the shuttle in the switch and actuate a warning light.

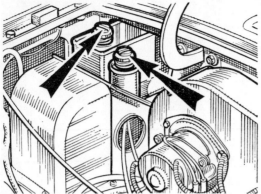

FIG 11 : 1 Master cylinder reservoirs, arrows indicate filler caps

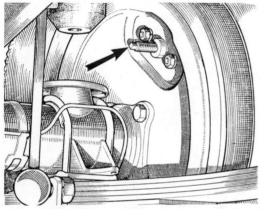

FIG 11 : 2 The rear brake adjuster point

11 : 2 Maintenance

At regular intervals check the fluid level in the master cylinder reservoir. The master cylinder is the one with the larger square tank arrowed in **FIG 11 : 1**. Before removing the filler cap wipe the top of the tank clean to prevent any dirt from falling into the reservoir. The correct level should not be higher than $\frac{1}{4}$ inch (6.35 mm) below the bottom of the filler neck and it should not be allowed to drop anywhere below half-full. If required, top up with clean fresh Lockheed Disc Brake Fluid (Series 329) to the correct level. The level will fall steadily as the disc brake pads wear but any sudden drop or increase in the rate of use of fluid must be investigated immediately as it can be caused by a leak in the system. **Leaks should be given urgent attention otherwise the brake system may fail.**

Adjust the rear brakes when the foot pedal travel becomes excessive. The adjuster is arrowed in **FIG 11 : 2**. Jack up each rear wheel in turn and turn the adjuster in a clockwise direction until the rear brake is locked. Turn back the adjuster one notch and check that the wheel now rotates freely without the brake binding. Do not confuse drag from the rear axle with binding on the brakes.

Regularly inject grease into the handbrake cable through the grease nipple fitted to the cable.

Preventative maintenance:

Never use any fluid but the recommended one, Lockheed Disc Brake Fluid (Series 329). Old and dirty fluid should be discarded and the system filled with fresh clean fluid which has been stored in a sealed container.

Observe absolute cleanliness when working on any part of the hydraulic system.

Regularly examine friction pads, rear brake linings and all pipes, unions and hoses. If one friction pad is worn more than the other on a brake they may be interchanged to even the wear.

When bleeding or draining the system the used fluid should be discarded unless it is perfectly clean. If the fluid is clean, do not return it to the reservoir but allow it to stand for 24 hours in a sealed container so that all the minute air bubbles can have time to disperse. Brake fluid should always be kept in sealed containers as it absorbs moisture from the air thus lowering its boiling point.

It is recommended that the fluid be drained out and discarded at 24,000 mile intervals and the system filled and bled with new fluid. At 40,000 mile intervals the system should be stripped and all seals renewed. This also gives an opportunity for examining the bores of all the cylinders, and renewing any suspect parts.

11 : 3 Front disc brakes

The front disc brake details are shown in **FIG 11 : 3**.

Renewing the friction pads:

The pads must be renewed if the friction material has worn down to a minimum thickness of $\frac{1}{16}$ inch (1.6 mm).

1 Apply the handbrake, securely jack up the front of the car and remove the front road wheels.
2 Press in the retaining springs 13 and remove the splitpins. The positions of the splitpins are arrowed in **FIG 11 : 4**. Withdraw the pads from the caliper.
3 Thoroughly clean out the recesses in the caliper and the exposed faces of the pistons.
4 Press the pistons back into the calipers, using a clamp. The method using the clamp 18G.590 is shown in **FIG 11 : 5**. As the pistons are pressed back, the level of the fluid in the reservoir will rise and some fluid may have to be syphoned off to prevent it from overflowing. **Avoid spilling brake fluid onto paintwork as the fluid will quickly soften and remove the paint.**
5 Check that the cutaway portion of the pistons is positioned at the inner end of the caliper, towards the hub, as shown in **FIG 11 : 6**. Refit the new friction pads, checking that they move freely in the caliper recesses. Any high spots on the pad backing plate may be removed by careful filing. Secure the pads in place with the retaining springs and splitpins. Pump the brake pedal several times to adjust the front brakes.

Servicing a brake caliper:

Securely raise the front of the car and remove the road wheel. Free the tabwasher 17 and take out the two bolts 16 securing the caliper to the swivel axle. Do not disconnect the flexible hose, and support the caliper so that

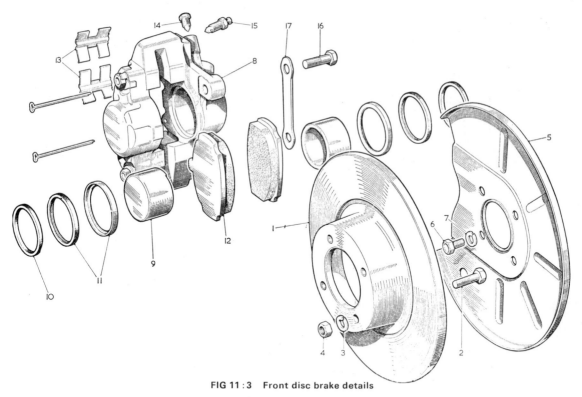

FIG 11 : 3   Front disc brake details

Key to Fig 11 : 3   1 Disc   2 Bolt   3 Washer   4 Nut   5 Dust cover   6 Bolt   7 Washer   8 Caliper   9 Piston
10 Inner seal   11 Dust seal with retainer   12 Pad assembly   13 Clip   14 Plug   15 Bleed nipple   16 Bolt   17 Washer

the hose is not twisted or strained. Remove the friction pads 12.

1 Clean the caliper assembly all over using methylated spirits or hydraulic cleaning fluid. Do not use any other solvents. Use a small brush to wash dirt out of all the recesses.

2 Apply a clamp to hold the mounting half piston in place and apply gentle pressure to the footbrake so as to press out the other piston far enough for it to be removed by hand. Carry out this operation over a wide-necked container or drip tray in order to catch the fluid that will be spilt.

3 Use a small blunt tool to prise out the fluid seal 8 (shown in **FIG 11 : 7**), taking great care not to score or damage the bore of the cylinder. Gently prise the retainer 6 out and remove the dust seal 7.

4 Clean out the bore in the cylinder and the piston with methylated spirits or hydraulic cleaning fluid. **Do not use any other solvents.**

5 Coat a new fluid seal with clean hydraulic fluid and fit it into the recess in the bore. Use no tools but the fingers and work the seal around until it is fully and squarely in its bore. Slacken the bleeder screw, coat the piston working surfaces with hydraulic fluid and very carefully press the piston back into place, so that the cutaway portion faces as shown in **FIG 11 : 6** and the piston is left protruding $\frac{5}{16}$ inch (8 mm). Take great care not to allow the piston to tilt during this operation.

6 Coat a new dust seal 7 with clean hydraulic fluid and fit it into the retainer. Press the seal assembly onto the protruding portion of the piston making sure that it is squarely in place, and use the clamp 18G.590 to press both the seal and the piston into place as shown in **FIG 11 : 5**.

7 Tighten the bleed screw and leave the clamp holding the piston assembly that has just been serviced. Remove the other piston assembly by applying gentle pressure to the brake pedal and service it in a similar manner to the mounting half piston.

Normally the caliper should not be dismantled further, except for removing the bleed nipple and pipeline and then blowing through with compressed air. Only if it is absolutely essential should the caliper be dismantled further, and in this event the owner should bear in mind that mating faces must be scrupulously clean and that the special clamping bolts, fluid seal and lockplates must be renewed on reassembly. Tighten the clamping bolts to a torque of 35.5 to 37 lb ft (4.9 to 5.1 kgm).

Refit the caliper in the reverse order of removal. Fill and bleed the hydraulic system and pump the pedal several times to adjust the front brakes.

Brake disc:

Remove the front hub and disc assembly from the car as described in **Chapter 9, Section 9 : 3**. The brake disc can then be removed from the wheel hub by removing the nuts 4, washers 3 and bolts 2.

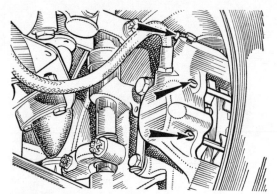

FIG 11:4 Friction pad retaining pins and bleed nipple location

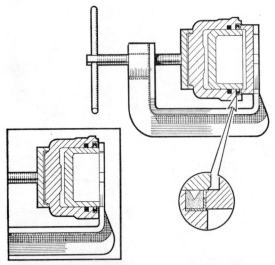

FIG 11:5 Using clamp No. 18G.590 to refit the dust seal assembly to a caliper. The square inset shows the tool, less adaptor being used to reset or hold a piston

Refit the hub and disc in the reverse order of removal. After the wheel hub end float has been correctly set, check the runout on the disc. Press the hub firmly in to avoid end float from confusing the measurements, and use a DTI (Dial Test Indicator) to check that the runout does not exceed .003 inch (.076 mm). If the runout is excessive, remove the disc and check that there is no dirt between the mating faces of the hub and disc. Turn the disc relative to the hub so that different sets of securing holes are aligned.

If the runout is still excessive or the disc is badly scored the disc can be sent to a specialist firm for truing up by grinding. The maximum that may be machined off both sides is calculated so that the total removed does not reduce the original thickness, .350 to .340 inch (8.89 to 8.63 mm), by more than .040 inch (1.016 mm).

11:4 Rear drum brakes

The details of a rear brake are shown in **FIG 11:8** and a rear brake correctly assembled is shown in **FIG 11:9**.

Removing rear brake shoes:

1 Jack up the rear of the car, with the front wheels chocked, and place it securely on blocks or stands. Remove the rear road wheel.
2 Slacken back the adjuster wedge spindle 13 to free the brake shoes from the drum. Remove the two counter-sunk screws 25 for disc wheels or the nuts 26 for wire wheels. Withdraw the brake drum 24 from the brake assembly.
3 Hold the steady pins 8 from behind the brake back-plate 1. Grip the retaining washers 10 with a pair of pliers, press them in against the pressure of the spring 9 and rotate the washer through 90 degrees so that it

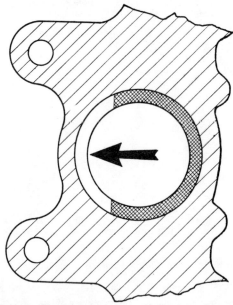

FIG 11:6 The cutaway portion of the piston (arrowed) must be fitted towards the inner edge of the caliper

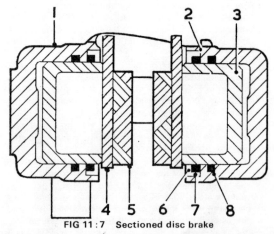

FIG 11:7 Sectioned disc brake

Key to Fig 11:7 1 Caliper—mounting half   2 Caliper—rim half   3 Hydraulic piston   4 Pad backing plate
5 Friction pad   6 Dust seal retainer   7 Dust seal
8 Fluid seal

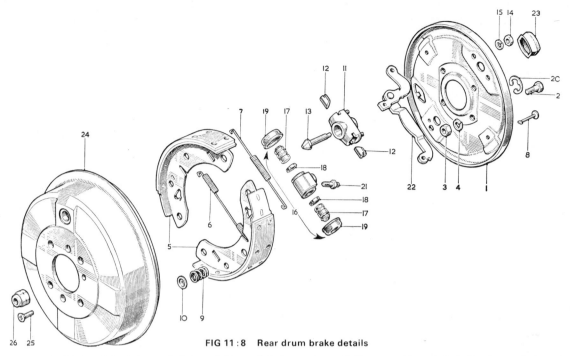

FIG 11 : 8   Rear drum brake details

Key to Fig 11 : 8   1 Backplate   2 Bolt   3 Nut   4 Spring washer   5 Shoe assembly   6 Pull-off spring—cylinder end
7 Pull-off spring—adjustment end   8 Brake shoe steady pin   9 Brake shoe steady spring   10 Retainer washer   11 Adjuster
assembly   12 Tappet   13 Wedge spindle   14 Nut   15 Spring washer   16 Wheel cylinder assembly   17 Piston
18 Piston seal   19 Dust cover   20 Wheel cylinder retaining clip   21 Bleed nipple   22 Handbrake lever   23 Dust cover
24 Brake drum   25 Drum to hub screw   26 Drum retaining nut (wire wheels)

comes free of the T-head on the retaining pin. Remove
the washers 10, springs 9 and retaining pins 8.
4 Pull or lever the trailing shoe (the shoe on which the
trailing end of the shoe is pushed into contact with the
drum when the drum is rotating in a forward direction)
out of its mounting slots against the pull of the springs.
Take care not to damage the rubber dust cover 19 as
the shoe comes free. Either disconnect the return
springs 6 and 7 from the shoe, (in which case the other
shoe will fall free), or else similarly remove the other
shoe so all spring tension is gone and the springs can
easily be disconnected.

Relining the brakes :

**Exchange shoes must be fitted if the old linings
are either so worn that the rivet heads are nearly
flush with the working face or if the linings are
contaminated with oil or grease.** Whatever method is
used for cleaning the linings some grease or oil will always
remain in the material to cause poor braking.

If relining is required then renew all four brake shoes,
otherwise uneven braking will be produced.

New linings must be concentric with the brake drum
and there must be no gaps between the linings and the
shoes so, unless the owner is experienced in riveting on
new linings, exchange shoes should always be fitted.

Refitting the brake shoes :

Before refitting the linings, remove all loose dust and
dirt from inside the brake and brake drum, using a

stiff brush and air either from an airline or tyre pump.
Scuff the linings lightly to remove and break the glazed
surface. A small chamfer should be carefully filed on the
leading and trailing edges of the linings as this helps to
prevent squeal and grabbing. Slacken the adjuster right
off.

Use white zinc-based grease to lightly lubricate the
pivot points and refit the shoes in the reverse order of
removal. It is probably easiest to reassemble the shoes and
return springs loosely behind the hub and then to pull the
shoes into the slots using a length of cord. Refit the brake
drum after tapping the shoes into place so that they are
concentric with the drum. Tighten up the adjuster and
pump the brake pedal hard so as to centralize the shoes
before adjusting the brakes fully.

Brake drum :

Clean out all dust and dirt. Solvents may be used to
remove any grease or contaminant but they must be
allowed to dry off before refitting the brake drum.

Renew the brake drum if it is badly scored or cracked.
Cracks are most easily detected if the drum is hung on a
wooden handle through the centre aperture and then
tapped with a light metallic object. A cracked drum will
sound flat.

Minor scoring may be skimmed off in a lathe, provided
that the drum is mounted on an arbor and not in a chuck,
which will distort the drum causing it to be cut non-
circular.

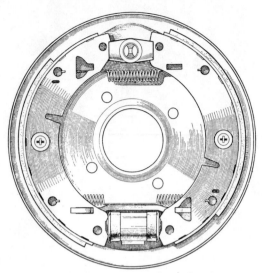

FIG 11:9   The rear brake assembly

Wheel cylinder and adjuster:

Before the wheel cylinder is removed, the brake shoes must be removed, and the flexible hose disconnected (see **Section 11 : 5**).

1 Remove the clevis pin securing the handbrake cable to the handbrake lever 22. Remove the circlip 20 and the retaining washer and draw the wheel cylinder assembly 16 out from the backplate. Take off the dust cover 23 and remove the handbrake lever 22.

2 Remove the dust covers 19 and pull out the two pistons 17 complete with their seals 18. Remove and discard the seals 18. Wash the metal parts in any suitable degreasing solvent, although only methylated spirits or hydraulic fluid may be allowed to come into contact with the rubber seals. Allow the metal parts to dry completely and then examine the parts. If the bore of the cylinder shows any signs of corrosion, wear or scoring, the complete assembly must be renewed.

Dip new seals 18 into clean hydraulic fluid and refit them to the pistons so that their lips face into the cylinder. Use only the fingers and work the seals around to make sure that they are squarely and fully

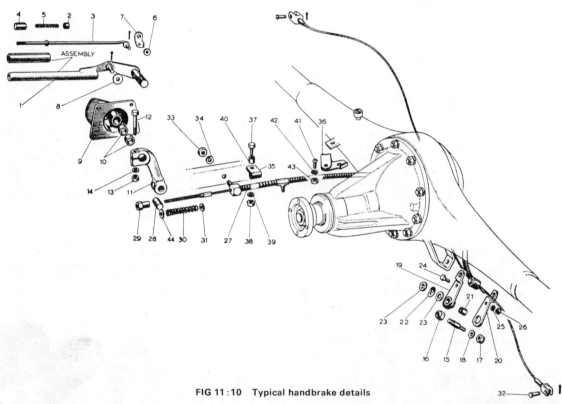

FIG 11 : 10   Typical handbrake details

Key to Fig 11 : 10   1 Handle assembly   2 Bush   3 Pawl rod assembly   4 Knob   5 Spring   6 Washer—plain   7 Pawl
8 Washer   9 Fulcrum and ratchet assembly   10 Bush   11 Operating lever   12 Bolt   13 Nut   14 Washer—spring
15 Fulcrum—handbrake compensator   16 Nut—fulcrum to axle   17 Nut—compensator to fulcrum   18 Washer   19 Lever—
inner compensating   20 Lever—outer compensating   21 Bush—compensating lever   22 Washer—anti-rattle   23 Washer—
plain   24 Screw   25 Washer—spring   26 Nut   27 Cable—handbrake   28 Trunnion   29 Adjuster nut   30 Spring—
cable   31 Washer—plain   32 Clevis pin   33 Abutment nut   34 Washer—spring   35 Clip—cable to battery carrier
36 Clip—cable to 3-way piece—axle brackets   37 Screw   38 Nut   39 Washer—spring   40 Distance tube   41 Screw—
clip—3-way piece   42 Washer—spring   43 Nut   44 Washer—plain

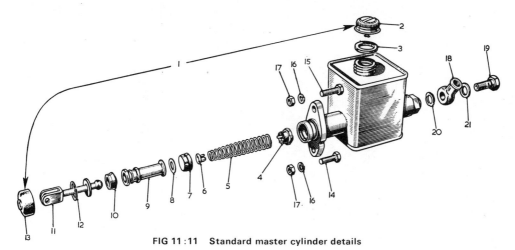

FIG 11:11 Standard master cylinder details

Key to Fig 11:11   1 Cylinder and supply tank assembly   2 Filler cap   3 Seal   4 Valve assembly   5 Spring—piston return   6 Retainer   7 Cup—main   8 Washer   9 Piston   10 Cup—secondary   11 Pushrod   12 Circlip   13 Boot   14 Bolt   15 Bolt   16 Washer   17 Nut   18 Banjo—master cylinder   19 Banjo bolt   20 Gasket   21 Gasket

seated. Very carefully press the piston back into the bore, taking great care not to damage or bend back the seals. Refit the dust covers and then the cylinder is ready for replacement to the backplate.

3 The adjuster assembly is secured to the backplate by the nuts 14 and washers 15. The adjuster can be left fitted for servicing. Pull out the tappets 12 and turn the square head of the wedge spindle 13 in a clockwise direction to unscrew the spindle from the body. If the spindle is stiff to turn, use a wire brush to scrub the corrosion from the exposed threads and then use a few drops of penetrating oil. Wash the parts in clean fuel and reassemble the adjuster using white zinc-based grease or Lockheed Expandor Lubricant. In cases where the squared head has been damaged so that it cannot be turned with a spanner, or the special spanner 18G.619A, drive a tight fitting nut onto the remains of the head and use a spanner on this to adjust the brakes.

4 Refit the wheel cylinder assembly and the remainder of the parts in the reverse order of removal. Fill the hydraulic system and bleed the brakes, as described in **Section 11:9**.

11:5 Flexible hoses

If a flexible hose appears blocked never try to clear it by using a length of wire or similar material. If compressed air will not clear the obstruction then the hose must be renewed. The hose must also be renewed if it is perishing, cracking, has been chafing enough to wear the hose, or if it feels soft in places. Twisting the flexible portion or leaving the hose fitted in a twisted condition will also damage the hose.

Removal:

Do not twist the flexible portion. Undo the metal pipeline union and then remove the locknut securing the flexible hose to its bracket, while holding the adjacent

hexagon on the flexible hose with a spanner. Be prepared for hydraulic fluid to leak out when the pipeline union is disconnected. Remove the end of the hose from its bracket and then unscrew the hose at the other end using a spanner on the hexagonals at the fixed end.

Replace the hose by reversing the removal instructions.

11:6 The handbrake

The details of the MGA handbrake are shown in **FIG 11:10**. The system is similar enough to be used as a guide.

When the handbrake is operated the compensator lever assembly allows the free end of the outer cable to move until the load is shared equally between the inner and outer cables, and the handbrake levers on the brakes are therefore applied with equal pressure. Thus the inner cable is under tension and the outer cable is under compression when the handbrake is applied.

Adjustment:

Normally, adjusting the rear brakes should also set the handbrake. If the handbrake lever still moves excessively after the rear wheel brakes have been adjusted, check through the system for wear. The most likely points are worn clevis pins securing the cables to the levers on the brakes, or a defective compensator lever. Renew any worn parts. Only when the system has been checked through should the handbrake cable be adjusted. Make sure that the rear brakes are correctly adjusted and rotate the adjuster nut 29, accessible underneath the car, until the handbrake is fully on when the handbrake lever is pulled up three or four notches.

Removal:

1 Unscrew the adjuster nut 29, pull the end of the cable out of operating lever 11 and remove the washers 31 and 44 as well as the spring 30. Disconnect the clips securing the cable to the body and rear axle. The nut 33 and washer 34 are accessible from inside the car

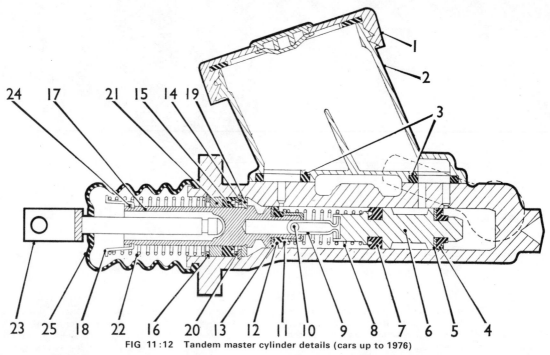

FIG 11:12 Tandem master cylinder details (cars up to 1976)

Key to Fig 11:12
1 Filler cap
2 Plastic reservoir
3 Reservoir seals
4 Main cup
5 Piston washer
6 Piston
7 Main cup
8 Spring
9 Piston link
10 Pin
11 Pin retainer
12 Main cup
13 Piston washer
14 Circlip
15 Cup
16 Circlip
17 Piston
18 Spring retainer
19 Stop washer
20 Washer
21 Bearing
22 Spring
23 Pushrod
24 Spirolox ring
25 Rubber boot

after lifting the carpet. Extract the splitpins and remove the clevis pins securing the cables to the brake levers. Slacken the nut 17 until the compensator levers can be sufficiently separated to free the cable trunnion from between them. Lift out the handbrake cable.

2 The handbrake lever and parts can be removed if required. Remove the bolt 12, nut 13 and washer 14 securing the operating lever 11 to the spindle of the hand lever and withdraw the hand lever assembly from inside the car, after having removed the operating lever 11. The ratchet plate 9 is secured to the transmission tunnel by three screws.

Replace the parts in the reverse order of removal and adjust the nut 29 until the handbrake is fully on with the lever at the third or fourth notch.

11:7 The master cylinder

Single master cylinder:

The details of the master cylinder fitted to single-system standard cars are shown in **FIG 11:11**. This master cylinder, apart from having a larger reservoir and the check valve assembly 4 fitted, is of the same design and construction as the master cylinder fitted to the clutch system and is dealt with in exactly the same manner (see **Chapter 5, Section 5:3**).

The remainder of this section will deal only with the tandem master cylinder.

Tandem master cylinder (cars up to 1976):

The details of this are shown in **FIG 11:12**. The reservoir is divided by a baffle to prevent loss of fluid from

one half of the system depleting the other half. The pushrod 23 is connected to the brake pedal and moves the piston 17 down the bore of the cylinder when the pedal is pressed. The bypass port to the reservoir is then connected to the back of the piston 17 and fluid is prevented from leaking out by the cup seal 15. When the pedal is released the piston 17 is returned by the action of the return spring 22. The secondary piston 6 is also drawn back up the bore by the link 9 and pin 10 but the two pistons are normally kept apart by the spring 8. When the secondary piston 6 moves down the bore its bypass port is connected to the annulus in the piston and fluid leakage is prevented by the seals 4 and 7. As the piston 17 moves down the bore hydraulic pressure rises in the chamber in front of it and this pressure is fed to operate one half of the brake system. The pressure also causes the secondary piston 6 to move down the bore, pressurizing the fluid in the chamber in front of it and this pressure then operates the other half of the braking system.

If the half of the system fed by the front chamber fails, then the piston 6 will move down the bore until it hits the end of the cylinder and pressure can build up normally in the rear chamber. If the rear chamber system fails then the two pistons physically contact each other and pedal pressure is transmitted directly to the secondary piston 6.

Removal:

1 Drain both the clutch and the brake hydraulic systems. This is best done by attaching a length of tube to a suitable bleed nipple, either on the front brakes, rear brakes or clutch slave cylinder depending on which

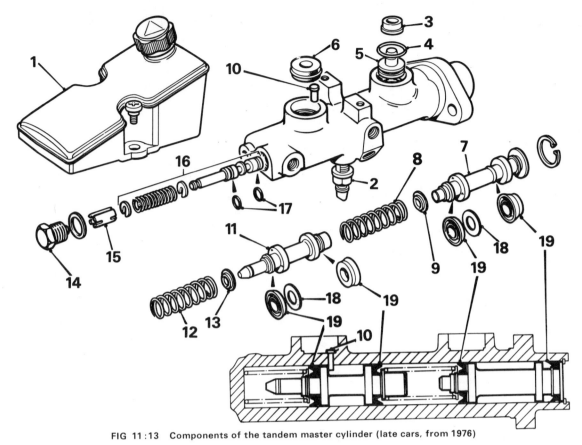

FIG 11:13 Components of the tandem master cylinder (late cars, from 1976)

Key to Fig 11:13 1 Reservoir 2 Pressure failure warning switch 3 Primary feed port seal 4 'O' ring 5 Adaptor 6 Secondary feed port seal 7 Primary piston 8 Return spring 9 Cup 10 Stop pin 11 Secondary piston 12 Return spring 13 Cup 14 End plug 15 Distance piece 16 Pressure differential piston assembly 17 'O' ring 18 Shim 19 Seal

part of the system is being bled. Open the bleed nipple and fully depress the appropriate pedal. Tighten the bleed nipple and release the pedal. Carry on pumping by this method until the appropriate reservoir is empty. **Discard the first fluid that comes out of the bleed nipple.** The remainder of the fluid should be collected in a clean container for possible re-use though this too should be discarded if it is at all dirty.

2 Remove the master cylinder cover. Disconnect and plug all the pipelines to the master cylinders. Use rubber plugs which are easily removable to prevent dirt entering the pipelines.

3 Disconnect the pedals from the master cylinders by removing the splitpins and clevis pins and disengage the pedal springs.

4 Remove the lefthand lower facia panel and unscrew the two bolts securing the pedal box to the toe plate. Unscrew the nut securing the pedal pivot bolt, withdraw the bolt, remove the spacer and temporarily refit the bolt.

5 Undo the six bolts securing the pedal box to the bulkhead and lift out the pedal box complete with the pedals and master cylinders. The master cylinder is secured to the pedal box by two bolts.

The pedal box and parts are replaced in the reverse order of removal. After they have been replaced both the clutch and brake hydraulic systems must be filled and bled (see **Section 11:9** and **Chapter 5, Section 5:5**), and the brake pedal clearance set.

Dismantling:

Clean the outside of the master cylinder with methylated spirits (denatured alcohol) before dismantling.

1 Remove the rubber boot 25 and withdraw the pushrod 23. Support the master cylinder in the padded jaws of a vice, with the opening in the bore uppermost. Push down the spring 22 and carefully remove the Spirolox circlip 24, taking great care neither to damage the bore or distort the coils of the circlip. Remove the retainer 18 and spring 22.

2 Remove the circlip 16, preferably with special pliers 18G.1112 and taking great care not to score the bore. Work the piston 17 up and down so that the nylon bearing 21, seal 15 and washer 20 are eased up until they can be withdrawn.

3 Carefully remove the circlip 14 and withdraw the piston assemblies complete with the stop washer 19.

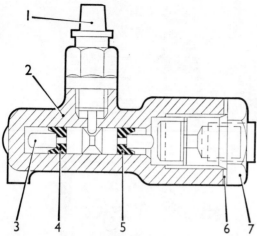

FIG 11:14   Pressure failure switch details (cars up to 1976)

Key to Fig 11:14   1 Nylon switch assembly   2 Body
3 Shuttle valve piston   4 Piston seal   5 Piston seal
6 Copper washer   7 End plug

Remove the stop washer. Compress the spring 8 and drive out the roll pin 10 to free the two piston assemblies from each other.

4 Accurately note the positions of all the seals, paying particular attention to the directions that they face. Remove the seals and preferably discard them.

5 Remove the reservoir by unscrewing the four screws that hold it in place. Extract the sealing rings 3. Unscrew the front brake pipe adaptor and discard the copper gaskets. Remove the springs and trap valves from the ports.

Inspection:

Wash all the parts in methylated spirits or hydraulic cleaning fluid. **Do not allow even traces of any other solvent to come into contact with the seals.** Renew the master cylinder assembly if the bore shows any signs of pitting, wearing or scores.

All the seals should be renewed unless they are in excellent condition. When examining a seal, check that the lips are not scored or worn but do not bend back the lips.

Reassembly:

The parts are reassembled in the reverse order of dismantling but noting the following points:

1 All the internal parts, including seals, should be dipped in clean hydraulic fluid and reassembled wet.

2 Only the fingers may be used for refitting seals. Stretch them carefully into place and work them around so that they are squarely and fully seated. Make sure that the seals are fitted facing in the correct direction. The washer 5 is fitted with its convex face towards the piston.

3 Take very great care not to damage or bend back the seals when refitting the internal parts into the bore.

Tandem master cylinder (cars from 1976):

The unit is shown in **FIG 11:13** and its operation is similar to that of the earlier unit detailed in this section and differs mainly in being mounted on the front of the servo unit and operated directly by the servo unit through a pushrod. The pressure failure switch and differential valve are incorporated into the unit as shown in the illustration.

Removal:

1 Drain the brake fluid from the system in the same manner described for the earlier tandem master cylinder.

2 Unscrew the brake pipe unions from the master cylinder and disconnect the two leads from the pressure failure warning switch 2.

3 Unscrew the two nuts securing the master cylinder to the servo unit and remove the master cylinder.

Refitting is the reversal of removal, bleeding the brakes on completion as detailed in **Section 11:9.**

Dismantling:

1 Unscrew and remove the pressure failure warning switch 2, collecting the sealing washer if it becomes detached.

2 Hold the master cylinder between the padded jaws of a vice, remove the two shouldered screws securing the plastic reservoir 1 and detach the reservoir.

3 Pull off the seal and adaptor assembly 3, 4 and 5 from the primary feed port. Similarly, extract the seal 6 from the secondary feed port.

4 Use a pair of circlip pliers to remove the circlip from the end of the master cylinder bore.

5 Withdraw the primary piston 7, cup 9 and return spring 8.

6 Insert a wooden or soft metal bar into the bore and depress the secondary piston 11 a little. Extract the secondary piston stop pin 10 while the piston is depressed and then withdraw the secondary piston. If necessary, apply air pressure to the secondary port outlet, or tap the cylinder gently against a block of wood to dislodge the secondary piston from the bore to facilitate withdrawal.

7 Unscrew the end plug 14. Remove the end plug and sealing washer, leaving the distance piece 15 on the end plug spigot.

8 Withdraw the pressure differential piston assembly 16, applying air pressure if necessary to the primary outlet port to dislodge the assembly.

Inspection and overhaul:

Wash all components in industrial alcohol or fresh brake fluid and dry them.

Examine the bore of the cylinder and renew the complete unit if the bore is scratched, scored or damaged.

Renew all the seals, 'O' rings and cups which are obtainable in kit form.

Check the outlet bores for blockages or damage, including damage to the threaded portions and repair or renew the unit as necessary.

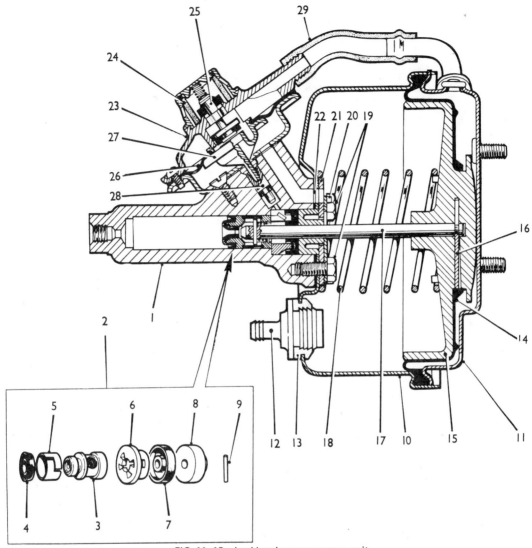

FIG 11:15 Lockheed vacuum servo unit

Key to Fig 11:15   1 Slave cylinder   2 Slave piston components   3 Slave piston*   4 Piston seal*   5 Retaining clip*
6 Spacer*   7 Cup*   8 Bearing*   9 Connecting pin*   10 Servo shell   11 End cover   12 Non-return valve
13 Rubber mounting   14 Main servo diaphragm   15 Diaphragm support   16 Retaining key   17 Pushrod
18 Main return spring   19 Servo shell retaining bolts   20 Locking plate   21 Abutment plate   22 Joint washer
23 Air valve cover   24 Air filter   25 Air valve   26 Air valve diaphragm   27 Diaphragm support   28 Air valve piston
29 Rubber pipe
Shown inset

Reassembly:

Lubricate the cylinder bores and all components in fresh brake fluid and ensure scrupulous cleanliness. Assemble while the components are wet.

Fit new 'O' rings 17 to the pressure differential piston and new shims 18 to the primary and secondary pistons. Use the fingers only and fit new seals 19 to the primary and secondary pistons so that the wider lip of each seal is positioned as clearly shown in the illustration.

Refit the return spring 12 and a new cup 13 to the secondary piston. The return spring 12 is shorter than the primary piston return spring 8 in case of confusion.

Refit the secondary piston assembly into the cylinder taking care not to cause the seal lips to be turned back as the piston is pushed in. Depress the piston using a wooden or soft-metal bar and refit the stop pin 10 to secure the piston as shown in the lower portion of the illustration.

Refit the primary piston and secure it with the circlip. Refit the pressure piston assembly 16 followed by the distance piece 15 and end plug 14, using a new sealing washer on the end plug and tightening the plug to 33 lb ft (4.6 kgm).

Refit the feed port seals and 'O' ring. Refit and tighten the pressure failure warning switch 2 and then refit the reservoir 1 securing it with the screws.

Refitting:

Refit the master cylinder to the servo unit but do not tighten the securing nuts. Refit the brake fluid pipes and then tighten the master cylinder securing nuts. Tighten the brake pipe unions and reconnect the two leads to the pressure failure warning switch. On completion bleed the brakes as detailed in **Section 11:9**.

11:8 The pressure failure switch

This is only fitted to cars equipped with tandem master cylinders, and the details are shown in **FIG 11:14**.

Removal:

1 Disconnect the batteries and then disconnect the wiring from the switch.
2 Disconnect and plug the hydraulic pipelines. Remove the securing bolt and lift the assembly out of the car.
The switch is replaced in the reverse order of removal. Once the switch has been refitted both halves of the brake system must be filled and bled (see **Section 11:9**).

Dismantling:

1 Remove the end plug 7 and discard the copper washer 6. Unscrew the nylon switch assembly 1.
2 Withdraw the shuttle valve piston 3, using air pressure to blow it out if required. Remove and discard the two seals 4 and 5.

Inspection:

Clean the parts with methylated spirits or hydraulic cleaning fluid. Renew the assembly if the bore is scored, worn or pitted.

Check the operation of the switch 1 by reconnecting it back into the circuit, connecting the batteries and pressing the plunger firmly against an earthed metal surface on the car. The warning light should operate when the ignition is switched on.

Reassembly:

1 Use only the fingers and fit new seals 4 and 5 to the shuttle 3, so that their lips face outwards.
2 Press the shuttle assembly back into the bore, taking great care not to damage the seal 4. Refit the end plug 7 using a new copper washer 6 and tightening it to a torque of 200 lb in (2.3 kgm). **Make sure that the annular groove in the shuttle is situated under the hole for the switch plunger.**
3 Refit the nylon switch assembly, tightening it to a torque load of 15 lb in (.173 kgm).

11:9 Bleeding the brakes

This is not routine maintenance and is only required when air has entered the system, either by dismantling parts or allowing the fluid level in the reservoir to fall so low that air has been drawn into the master cylinder.

Before bleeding the brakes, fill up the master cylinder with fresh brake fluid and keep it constantly topped up

during the operation. If the level is allowed to fall too far air will again be drawn into the system.

If only one half of the system has been dismantled then only that half of the system requires bleeding when a tandem master cylinder is fitted.

Single master cylinder:

1 Start bleeding at the bleed nipple furthest from the master cylinder, nearside rear on righthand drive cars. Attach a length of plastic or rubber tube to the bleed nipple and put the free end of the tube into a little clean hydraulic fluid in a clean glass container.
2 Open the bleed nipple part of a turn and have a second operator pump the brake pedal with full slow strokes allowing the pedal to return unaided.
3 When the fluid comes out free from any air bubbles, tighten the bleed nipple either on a downstroke or when the pedal is held fully down.
4 Transfer the tube and bleed the remaining nipples in a similar manner, always ending on the bleed nipple nearest to the master cylinder.
5 Top up the reservoir to the correct level.

Tandem system (early—up to 1976):

The brake pedal must only be moved with gentle pressure and the pedal must never be 'tried' until bleeding is completed. Failure to observe these precautions will mean that the shuttle in the pressure failure switch will move and the switch will have to be centralized.

1 If there is a great deal of air in the system it is best to let the fluid run through on its own. Attach the bleed tube to each bleed nipple in turn, open the nipple and allow fluid to run through until it comes out fairly air free.
2 Bleed the nipples as described for the standard system, taking great care not to use excessive pressure on the pedal.

Centralizing the pressure failure switch shuttle:

The procedure described next applies only to early tandem systems employing a separate pressure failure switch (**FIG 11:14**), and the master cylinder shown in **FIG 11:12**.

1 Complete the bleeding operation.
2 Transfer the bleed tube to a bleed nipple on the opposite half of the system and partially open the bleed nipple.
3 Switch on the ignition. The warning light will come on. Apply a steadily increasing pressure to the brake pedal. The shuttle will centralize with a click and the warning light will go out. **Do not press the pedal beyond this point** or the shuttle will move to the other side and have to be centralized by opening a bleed nipple on the original half of the system.

Tandem system (cars from 1976 onwards):

1 Fill the reservoir with fresh brake fluid and keep it at least half full throughout the bleeding operation.
2 Attach a tight fitting rubber or plastic hose to the bleed screw on the lefthand rear brake and immerse the free end of the hose into a glass jar containing an inch or two of brake fluid.
3 Refer to **FIG 11:13**. Disconnect the two leads from

the pressure failure warning switch 2 and unscrew the switch by three-and-a-half complete turns to break the contact between the switch plunger and pressure differential piston.

4 Open the rear lefthand bleed screw about half a complete turn. Depress the brake pedal slowly through its full stroke and then allow it to return unassisted. Pause for two or three seconds and then depress the pedal again, allowing it to return unassisted.

5 Continue this pumping operation, keeping the reservoir topped up and observing the fluid being expelled. When no more air bubbles emerge at the glass jar, close the bleed screw during a downward stroke of the pedal.

6 Repeat the process for the remaining three brake assemblies until all air is expelled from the system.

7 When a firm pedal is finally obtained, check the system for leakage by holding the pedal down for two to three minutes with all bleed screws closed. Any leakage will then be evident at the master cylinder, pipe unions or disc calipers and rear wheel cylinders.

8 On completion, top up the master cylinder, retighten the pressure failure warning switch and remove the glass jar and bleed hose.

11:10 Lockheed Type 6 servo unit

In order still further to improve the braking and to reduce the effort required of the driver a Lockheed vacuum servo unit is offered as an optional extra. This is shown in the sectional view of **FIG 11:15** from which it will be seen that there are three main components, the vacuum cylinder 10, the air-valve assembly 23 and the slave cylinder 1, which is connected in the hydraulic circuit between the master cylinder and the wheel cylinders.

Under light braking the fluid passes directly to the wheel cylinders through the hollow centre of the slave piston 3 and no assistance is obtained.

With heavier pressure on the brake pedal the air valve piston 28 is moved upwards, so opening the air valve 25 and allowing air to pass through into the chamber behind the main diaphragm 14, thus destroying the vacuum there. This causes the pushrod 17 to be moved to the left, sealing the hollow centre of the slave piston and pushing it down the bore and increasing the fluid pressure at the wheel cylinders.

When the brake pedal is released the pressure beneath the air valve piston is reduced, the diaphragm 26 re-opens and the air valve closes. A vacuum is re-created in the main chamber on each side of the main servo diaphragm which is then pushed back to the right by the spring 18 together with the pushrod and slave piston and so releasing the pressure at the wheel cylinders.

Air valve and filter:

The only item of maintenance work which should concern the home operator is the inspection and periodic renewal of the air filter element to which access is obtained by lifting off the domed cover shown in **FIG 11:16**.

In the event of suspected air valve failure the whole assembly must be renewed as a unit. This may be done

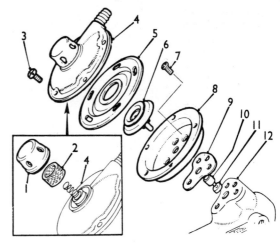

FIG 11:16   Air filter element

Key to Fig 11:16   1 Domed cover for filter   2 Air filter
3 Air valve cover securing screws   4 Air valve cover
5 Diaphragm   6 Diaphragm support   7 Valve housing
securing screws   8 Valve housing   9 Joint washer
10 Piston   11 Piston cup   12 Slave cylinder

by removing the five securing screws 3 and lifting off. This is also necessary if it is required to clean the interior of the valve housing.

Removing the unit:

If the servo unit should fail it is recommended that it should be taken to a service station for attention. Removal is as follows:

Disconnect the battery and remove the screw securing the base of the servo cylinder bracket (two screws on lefthand drive cars). Remove the bolt securing the vacuum hose clip to the bracket.

Disconnect the seal off the hydraulic feed from the master cylinder. Then on:

Righthand drive cars:

Remove the three nuts securing the servo to the rear bracket, take off the vacuum hose connections and lift away.

Lefthand drive cars:

From inside the car, remove the bulkhead grommet and three nuts securing the servo unit. Lift off the unit and disconnect the vacuum hose.

Refitting is a reversal of the above sequence after which the brake system must be bled as described in **Section 11:9**.

Cars from 1976:

Later cars (from 1976 onwards) are fitted with a servo unit which is directly operated by the foot pedal pushrod. The master cylinder is mounted at the front of the servo and this will have to be removed if the servo unit is being removed.

11 :11 Fault diagnosis

(a) 'Spongy' pedal

1 Leak in the fluid system
2 Air in the fluid system
3 Worn master cylinder
4 Leaking wheel cylinders
5 Gaps between shoes and underside of brake linings

(b) Excessive pedal movement

1 Check 1 and 2 in (a)
2 Excessive lining wear
3 Very low fluid level in reservoir
4 Too much free pedal movement (tandem brakes only)

(c) Brakes grab or pull to one side

1 Seized piston in wheel cylinder
2 Seized handbrake compensator lever
3 Wet or oily friction linings
4 Broken shoe return springs
5 Mixed linings of different grades
6 Unbalanced shoe adjustment
7 Defective suspension
8 Scored, cracked or distorted brake drums or brake discs
9 Uneven tyre pressures
10 High spots on brake drum
11 Worn steering connections

CHAPTER 12

THE ELECTRICAL SYSTEM

12:1 Description

All the models covered by this manual are fitted with a negatively earthed electrical system. The electrical system also contains polarity sensitive items which may be irreparably damaged if incorrectly connected.

An alternator, driven by a belt from the engine, supplies the necessary power for the system when the engine is running and two 6-volt lead/acid batteries connected in series supply the power for the starter motor and ancilliaries when the engine is not running.

The oil pressure gauge is electrically operated, as is the tachometer. The fuel contents and coolant temperature gauges are electrically operated, using a special supply from a voltage stabilizer unit instead of directly from the battery.

There are wiring diagrams in Technical Data at the end of this manual to enable those with electrical experience to trace and correct wiring faults. A simple voltmeter, or even a 12-volt test bulb, may be used to check continuity of wiring or to determine the terminals up to which electrical power is reaching, by connecting it between the suspect terminal and a good earth. Only high-grade instruments may be used for testing or adjusting components since cheap instruments will not be able to measure to the accuracy required.

Detailed instructions for the servicing of the electrical equipment will be found in this chapter, but it must be pointed out that it is a waste of time and money to try to repair items that are seriously defective, either electrically or mechanically. Such items should be returned and new or reconditioned units fitted in their place. Most items can be renewed on an exchange basis.

Do not make or break any connections in the charging circuit while the engine is running or components may be damaged.

Excessive voltage will damage diodes or transistors, so disconnect the circuit from any items containing these (alternator, radio, self-dipping mirrors etc), before carrying out any arc welding repairs to the car or boost charging the batteries.

12:2 The batteries

These are mounted in trays under the rear cockpit floor and each battery is held in place by a clamping plate and two bolts. The batteries are accessible after removing the panel in the rear floor. The panel is held in place by five quick-release fasteners.

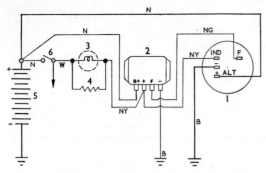

FIG 12:1 16 AC alternator charging circuit details

Key to Fig 12:1 1 Alternator 2 Control box
3 Warning light 4 Resistance 5 Battery 6 Ignition
switch

Maintenance:

Heavy demands are made on the battery, especially in winter, and if battery maintenance is neglected then the performance of the whole electrical system will suffer.

1 Regularly check the level of the electrolyte in each battery. Remove the battery vent cover, using the grip at the centre of the cover. If no electrolyte is visible in the battery, add pure distilled water until the three filling tubes and trough are full. Replace the cover and the levels will automatically be correct. **The cover must always be fitted, except when testing or filling.**

2 Always keep the tops of the batteries clean and dry. Moisture and dirt will provide a leakage path for the battery voltage. If the metal surrounds and clamp plate for the batteries are corroded, either by acid spillage or galvanic action, remove the batteries and wash the parts with dilute ammonia followed by plenty of clean water. When the metal parts are dry, paint them with anti-sulphuric paint.

3 Keep the battery connectors clean and tight. A high-resistance at the connectors is a common cause for the car failing to start. Wash off any corrosion using dilute ammonia followed by clean water. Smear the terminal posts and connectors with petroleum jelly before remaking the connections.

4 If the car stands idle for long periods, or the batteries have been removed for storage, the batteries should be given a freshening up charge every month. Failure to do this will cause the battery plates to sulphate, thus ruining the batteries. **Leave the vent covers in place when charging the batteries otherwise the gases will cause the electrolyte to flood out.**

Testing:

Remove the batteries and check that their casings and tops are free from cracks or damage. Only when electrolyte has been spilled or lost through leakage should electrolyte of the correct specific gravity be used to fill the batteries. **Never add concentrated acid.**

Use a hydrometer to test the specific gravity of the electrolyte in each cell. If the level is too low to allow sufficient electrolyte to be drawn up into the hydrometer, fill the battery and charge it for 30 minutes to throughly mix the water and electrolyte.

The indications from the hydrometer readings are as follows:

Specific gravity	*Cell state*
For climates below 32°C (90°F)	
1.270 to 1.290	Fully charged
1.190 to 1.210	Half-charged
1.110 to 1.130	Completely discharged

Replace spillage with electrolyte of 1.270 specific gravity.

For climates above 32°C (90°F)	
1.210 to 1.230	Fully charged
1.130 to 1.150	Half-charged
1.050 to 1.070	Completely discharged

Replace spillage with electrolyte of 1.210 specific gravity.

The above figures are given assuming a standard electrolyte temperature of 16°C (60°F). Correct to standard temperature by adding .002 to the reading for every 3°C (5°F) increment that the electrolyte temperature is above standard. Similarly subtract .002 for every increment that the electrolyte is below standard temperature.

All three cells of each battery should be within .040 specific gravity of each other and both batteries should give approximately the same readings. If one cell varies by more than this it indicates an internal defect. This will be confirmed if the electrolyte from that cell appears dirty or full of specks.

Electrolyte:

Electrolyte of the correct specific gravity may be prepared by adding concentrated acid to distilled water, in a glass or earthenware container. Heat will be produced so allow the mixture to cool before taking specific gravity readings. **Never add water to concentrated acid as the acid will sputter dangerously.**

12:3 The alternator

The alternator replaces the generator in the conventional electrical system. The advantages of an alternator are that it has greater reliability and will produce charging current for a greater speed range than a generator.

The alternator produces an AC voltage which is then changed into DC by an internal rectifier pack. On cars fitted with a Lucas 16 AC alternator the control is by a separate 4 TR control box and this charging circuit is shown in **FIG 12:1**. Some cars may be fitted with a Lucas 16 ACR alternator where the control unit is embodied in the alternator itself. The main current runs through the stator while the controlling field current runs through the revolving rotor. Complex commutators and brush gear are avoided and the field current is taken through two brushes and slip rings which do not need to take a heavy current.

Alternator tests:

If the alternator is not charging the following checks should be made before testing or dismantling the alternator.

1 Check that the driving belt is not slipping and if necessary adjust it as described in **Chapter 4, Section 4:4.**

2 Check the wiring system for loose connections or defective insulation. Pay particular attention to the battery connectors as if these are dirty or corroded they will prevent the alternator from charging the battery and will also stop the full output of the battery from being used. Make sure that the multi-socket connectors are securely in place.

3 Test the battery as described in **Section 12:2** to make sure that it is capable of holding a charge, and ensure that it is fully charged if further tests are to be made.

4 Connect a high-grade voltmeter between the positive terminal of the alternator and the positive terminal of the battery. Start the engine and run it at 3300 rev/min. Switch on the headlamps and check the voltage drop. Repeat the test with the voltmeter connected between the negative terminals of the battery and alternator.

On 16 AC alternators the voltage drop should not exceed .2 volts in either test, and on the 16 ACR alternator the voltage drop should not exceed .5 volts between the positive terminals and .25 volts between the negative terminals. If the voltage drop is exceeded then there is a high resistance in the charging circuit which must be traced and cured.

Provided that the previous checks are satisfactory, test the 16 AC alternator as follows:

1 Start the engine and run it until the alternator has reached its normal operating temperature. Stop the engine and withdraw the multi-socket connector from the alternator. Connect up a test circuit as shown in **FIG 12:2**. Do not connect the variable resistor 4 into the circuit until the test is ready to begin otherwise it will drain the battery. Make sure that the correct polarity of all connections is observed otherwise components will be seriously damaged.

2 Start the engine and gradually increase its speed. At 850 rev/min the test bulb 3 should go out. Increase the engine speed to 3300 rev/min and adjust the variable resistor 4 until the voltmeter reads 14 volts.

3 At these settings the ammeter should give a reading of approximately 34 amps and the test bulb should be extinguished. If the ammeter is not at the correct reading, fluctuates or the test bulb fails to extinguish fully, or the alternator operates noisily or overheats,

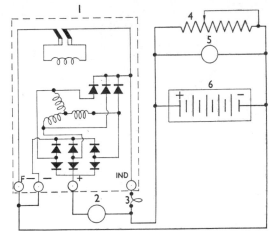

FIG 12:2 Test circuit for checking 16 AC alternator output

Key to Fig 12:2 1 Alternator 2 0-40 amp ammeter 3 12-volt, 2.2 watt bulb 4 0-15 ohm, 35 amp variable resistance 5 0-20 volt voltmeter 6 12-volt battery

then there is a defect and the alternator will have to be removed for further examination.

Test the 16 ACR alternator as follows:

1 Disconnect both connector blocks from the alternator and connect a voltmeter to each connector tag of the two connector blocks in turn and positive earth. With the ignition switched on the voltmeter should read battery voltage at each tag. If battery voltage is not obtainable trace through and cure the fault.

2 Remove the alternator end cover, which will then leave the alternator as shown in **FIG 12:3**. Bridge the green connector F3, on the alternator to earth. Refit the three-way connector to the alternator and connect an ammeter between the positive output terminal 2 and the positive lead in the two-way connector. Start the engine and run it at 3300 rev/min. If the ammeter does not register 34 amps or there are any other defects, then the alternator is defective and must be removed for further examination.

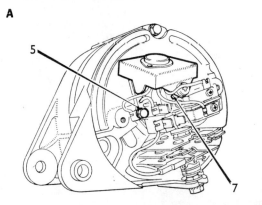

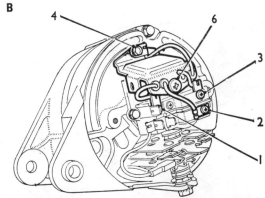

FIG 12:3 Control unit attachments on 16.ACR alternators

Key to Fig 12:3 **A** 11.TR unit **B** 8.TR unit 1 Battery + (B+) 2 Positive (+) 3 Field (F) 4 Negative earth (—) 5 Brush box retaining screw 6 Upper mounting screw 7 Spacer (11.TR only)

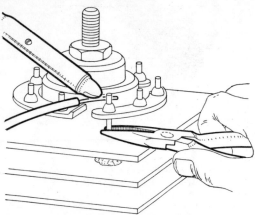

FIG 12:4 Using a pair of long-nosed pliers as a heat sink for the diodes

carried out instead. A diode check should also be carried out if the previous tests indicate a fault in the alternator.

Faulty diodes will affect the alternator output, and in certain circumstances will cause it to overheat as well as running with excessive noise.

1 Remove the end cover. Unsolder the three stator wires, carefully noting their positions, and using a pair or long-nosed pliers to prevent the heat from reaching the diodes, as shown in **FIG 12:4**. Remove the two brush moulding screws, slacken the rectifier pack securing nuts and remove the rectifier pack. On 16 ACR alternators the control unit attachments are shown in **FIG 12:3**.

2 Use a 12-volt battery (or the two car batteries in series) and a 1.5 watt test bulb to check each diode in turn. Connect the bulb in series with the battery to each diode pin and its corresponding heat sink, then repeat the test reversing the polarity. The bulb should light with the current flowing in one direction only. If the bulb either lights in both directions or does not light in either direction then the diode is faulty.

Any faulty diodes mean that the complete rectifier pack must be renewed.

3 Replace the parts in the reverse order of removal. Solder the stator wires back to their correct connections as rapidly as possible, again using a pair of long-nosed pliers as a heat sink.

3 Stop the engine and remove the bridge between F and earth. Connect a voltmeter across the battery terminals. Start the engine and again run it at 3300 rev/min. If the ammeter reads zero then the regulator pack is defective and must be renewed. Adjust the engine speed until the ammeter reading falls below 10 amps and at this speed the voltmeter should read 14.0 to 14.4 volts. If the voltmeter reading is not within these limits either the regulator pack is defective or else there is a high resistance in the charging leads.

Diode check:

If suitable instruments are not available to carry out the tests described previously, a diode check should be

Dismantling:

The details of the alternator are shown in **FIG 12:5**.

1 Remove the end cover, control unit (if fitted), brush-gear and rectifier pack as described for the Diode test.

2 Remove the through-bolts 3. Fit a tool, whose dimensions are shown in **FIG 12:6**, over the slip ring moulding 6 and carefully drive the bearing from its

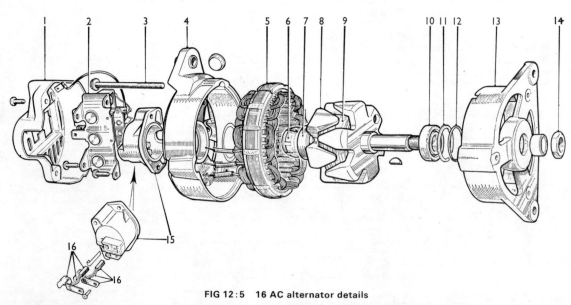

FIG 12:5   16 AC alternator details

Key to Fig 12:5   1 Cover   2 Rectifier pack   3 Through-bolt   4 Slip ring end bracket   5 Stator   6 Slip rings
7 Slip ring end bearing   8 Rotor   9 Field windings   10 Drive end bearing   11 Circlip   12 Oil sealing ring   13 Drive
end bracket   14 Shaft nut   15 Brush box moulding   16 Brush assembly

housing with the tool fitting against the outer track of the bearing 7. Solder may have to be carefully filed off the slip ring connections in order to allow the tool to pass over the moulding.

3 Remove the shaft nut 14 and withdraw the washer, pulley and cooling fan. Extract the key from the rotor shaft and press the drive end bracket off the rotor shaft. The bearing 10 can be removed from the drive end bracket 13 after removing the circlip 11.

4 The slip ring end bearing 7 can be removed after unsoldering the field coil connections and withdrawing the moulding.

Rotor:

Check the rotor for obvious signs of damage. Connect either an ohmmeter or a 12-volt supply in series with an ammeter across the slip rings. The ohmeter should read

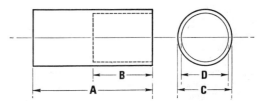

FIG 12:6 Dimensions for tool for dismantling alternator
Key to Fig 12:6   A= 3 inch (76 mm)   B= 1.5 inch (38 mm)   C= 1.32 inch (33.5 mm)   D= 1.24 inch 31.5 mm)

4.3 ohms while the ammeter should read 3 amps for the field coils to be satisfactory.

A 110 AC volt supply is required to check the insulation. Use a 15 watt test bulb between each slip ring and the rotor metal parts, and if the lamp lights then the insulation is defective. Renew a defective rotor.

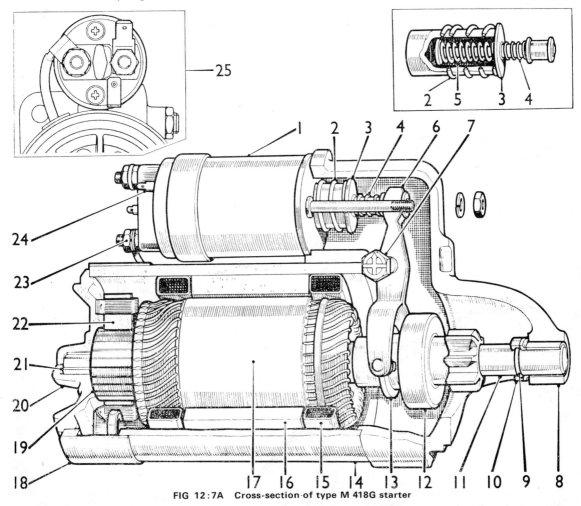

FIG 12:7A   Cross-section of type M 418G starter

Key to Fig 12:7A   1 Solenoid   2 Plunger return spring   3 Plunger   4 Lost motion spring   5 Drive engagement spring
6 Engaging lever   7 Pivot pin   8 Fixing bracket   9 Retaining ring   10 Thrust collar   11 Armature shaft extension
12 Clutch   13 Drive operating plate   14 Yoke   15 Field coils   16 Pole shoes   17 Armature   18 Cover band
19 Commutator   20 End bracket   21 Bush bearing   22 Brushes   23 Solenoid 'STA' terminal   24 Solenoid operating terminal
25 Repositioned solenoid (later cars)

Stator:

Connect a 12-volt supply and 36 watt test lamp between any pair of stator wires. Repeat the test between one of the original wires and the third wire. If the lamp fails to light on either test then the stator is defective and must be renewed. Check the stator insulation using a 110 AC volt 15 watt test lamp.

Slip rings and brushgear:

Clean the slip ring surfaces using a cloth moistened in fuel. Light burn marks may be polished away using fine glasspaper. **Never use emerycloth on the slip rings,** as particles will be imbedded in the rings, and **never machine the slip rings** as the high speed performance of the alternator will suffer.

Renew the brushes if less than .2 inch (5 mm) of brush is protruding when the brushes are free.

Use a modified spring balance and check that the spring pressure is 7 to 10 oz (198 to 283 gramme) when the brush face is pressed flush with the face of the housing. Renew the brushes and springs if they are outside the limits given.

If the brushes are stiff to move in their housings, clean the parts with a petrol moistened cloth. The sides of the brushes may also be polished on a smooth file.

Reassembly:

The parts are reassembled in the reverse order of dismantling but note the following points:

1 Wash the bearings in clean fuel and renew them if they are worn. Pack the bearings with Shell Alvania RA.

The slip ring end bearing 7 must be fitted with its open side towards the rotor and pressed fully into place on the shaft.

2 The field connections should be resoldered with Fry's HT3 solder. Never use an acid-based flux on the alternator soldered connections.

3 Use a length of suitable diameter tube to support the inner track of the bearing 10 when refitting the rotor to the drive end bracket. The bracket may easily be damaged if it is the sole means of support for the pressure.

12:4 The starter motor

Up to 1972 the starter fitted to these cars was the Lucas type M 418G while later models have the model 2M100 which differs mainly in having a face type commutator in place of the older drum type. The M 418G type is illustrated in **FIG 12:7A** and described in this section. Differences in the construction of the later pattern can be seen in **FIG 12:7B**.

When the solenoid is first energized it moves the pinion into mesh with the flywheel ring gear and further movement of the solenoid then closes the contacts which allow current to flow to the starter motor. In the event of tooth to tooth abutment the springs compress allowing the solenoid to complete its range of movement and as soon as the motor rotates the teeth engage fully.

The solenoid contains two coils. A heavy duty coil is used for the initial engagement and this shorts out when the contacts close, leaving the solenoid held in position by a weaker holding-in coil.

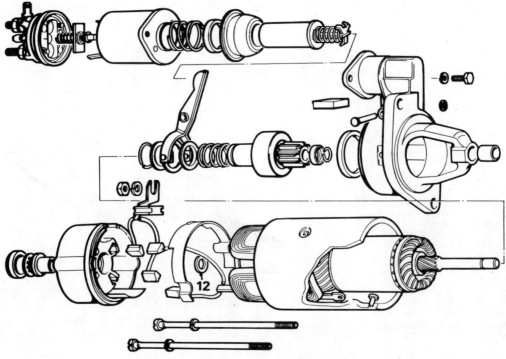

FIG 12:7B   Components of type 2M100 starter

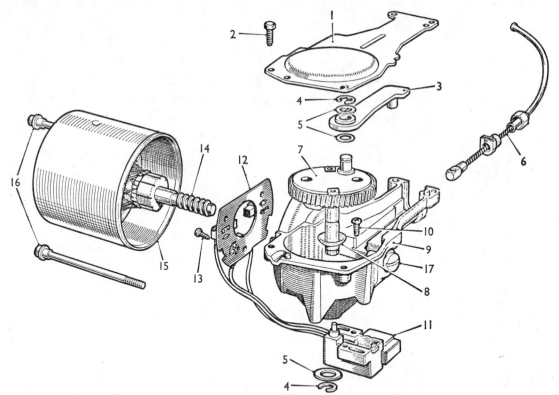

FIG 12:8   Windscreen wiper motor details

Key to Fig 12:8   1 Gearbox cover   2 Screw for cover   3 Connecting rod   4 Circlip   5 Plain washer   6 Cable assembly   7 Shaft and gear   8 Dished washer   9 Gearbox   10 Screw for limit switch   11 Limit switch assembly   12 Brush gear   13 Screw for brush gear   14 Armature   15 Yoke assembly   16 Through-bolts   17 Armature adjusting screw

Tests for a starter motor that does not operate:

1 Check the condition of the battery terminals and connectors. If these are dirty or loose then they will cause a high resistance which will prevent the starter motor from operating satisfactorily. At the same time check that the battery is fully charged, and capable of holding a charge.

2 Switch on the lights and again operate the starter. If the lights go dim this shows that the starter motor is taking current and is probably jammed. Engage a gear and rock the car backwards and forwards. If this does not free the starter motor, or the motor regularly jams, then it will have to be removed for further examination.

3 If the lights do not go dim then there is a fault either in the switch, wiring or solenoid. Use a voltmeter or 12-volt test lamp to trace the defect. If power is found to be reaching as far as the solenoid, but the motor still fails to operate, short across the heavy duty terminals on the solenoid with a thick piece of metal, such as an old pair of pliers, and if the motor now operates then the solenoid is defective. If the starter motor does not operate even though current is reaching it, it will have to be removed for further examination.

Removal:

Remove the distributor by taking out the bolts securing the clamp plate to the housing. **Do not slacken the distributor clamp plate pinch bolt or the ignition timing will be lost.** Remove the top starter motor securing bolt and disconnect the wiring from the solenoid terminals. Remove the bottom securing bolt and remove the starter motor from the car.

Replace the starter motor in the reverse order of removal.

Examining the commutator and brushgear:

Remove the coverband 18. Hold back each of the brush springs in turn and check that the brushes move freely by gently pulling on their flexible connectors. If the brushes are stiff they should be withdrawn and their sides lightly polished on a smooth file. Clean out the brush housings with a fuel-moistened cloth. If the brushes are worn to $\frac{5}{16}$ inch (8 mm) they must be renewed. Remove the commutator end bracket and carefully unsolder and open up the clips securing the flexible connectors. Solder the new brush connectors into place taking care to prevent solder from creeping up the flexible connectors. New brushes do not require bedding-in, but brushes that have been in use should be replaced in their original positions and facing in the original direction.

Use a spring balance to check the brush spring tension. Renew the springs if their tension is less than 36 oz (1.02 kg) when acting on new brushes.

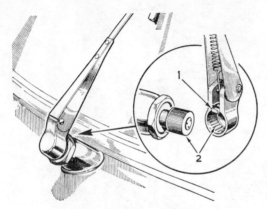

FIG 12:9 Wiper arm attachments

Key to Fig 12:9   1 Retaining clip   2 Splined drive

The commutator can be cleaned by wiping it with a fuel-moistened cloth. If the commutator shows burn marks or wear, dismantle the starter motor and rotate the commutator in a strip of glasspaper, **never use emery-cloth or other abrasives.** If the damage is too deep to be polished off, the armature will have to be mounted in a lathe and the damage skimmed off at high-speed with a very sharp tool. Ideally a light finishing cut should be given using a diamond-tipped tool, but an adequate finish is obtainable by polishing with fine glasspaper. The minimum diameter to which the commutator may be skimmed is $1\frac{17}{32}$ inch. **Do not undercut the insulation between the copper segments.**

Dismantling the starter motor:

1 Disconnect the cable between the motor and the STA terminal on the solenoid. Remove the solenoid securing nuts and withdraw the solenoid while disengaging the solenoid plunger 3 from the engagement lever 6.

2 Remove the coverband 18, hold back the springs and withdraw the brushes from their housings. Take out the long through-bolts and remove the commutator end bracket 20. Slacken the locknut and unscrew the pivot pin 7.

3 Carefully support the yoke 14 and gently tap off the fixing end bracket 8, remove the engaging lever 6 and withdraw the armature assembly and collect the thrust washer from the drive end of the armature shaft.

4 Use a $\frac{5}{8}$ inch diameter tube to drive the thrust collar 10 off the retaining ring 9 and towards the armature. Prise out the retaining ring 9 and withdraw the collar 10, drive assembly 12 and operating plate 13 from the armature shaft.

The solenoid:

Normally if this is defective it should be renewed. Check that the plunger assembly moves freely in the solenoid bore and use fine emerycloth to remove any dirt or corrosion. Check the springs 2, 4 and 5.

The solenoid can be partially dismantled, though it is not recommended. Remove the waterproof tape from around the body. Take off all the nuts and washers from the heavy duty terminals and remove the two cross-headed screws. Apply a hot soldering iron to the unmarked terminal tag and, when the solder is molten, free the wire and remove the plastic contact assembly. Take great care not to lose the springs from the contacts. File the contacts clean and smooth, finally polishing them with fine glasspaper. Reassemble the solenoid in the reverse order of dismantling.

Checking the armature:

Examine both the commutator and armature to check that no segments have lifted because of overspeeding. If this has occurred then the clutch 12 should be examined as it is probably defective.

Apart from servicing the commutator, very little can be done to the armature. Special equipment is required to check the armature coils and if the armature is damaged or bent it must be renewed, as it must not be machined and it is impossible to straighten a bent shaft with sufficient accuracy and without damaging the laminations. If the armature is suspect, either have it checked at an electrical specialist or fit a satisfactory armature as a comparison.

Field coils:

These are secured in place by the polepieces which are in turn held by special screws. A special wheel screwdriver is required to undo and tighten these screws, so if the field coils are defective they should be renewed by a garage. Loose polepieces will damage the armature so if the securing screws can be turned by an ordinary screwdriver they must be resecured by a garage.

Connect a test lamp and 12-volt supply between the STA cable and each of the field coil brushes in turn, taking care not to earth the brushes or their connectors onto the yoke. If the lamp does not light then the coils are defective. Connect the test lamp between each brush in turn and the yoke and if the lamp now lights then the insulation is defective. If possible use a 15 watt 110 AC test lamp for insulation tests.

Commutator end bracket:

Brush away all loose dirt and check the insulation between the insulated brushboxes and the bracket, preferably using a 15 watt 110 AC volt test lamp. Renew the bracket if the insulation is defective.

Drive clutch:

Wipe away any external dirt or grease but do not wash the unit in solvents or the internal lubrication will be removed. The unit must instantaneously take up drive but must rotate freely in the opposite direction. Check that the unit slides freely on the armature shaft splines.

Renewing the bearings:

These must be renewed if they are so worn that they allow sideways movement of the armature. Remove the old bushes by squarely screwing a $\frac{9}{16}$ inch tap partially into them and then withdrawing them on the tap.

Before refitting, new bushes must be soaked in engine oil for a period of 24 hours. In an emergency the period can be reduced by heating the oil to 100°C (212°F) over a bath of boiling water, leaving the bushes to soak for two hours in the heated oil and then fitting the bushes when the oil has cooled down.

Press the new bushes into place, using a stepped mandrel whose highly polished spigot is of the same length as the bush and .0005 inch (.013 mm) greater in diameter than the shaft which is to fit into the bush. **Do not ream or bore the bushes after they have been fitted as this will destroy the porosity of the material.**

Reassembling the starter motor:

The motor is reassembled in the reverse order of dismantling but note the following points:
1 Lubricate all bearing surfaces lightly with Shell Retinax A grease or the equivalent.
2 The pivot pin 7 need only be screwed far enough in to keep it in position safely but make sure that the arrow on the head points in the upper 180 degree arc of movement.
3 Make sure that the thrust collar 10 is pressed firmly over the retaining ring 9 and do not forget to refit the thrust washer.
4 When the motor has been reassembled then the pinion travel must be set as follows.

Adjusting pinion travel:

1 Connect a 6-volt supply (one of the car batteries) and a switch between the unmarked terminal tag on the solenoid and the yoke or an earth point on the motor. Slacken the locknut on the pivot pin 7 and screw the pivot pin home, then unscrew it sufficiently to ensure that the full arc of adjustment is available.
2 Energize the circuit so that the drive is thrown out into mesh. **Keep the energized period as short as possible to prevent overheating of the coils.** Press the pinion towards the armature to take up any slack and accurately measure the distance between the pinion and thrust collar with feeler gauges.
3 The correct distance should be .005 to .015 inch (.13 to .4 mm). If the distance is incorrect adjust the pivot pin 7 until the distance is within limits. **The arrow on the pivot pin must be pointing in the upper arc indicated by the arrows cast in the casting.**
4 When the adjustment is correct, disconnect the battery and switch.

Testing the motor:

Connect a 10-volt supply and switch across the un-marked tag on the solenoid and the yoke of the motor (10 volts is obtainable by using 5 cells of a lead/acid battery). Connect a test lamp and separate battery across the solenoid heavy duty terminals of the solenoid.

Fit a stop to prevent the pinion from moving beyond its normal out of mesh position and briefly close the switch. The test lamp should glow steadily and continuously while the solenoid is energized.

Repeat the test with the stop removed and when the switch is again opened hold the pinion to prevent it returning. The test lamp should go out. If the lamp does not light and go out as it should do then the solenoid is defective and must be renewed.

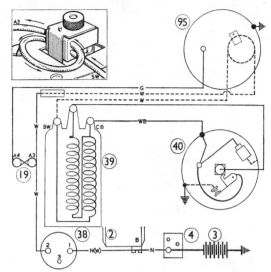

FIG 12:10   Impulse tachometer circuit. Inset shows the correct routing for the impulse lead

Key to Fig 12:10	2 Control box	3 Batteries (12-volt)
4 Starter solenoid	19 Fuse	38 Ignition switch
39 Ignition coil	40 Distributor	95 Tachometer

The starter motor can be tested by mounting it in a vice and connecting it by heavy duty cables to a 12-volt battery. The motor should rotate rapidly and freely. Test data figures are given in Technical Data.

12:5 The alternator control unit:

On 16 AC alternators a separate 4TR unit is fitted to control the alternator output.
1 Check that the alternator is performing satisfactorily (see **Section 12:3**).
2 Connect a voltmeter across the battery terminals and an ammeter in series with the alternator main output cable.
3 Start the engine and run it at a speed of 2750 rev/min until a steady ammeter reading of 5 amps is obtained. If the voltmeter reading is unsteady or outside the limits of 14.3 to 14.7 volts the control unit is defective and must be renewed.

12:6 The windscreen wipers

A two-speed motor is fitted as standard equipment, and the details of the motor are shown in **FIG 12:8**. The cable assembly 6 passes through tubing mounted to the body and operates the wheelboxes mounted under the facia.

Routine maintenance is confined to renewing the wiper blades when they no longer give a clean sweep, and occasionally lubricating the rubber grommets around the wheelbox spindles with a few drops of glycerine. The cable rack and motor gearbox are packed with grease on assembly and require no routine maintenance.

Poor or no operation:

Check the fuse. If this has blown then trace through the wiring for faults such as damaged insulation. If no fault is found then renew the fuse, using one of the correct

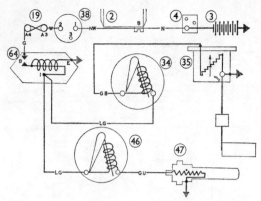

FIG 12:11   Voltage stabilized instruments circuit

Key to Fig 12:11   2 Control box   3 Batteries (12-volt)
4 Starter solenoid   19 Fuse   34 Fuel gauge   35 Fuel
tank unit   38 Ignition switch   46 Coolant temperature
gauge   47 Coolant temperature transmitter   64 Voltage
stabilizer

rating. If the fuse blows again and there is no fault in the
wiring then the motor will have to be removed for further
examination.

If the wipers operate sluggishly then check through
the wiring for faults such as poor connections. Use a
voltmeter or 12-volt test bulb to check the wiring. The
voltmeter should read battery voltage and the bulb glow
brightly at all points.

Remove the gearbox cover 1 and disconnect the
connecting rod 3 from the cable rack 6 by removing the
circlip 4. Connect an accurate ammeter into the circuit
and switch on the motor. Allow the motor to run for one
minute before taking readings. The current consumption
should be 1.5 amps at normal speed and 2.0 amps at high
speed, while the motor should operate at a speed of 46 to
52 cycles/minute at normal speed and 60 to 70 cycles/
minute at high speed.

If the motor operates satisfactorily when disconnected
from the cable but the overall operation of the wipers is
sluggish, then there is a fault in the wiper boxes or cables.
Remove the wiper arms and use a spring balance to check
that the force required to move the cable does not exceed
6 lbs (4 kg). If this force is exceeded then either the tubes
are damaged or misaligned or the wheelboxes are
damaged.

Abnormal current demands by the motor can be
caused by defective brushgear or faulty armature, and a
high current consumption will also be caused by internal
shortcircuits or excessive internal friction. No field coils
are fitted as the exciting field is produced by a permanent
magnet in the yoke assembly 15.

Dismantling the motor:

1 Remove the motor from the car. Disconnect the wiring
and battery connections (motor connections accessible after removing the righthand panel under the
facia). Remove both wiper arms complete. Take
out the two motor mounting bolts, unscrew the large
nut securing the tubing to the motor body and withdraw the motor complete with the cable rack 6.

2 Remove the gearbox cover 1 and disconnect the connecting rod 3 by removing the circlip 4 and carefully
noting the positions of the plain washers 5. Remove
the circlip 4 and other plain washer 5. Check that the
end of the shaft is free from burrs or sharp edges,
cleaning it with emerycloth or by careful filing if
required. Withdraw the shaft and gear 7, noting the
position and direction of the dished washer 8. Do not
remove the crankpin mounting plate from the gear
unless it is necessary and not until the relation of the
crankpin to the gear has been carefully marked.

3 Mark indelibly across the yoke 15 and gearbox flange 9
so that they will be reassembled in the same relative
positions. If this precaution is omitted then the motor
may run in reverse on reassembly. Take out the two
through-bolts 16 and withdraw the yoke. The
armature 14 will be drawn out with the yoke by the
permanent magnet, so do not withdraw them further
than $\frac{3}{16}$ inch. Ease the brushes off the commutator 4

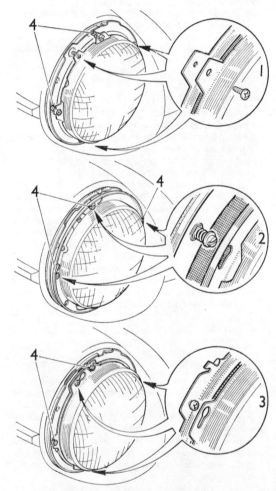

FIG 12:12   Headlamp unit attachments

Key to Fig 12:12   1 Removable screw   2 Combined
adjusting/retaining screw   3 Captive retaining screw
4 Beam setting adjusting screws

and then completely withdraw the parts, taking care not to contaminate the brushes with grease.

4 Remove the screws 10 and 13 to free the limit switch 11 and brushgear assembly 12.

Brushgear:

Renew the assembly if the normal brushes are worn down to a length of $\frac{3}{16}$ inch (4.8 mm) or if the high speed brush is so worn that the narrow portion is nearly worn away.

Use a modified spring balance to check the spring pressure. The spring pressure should be 5 to 7 oz (140 to 200 gramme) when the brush is pressed in so that the bottom of the brush is flush with the bottom of the slot in the brushbox. Renew the assembly if the springs are weak.

Commutator and armature:

Clean the commutator with a fuel-moistened cloth. Light burn marks or wear can be polished off using fine glasspaper.

If the armature is suspected, the motor should be reassembled and tested with an armature of known satisfactory performance, as this is the best test readily available. Renew the armature if it shows obvious signs of damage such as charring, loose laminations or lifted commutator segments.

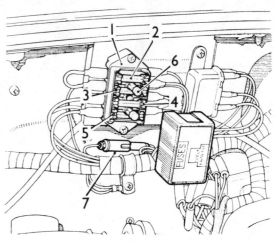

FIG 12:14   Fuse box details

Key to Fig 12:14   1 Fuse block   2/3 Side and tail lamps   4 Ignition switch circuits   5 Independent circuits   6 Spare fuses   7 Line fuse

Reassembling the motor:

The motor is reassembled and refitted in the reverse order of dismantling and removal. Check that the self-lubricating bearings move freely in their spring clips. Lubricate all the shafts and bearings with Shell Turbo 41 oil and pack the gearbox and cable rack with Ragosine Listate grease. Take great care to prevent oil or grease from contaminating the brushes or commutator.

Armature end float:

The screw 17 controls the armature end float, which is correct at .004 to .008 inch (.1 to .21 mm). If the end float is insufficient, fit packing washers under the screw to correct. If the end float is excessive, the underside of the screw head will have to be turned down in a lathe.

Reconditioned armatures are supplied with a screw and locknut so that the end float can be adjusted without shimming or machining.

Wheelboxes:

Remove the motor and cable rack. From outside the car unscrew the nut securing the unit and remove the washer and rubber bush. Working under the facia, slacken the wheelbox backplate screws so that the tubing can be freed from them and withdraw the wheelboxes from the car.

The wheelboxes are replaced in the reverse order of removal. Take care to align the tubing with the wheelboxes. An oversize cable rack gauge is available at Lucas agents and, provided that this gauge moves freely through the tubing with the wheelboxes removed, then the tubing is satisfactory.

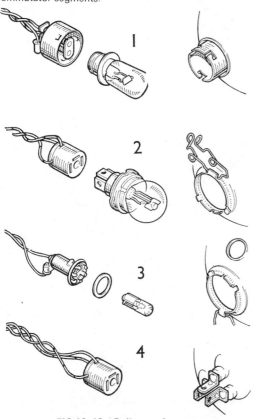

FIG 12:13   Bulb attachments

Key to Fig 12:13   1 Cap type holder   2 Spring clip type   3 Headlamp pilot lamp   4 Sealed beam unit

Wiper arms:

The two types of attachment of the wiper arms are shown in **FIG 12:9**.

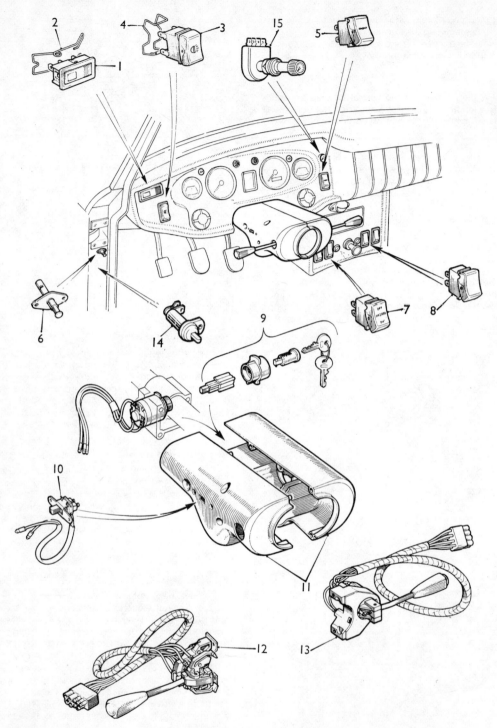

FIG 12:15   Switches for USA model cars

Key to Fig 12:15   1 Brake pressure—warning light/test push   2 Retaining clip   3 Lighting switch   4 Retaining clip
5 Heater blower switch   6 Door switch—interior light   7 Hazard warning switch   8 Map light switch   9 Ignition switch
10 Panel light switch   11 Steering column switch cowl   12 Direction indicator/headlight flasher—low/high beam/horn switch
13 Windshield wiper/washer and overdrive switch   14 Audible warning door switch   15 Panel lamp rheostat switch

12:7 Instruments

Tachometer (rev counter):

An electrical impulse type of tachometer is fitted to the models covered by this manual. The circuit for the tachometer is shown in **FIG 12:10**. Note that the inset shows the correct method of fitting the pulse lead so that it forms a symmetrical loop without being pulled tight.

If the tachometer fails to operate, check the appropriate fuse and if it has blown trace the cause. Loose or poor connections will result in faulty readings.

Voltage stabilized instruments:

The fuel contents and coolant temperature gauges take their supply from a bi-metallic voltage stabilizer unit. The stabilizer unit produces a varying voltage which, over a period of time, allows exactly the same current to flow as a stable 10-volt supply would have given over the same period. Since the voltage is not constant the performance of the components cannot be checked with ordinary instruments and a special tester must be used. The circuit for the instruments is shown in **FIG 12:11**.

If a fault develops do not test the instruments by connecting them directly across full battery voltage. Check through the wiring for loose or broken connections and faulty insulation. Without the correct Smiths tester, the instruments and transmitters will have to be checked by substitution and a process of elimination.

12:8 The headlamps

The light retaining screws are shown in **FIG 12:12**. Remove the rim, press the unit slightly inwards and rotate it anticlockwise to free it from the retaining screws. Do not turn the adjusting screws 4 (also shown in inset 2) when these secure the unit.

The bulb attachments are shown in **FIG 12:13**. On the sealed-beam type of unit shown at 4 the complete unit must be renewed if a filament burns out.

Beam setting:

The beam alignment is set by adjusting the screws 4 on all types of headlamp. The main beams are usually set to be parallel with the road and running parallel to the centre line of the car. This can be checked by standing the car squarely on to a whitewashed line and measuring the positions of the beam centres. However, to conform with local regulations it is best to have the headlamps set on a beamsetter gauge by a garage as there can then be no doubt as to the accuracy of the adjustments.

12:9 Fuses

The fuse box, shown in **FIG 12:14**, is fitted to the righthand wing valance. The circuits that the fuses protect are easily traced by reference to the appropriate wiring diagram (see Technical Data).

A blown fuse is indicated by the circuits that it protects failing to operate. After a period of time fuses will blow for no reason, but the systems should be briefly checked before fitting a new fuse. Switch on the circuits separately and check that the fuse does not blow. If the fuse blows again some idea of where the fault lies will have been gained. The fault must be traced and cured before fitting

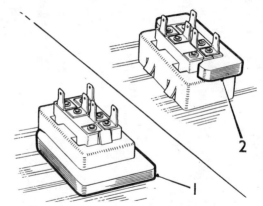

FIG 12:16 Removing rocker-type switches from USA models, using special tool No. 18G.1145

Key to Fig 12:16   1 Switch complete with bezel
2 Switch interior only

another new fuse. **Do not be tempted to fit fuses of a higher rating as this may cause damage to components or wiring.**

A line fuse is fitted below the fuse box to protect heated backlights on GT models.

12:10 The horns

If the horns fail to operate first check the appropriate fuse and then the wiring. All the connections must be clean and tight as the horns take up to 7 amps between them. Check that the horn mountings are tight and that the horn itself is not fouling on any adjacent structure.

Disconnect each horn in turn, taking great care not to allow the loose cables to earth onto the car, and check the current consumption of the other horn. Each horn should take 3 to $3\frac{1}{2}$ amps for satisfactory operation.

Remove the cover and, if required, clean the contacts by carefully filing them and then wiping with a fuel-moistened cloth. Adjust each horn in turn with the other disconnected. Slacken the locknut on the fixed contact, and rotate the adjusting nut clockwise until the horn just fails to sound when the horn push is operated. Rotate the adjusting nut by half a turn anticlockwise and lock it in position with the locknut. Refit the cover and its strap.

12:11 The flasher unit

All the parts of the unit are contained in a sealed aluminium case. The unit operates by the alternate expansion and contraction of a wire caused by the heating and cooling as current passes through it and then is cut off by the opening of the contacts.

Handle the unit with care and do not connect it back into a live circuit as it is a delicate item and easily damaged. Once damaged it cannot be repaired and a new unit must be fitted in its place.

A warning light is fitted to the dash and this flashes at the same rate as the actual indicator lamps. A change in the flash rate or no operation of the warning light indicates a fault.

If the indicators fail to operate correctly first check that no bulbs are blown as this will alter the flash rate. With-

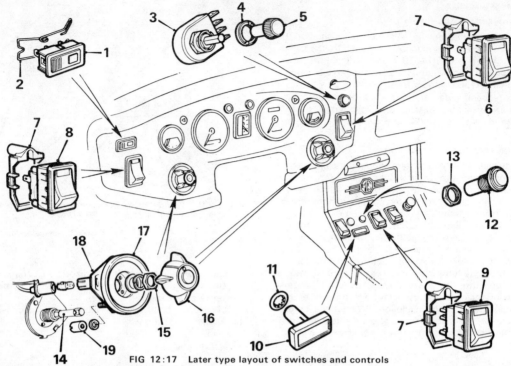

FIG 12:17   Later type layout of switches and controls

Key to Fig 12:17   1 Brake pressure warning light test-push   2 Retaining clip   3 Panel lamp rheostat switch
4 Retainer   5 Knob for rheostat switch   6 Heater blower switch   7 Retainer for rocker switch   8 Lighting switch
9 Hazard warning switch   10 Seat belt warning lamp   11 Retainer for seat belt warning lamp   12 Hazard warning lamp
13 Retainer for hazard warning lamp   14 Rotary control   15 Retaining nut   16 Rotary control knob   17 Dial assembly
18 Light box   19 Retaining nut

draw the flasher unit from its socket and check that battery voltage is reaching the B terminal with the ignition switched on. If battery voltage is present, bridge the B and L terminals with a short piece of wire. Operate the direction indicator switch in both directions and check that the appropriate indicator lamps light. If a lamp does not light but the bulb is satisfactory then check the earthing of the lamp. Correct operation of the lamps shows that the flasher unit is defective and must be replaced.

If battery voltage is not available, or the lamps do not light, then the circuit will have to be traced through and the fault found and rectified.

12:12 USA models

For safety and legal reasons these are fitted with extra circuits and rocker switches. The switches are shown in **FIG 12:15**.

Audible door warning:

The switch 14 operates a buzzer when the door is opened while the ignition key is in the lock. If the units are defective repair is made by replacing the defective component.

Brake failure warning:

The warning lamp 1 is actuated by the pressure warning switch (see **Chapter 11, Section 11:8**). The manual test should be operated at regular intervals to check that the bulb is still functioning and a brake failure is not masked by a blown bulb.

Hazard warning:

A separate switch and flasher unit operate all the indicator lamps together in case of hazard. The system is protected and should be used in the event of an accident, unless spilt fuel requires disconnection of the batteries.

Additional lights:

Front and rear side-marker lamps are fitted as standard.

Switches:

FIG 12:16 shows the method of removing switches, using special tool No. 18G.1145 to hold down the securing lugs. Note that the steering wheel has to be removed in order to take off the cowls 11 and gain access to the steering column mounted switches.

Later cars:

For 1973 models a revised layout for the switches on the instrument panel was adopted. A diagram showing the location of the switches, lamps and controls is given in **FIG 12:17**. Access to these may require the removal of the glove box, centre console or a facia panel, but otherwise there should be no difficulty for a reasonably competent home operator.

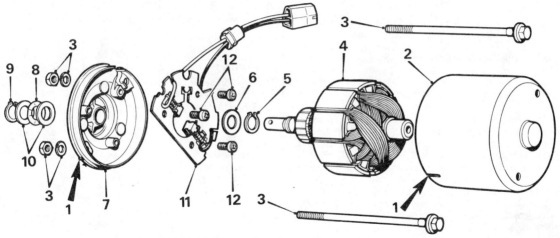

FIG 12:18 Radiator fan motor components

Key to Fig 12:18 1 Assembly marks 2 Yoke 3 Through bolts, spring washers, and nuts 4 Armature 5 Circlip
6 Thrust washer 7 End cover 8 Bowed washer 9 Circlip 10 Shims 11 Brush carrier 12 Screws

Steering column mounted switches:

In order to remove the two switches 12 and 13 in **FIG 12:15** the following procedure should be observed.
1 Withdraw the centre motif from the steering wheel, unscrew the retaining nut and pull off the steering wheel using a suitable extractor.
2 Remove the three retaining screws and lift off the left-hand half of the switch cowling 11.
3 Remove the retaining screw and lift off the righthand half of the switch cowling.
4 Remove the two screws retaining the windshield wiper/washer and overdrive switch, disconnect the switch wiring at the snap connectors and remove the switch together with the wiring.
5 Remove two retaining screws, disconnect the wiring and remove the direction indicator and flasher switch.
6 Reverse the above sequence to refit.

12:13 Warning and panel lamps

Instrument panel:

To gain access to the bulbs behind the panel, unscrew the three screws securing the bottom panel and pull it forwards from its retaining clips at the rear. The bulbs are housed in holders which are a press fit into the back of the panel.

Console:

On early cars the procedure is as follows: Release the carpet fastener behind the console, turn back the carpet covering the gearbox tunnel, remove the four console retaining screws and pull the console to the rear. The bulb holders can now be withdrawn from the warning lamps.
On later cars, first remove the screws retaining the trim ring for the gear lever gaiter, then remove the gear lever knob, the screw inside the arm rest box and the arm-rest centre console assembly complete. Remove the four vertical console retaining screws and draw the console

rearwards. The bulb holders are now exposed for withdrawal from their lamps.
When radio or ashtrays are fitted these will need to be removed before the console can be withdrawn.

Brake:

Withdraw the holder and test-push assembly from the panel to gain access. Gently press the switch rocker pivot lugs inwards and withdraw the rocker from the casing.

Seat belt warning system:

Later export model cars are equipped with a system which gives audible and visible warnings if an attempt is made to start the engine or engage a gear without having first correctly secured the seat belts. This may be coupled with a sequential control system which requires not only that the seat belts be fastened, but also that a set sequence of actions be followed.
Switches associated with this system are positioned under the seats, in the seat belt harnesses and on the gearbox. In normal use they require no maintenance and the control unit, located underneath the facia panel, is not suitable for home servicing, it is usually checked on the bench and a substitute unit installed.

12:14 Radiator fan motor

Test:

Remove the fan motor (see **Chapter 4**) and take off the blades.
Connect the motor to a 13.5-volt DC supply with a moving coil ammeter in series and check that the motor light running current does not exceed 3 amps after 60 seconds from cold.
Check that the light running speed is between 3500 and 4000 rev/min under these conditions.
A low consumption and speed indicates a dirty commutator or faulty brush gear.
A high consumption indicates a faulty armature.

Dismantling:

Remove the bolts 3 (see **FIG 12:18**), withdraw the end cover 7 complete with armature 4, from the yoke 2 noting the assembly marks 1 for reassembly. Remove the circlip 9, the two shims 10, and bowed washer 8, and withdraw the armature assembly from the end cover. Withdraw the thrust washer 6 and remove the circlip 5. Remove the three screws 12 and withdraw the brush carrier assembly 11 from the end cover.

The minimum brush length is $\frac{3}{16}$ inch (4.76 mm), renew the brush gear if necessary. Ensure that the black lead is connected to its correct brush and connector pin if the leads are renewed.

Reassemble in the reverse order of dismantling and retest. If current consumption is high after reassembly it may be caused by misalignment of the end cover bearing and can usually be cured by a few light taps with a soft-faced mallet on the side of the end cover, otherwise the armature is faulty.

12:15 Fault diagnosis

(a) Battery discharged

1 Terminals loose or dirty
2 Insufficient charging current
3 Shortcircuit or defective insulation in wiring or components
4 Battery defective internally

(b) Battery will not hold charge

1 Low electrolyte level
2 Battery plates sulphated or plate separators ineffective
3 Electrolyte leakage from cracked case or top sealing compound

(c) Alternator output low or nil

1 Driving belt broken or slipping
2 Defective control unit
3 No battery supply to field coils
4 Brushes excessively worn or slip rings dirty
5 Weak or broken brush springs
6 Multi-socket connectors not properly fitted
7 High resistance in charging leads
8 Diodes failed in rectifier pack (may include overheating and noisy operation)
9 Stator or field coils defective
10 Internal mechanical damage

(d) Alternator noisy

1 Defective or worn bearings
2 Shortcircuited live side output diode (alternator also overheats)

3 Open circuit earth side output diode
4 One phase winding shorted to earth
5 Shortcircuit in field diode

(e) Starter runs but does not turn engine

1 Pinion and clutch sticking or defective clutch
2 Broken teeth on pinion or flywheel ring gear
3 Broken springs in starter motor

(f) Starter motor lacks power or will not operate

1 Battery discharged, or terminal connectors loose or dirty
2 Starter pinion jammed in mesh
3 Defective starter switch
4 Defective starter solenoid
5 Brushes worn or sticking
6 Brush leads detached or shorting
7 Weak or broken brush springs
8 Dirty or worn commutator
9 Defective armature or field coils
10 Starter motor mechanically defective
11 Engine abnormally stiff

(g) Starter motor rough or noisy

1 Bent armature shaft
2 Loose polepieces
3 Excessively worn bearing bushes
4 Mounting bolts loose
5 Damaged pinion or ring gear teeth

(h) Lamps inoperative or erratic

1 Defective wiring or loose connections
2 Bulbs burned out
3 Poor earth points
4 Battery discharged or dirty battery connections
5 Lighting switch defective
6 Battery defective and incapable of holding a charge
7 Fuse blown (check for cause)

(j) Wiper motor sluggish

1 Defective wheelbox or cable rack
2 Insufficient armature end float
3 Seized bearings, or bearings not aligning
4 Worn brushes or weak brush springs
5 Dirty or worn commutator
6 Defective armature windings
7 Gearbox components badly worn

CHAPTER 13

THE BODYWORK

13:1 Bodywork finish

Large scale repairs are best left to expert panel beaters and the spraying on of the colour done professionally. Even small dents can be tricky, as too much or injudicious hammering will stretch the metal and make things worse instead of better. Filling minor dents and scratches is probably the best method of restoring the surface. The touching-up of paintwork and minor spraying is well within the powers of most owners, particularly as self-spraying cans of paint in the correct colours are now readily available. It must be remembered however, that paint changes colour with age and that it is better to spray a whole panel rather than to try touching up a small area.

Never apply cellulose paint over synthetic as the synthetic will lift off in blisters. If there is any doubt try a test on an area of the car where it will not show.

Before spraying it is essential to remove all traces of wax polish, with white spirits. If silicone-based polishes have been used then even more drastic treatment will be required. Paint will not stick to the polish and little craters will be left on the surface. Lightly scuff the area to be sprayed and rub down to bare metal on rust spots. Mask off the surrounding area with masking tape and news-paper to prevent spray dust from settling on the surface.

Use a primer filler or paste stopper according to the amount of filling required. Apply the stopper in thin layers, allowing each coat to dry out before applying the next, otherwise the thick mass will take a very long time to harden. Chemical setting pastes may be applied thickly as they do not depend on air-drying to harden. Try to keep the surface smooth and even as this will save rubbing down later. When the surface is dry, rub it down with 400 grade 'Wet or Dry' paper using plenty of water until the surface is smooth and flush with the surrounding areas. If required, use more coats of stopper or filler and spend plenty of time and patience in achieving the best possible surface. Small blemishes which are hardly noticeable on the matt surface will stand out glaringly on the final polished finish. Apply the retouching paint, evenly over a complete panel but lighter around the edges so as to feather in the paint on smaller areas. It is better to apply two thin coats, and rub down between each, rather than apply one thick coat which may run.

When the paint is fully dry and hard use a cutting compound to lightly polish the surface and remove any loose

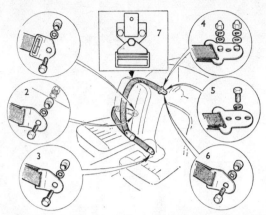

FIG 13:1   Seat belt attachments (Kangol magnet type belts)

Key to Fig 13:1   1 Sill   2 Drive shaft tunnel (early cars)   3 Drive shaft tunnel (later cars)   4 Wheel arch (early cars)   5 Wheel arch, first type belt (later cars)   6 Wheel arch, second type belt (later cars)   7 Stowage clip

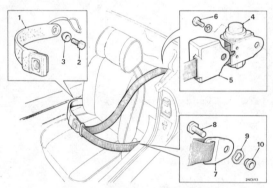

FIG 13:1A   Reel type seat belts

Key to Fig 13:1A   1 Short belt   2 Bolt   3 Spacer   4 Seat belt reel   5 Cover for reel   6 Bolt   7 Sill mounting   8 Bolt   9 Anti-rattle washer   10 Spacer

spray dust. Buff the paint with a mop and apply polish when the paint has had several days to harden.

13:2 Seat belts

The strong points for the belts are already fitted to the car so attaching the seat belts is merely a question of finding the strong points and attaching the belts correctly. It is unlikely that the models covered by this manual will not be fitted with the seat belts as well, as they are a legal requirement in most countries.

The attachments for early type belts are shown in **FIG 13:1**, while the intertia reel type of belt fitted to later cars is shown in **FIG 13:1A**.

If these belts have to be removed at any time, the procedure is as follows:

The short belt 1 is removed by lifting the carpet by the transmission shaft tunnel, disconnecting the electric wiring from the belt and then removing the single securing bolt 2 and spacer 3.

The long belt 7 is removed from the sill by unscrewing the securing bolt 8, the anti-rattle washer 9 and spacer 10.

The reel 4 is secured by the cover 5 and bolt 6 with a spring washer.

Refit in the reverse order of removal.

13:3 The doors

The doors are fitted with the window regulator mechanisms and the anti-burst lock parts.

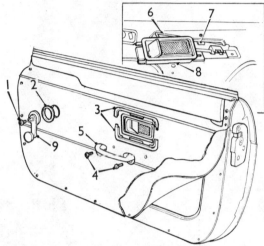

FIG 13:2   Door trim and handle attachments, inset shows remote control unit removal

Key to Fig 13:2   1 Window regulator handle screw   2 Fibre washer   3 Remote control unit bezel   4 Pull handle screw   5 Pull handle   6 Lock control rod   7 Anti-rattle clip   8 Remote control unit   9 Window regulator handle

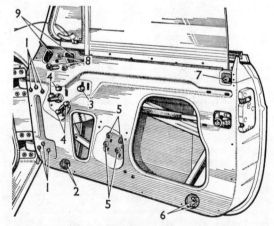

FIG 13:3   Door component attachments

Key to Fig 13:3   1 Door hinge securing bolts   2 Front door glass mounting bracket securing nuts   3 Regulator arm stop   4 Regulator securing bolts   5 Regulator extension securing setscrews   6 Rear door glass mounting bracket securing screw   7 Door glass channel securing screw   8 Door lock remote control securing bolts   9 Ventilator securing nuts

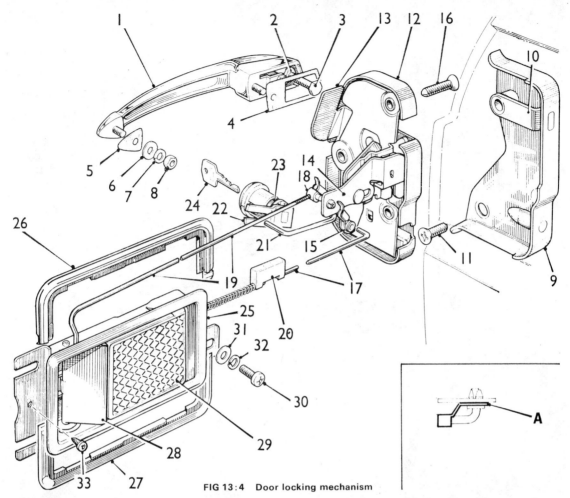

FIG 13:4   Door locking mechanism

Key to Fig 13:4   1 Exterior handle   2 Locknut   3 Push button plunger bolt   4 Sealing washer   5 Sealing washer
6 Plain washer   7 Spring washer   8 Nut   9 Striker   10 Anti-burst strap   11 Striker screw   12 Latch unit   13 Latch
contactor   14 Locking slide   15 Latch release lever   16 Latch unit screw   17 Latch release rod   18 Screwed pivot
19 Lock control rod   20 Plastic clip   21 Locking lever   22 Lock operating fork   23 Key operated lock   24 Key
25 Remote control unit   26 Remote control bezel—upper   27 Remote control bezel—lower   28 Locking latch   29 Inside
door handle   30 Remote control unit screw   31 Plain washer   32 Spring washer   33 Self-tapping screw

Door trim:

The details of the trim are shown in **FIG 13:2**.

1 Wind the window closed and take out the securing screw 1 to free the handle 9 and fibre washer 2 from the door.

2 Withdraw the top half of the plastic bezel 3 upwards and withdraw the bottom half downwards.

3 Take out the securing screws 4 and remove the pull handle 5. Unscrew the screws holding the waist rail and remove the rail.

4 Take out the screws securing the trim panel and remove the panel. Peel back the waterproof plastic cover as required.

The trim is replaced in the reverse order of removal, sticking or taping the plastic waterproof cover as required.

The attachments of the door components are shown in **FIG 13:3**. To remove a door, support it and take out the setscrews. Limited adjustment is provided to allow the door to be hung in line with the body when refitting the door. The hinge to body securing nuts are accessible after removing the splash panel.

13:4 The door lock mechanism

The details of the locking mechanism are shown in **FIG 13:4**. To gain access to the parts the door trim must first be removed (see **Section 13:3**).

Exterior handle:

With the trim removed, work through the access holes and remove the nuts 8 and washer 6 and 7. Withdraw the handle from outside the door complete with its seals 4 and 5.

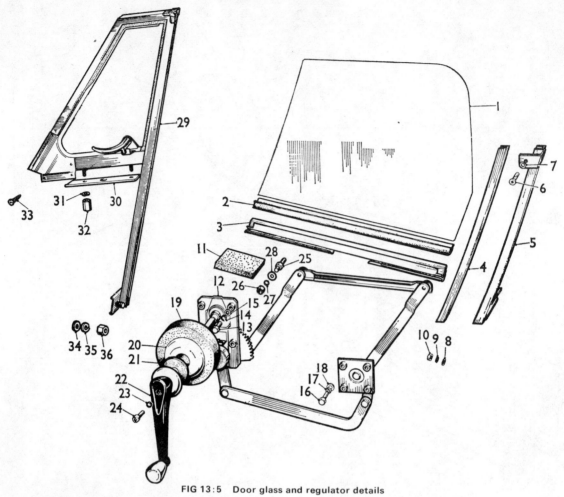

FIG 13:5 Door glass and regulator details

Key to Fig 13:5   1 Door glass   2 Glazing channel   3 Lower channel   4 Flexible channel   5 Channel   6 Screw
7 Cup washer   8 Plain washer   9 Spring washer   10 Nut   11 Buffer   12 Regulator   13 Setscrew   14 Spring washer
15 Plain washer   16 Setscrew   17 Spring washer   18 Plain washer   19 Pad   20 Escutcheon   21 Fibre washer
22 Handle and finisher   23 Spring washer   24 Screw   25 Stop   26 Nut   27 Spring washer   28 Plain
washer   29 Ventilator   30 Seating washer   31 Spring washer   32 Nut   33 Screw   34 Plain washer   35 Spring
washer   36 Nut

The handle is replaced in the reverse order of removal but the adjustment of the plunger bolt 3 should be checked first. Press the handle 1 and its seals 4 and 5 firmly into place against the outside of the door. Check visually through a door aperture that the gap between the plunger 3 and latch contactor 13 is $\frac{1}{32}$ inch (1 mm) minimum. **Do not attempt to check the clearance by pressing in the button on the handle as this is not sufficiently accurate.** If the gap is incorrect slacken the locknut 2 and adjust the plunger 3 until the gap is correct. Tighten the locknut, taking care not to turn the plunger, and refit the handle.

Remote control unit:

1 Free the latch release rod 17 and lock control rod 19 from their bushes and retaining clips on the latch unit 12 levers.

2 Remove the three securing screws 30 and their washers 31 and 32 as well as the self-tapping screw 33.

3 Withdraw the lock control rod 19 from its bush on top of the remote control unit and withdraw the unit from the door complete with the latch release rod 17. The rod 17 can be removed after drawing it downwards from the anti-rattle clip.

Refit the remote control unit in the reverse order of removal leaving the securing screws slack and omitting the self-tapping screw 33. Make sure that both the rods 17 and 19 are properly connected and clipped into place. Adjust the position of the unit as follows:

1 Move the remote control unit towards the latch until the latch release rod 17 contacts its stop, without compressing the spring. Tighten the securing screws.

2 Set the latch unit to the closed position and check that the striker is released before the inside door handle 29

154

is in its fully open position. If the remote control unit cannot be moved near enough towards the latch, it is permissible to extend the securing holes by carefully filing them.

3 Close the door and set the locking latch 28 to the locked position. Adjust the position of the screwed pivot 18 on the rod 19 so that the locking latch 28 overlaps the release handle 29. The pin on the pivot 18 fits freely into the bush on the locking slide 14 before being pressed into the spring clip.

Latch unit:

After the operating rods 17 and 19 have been disconnected the latch unit can be removed by taking out the three countersunk screws 16 securing it to the door.

The unit is replaced in the reverse order or removal. Lightly lubricate all the bearing surfaces with thin oil. Make sure that the plastic bushes on the release lever 15 and locking slide 14 are correctly fitted with their heads away from the centre of the latch and that the spring clip is then fitted under the head as shown in the inset A in **FIG 13:4**. When refitting the latch make sure that the locking lever 21 fits into the operating fork 22 on the private lock 23.

Private lock:

The unit can be removed after compressing the legs on the retaining collar from inside the door and withdrawing the lock 23 from the outside of the door.

When refitting the lock, position the retaining collar and press the lock into position so that the operating fork 22 is inclined away from the door shut face and engages with the locking lever 21 on the latch unit. **Lubricate the lock only with thin oil, never use grease.**

Striker:

The striker 9 is secured to the door aperture frame by the countersunk screws 11. **Never slam the door while the striker or door is out of adjustment.**

Check that the clearance between the striker and the latch face is $\frac{1}{32}$ to $\frac{1}{16}$ inch (1.0 to 1.6 mm) and fit or remove shims behind the striker to achieve this clearance when the door is closed.

1 Slacken the screws 11 sufficiently to allow the striker to be moved under pressure and yet leave them tight enough for the door to be shut.
2 Shut the door and pull or push the door inwards or outwards until it is aligned with the body. Carefully open the door and mark around the striker to mark its horizontal position.
3 Keeping the horizontal position by the marks, adjust the vertical position of the striker, by a process of trial and error, until the door shuts easily without being pulled up or down. Tighten the securing screws 11.
4 The striker is correctly adjusted when the door shuts easily, so make sure that the line of the striker plate is parallel with the line of the door closing, and the door can be fractionally pressed in against the seals.

13:5 The door glass

The details of the door glass and window regulator mechanism are shown in **FIG 13:5**. To gain access to the parts the door trim must first be removed (see **Section 13:3**).

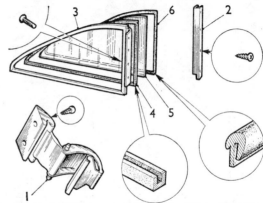

FIG 13:6   Rear quarterlight details, GT models only

Key to Fig 13:6   1 Toggle catch   2 Hinge   3 Frame
4 Glazing rubber   5 Glass   6 Sealing rubber

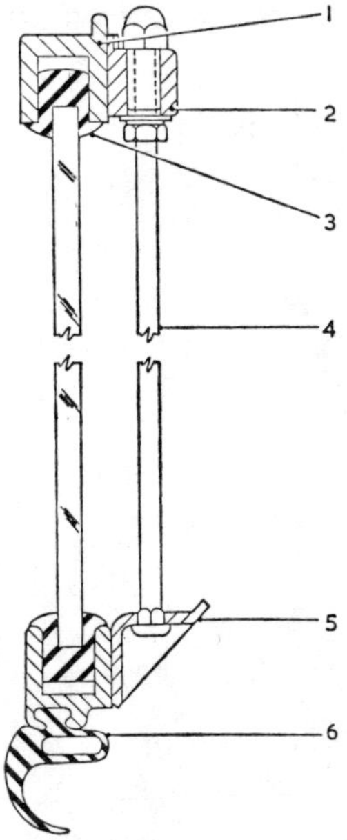

FIG 13:7   Sectioned view of tourer windscreen

Key to Fig 13:7   1 Top rail   2 Centre rod upper
bracket   3 Glazing rubber   4 Centre rod   5 Bottom
bracket   6 Seal

Door glass and regulator mechanism

1 Remove the setscrews 13 and the washers 14 and 15 securing the regulator 12 to the door and also remove the setscrew 16 and washers 17 and 18 securing the regulator extension to the door. These bolts and setscrews are also shown as items 4 and 5 in **FIG 13:3**.
2 Release the window regulator arc from the channel 3 on the bottom of the door glass. Raise the glass to clear it and remove the regulator mechanism through the aperture in the door panel.
3 If it is necessary to remove the glass, remove the nut 10 and washers 8 and 9 securing the channel 5 to the door and lift out the door glass.
4 Replace the parts in the reverse order of removal.

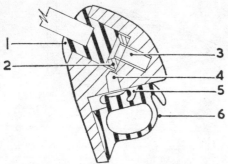

FIG 13:8 Sectioned view of tourer windscreen pillar

Key to Fig 13:8   1 Glazing rubber   2 Bottom reinforcement   3 Screw—reinforcement to pillar   4 Rivet —seal retainer   5 Seal retainer   6 Seal

Ventilator:

1 Remove the door glass assembly as described previously.
2 Remove the screws 33, the nuts 32 and washers 31 securing the ventilator to the top of the door.
3 Undo the nut 36 and remove the washers 34 and 35 securing the front glass channel to the door and lift out the ventilator assembly.
4 Refit the parts in the reverse order of removal.

13:6 The rear quarter-light (GT)

These are only fitted to GT models and the details are shown in **FIG 13:6**. The unit is easily removed by taking

out the screws securing the toggle catch 1 to the car body, finisher screws and the screw securing the hinge 2. Renew the sealing rubbers if they are defective and replace the assembly in the reverse order of removal.

13:7 Tourer windscreen

A section through the windscreen is shown in **FIG 13:7** and a section through the windscreen pillar is shown in **FIG 13:8**. The windscreen details are shown in **FIG 13:9**.

Removal:

1 Take out the two screws securing the bottom bracket 5 to the body.
2 Remove the facia panel (see **Section 13:11**) and remove the windscreen securing bolts.
3 Lift the windscreen assembly out of the car.

Dismantling:

1 Remove the domed nut from on top of the centre rod 4. Pull down the centre rod and remove the washers and plain nut, then withdraw the rod from the bottom bracket 5.
2 Remove the bottom sealing rubber 6 and take out the two screws securing the lower reinforcement pieces to each corner of the bottom rail.
3 Remove the three screws securing each end of the top rail to the pillars. Gently ease away the pillars followed by the rails from the glass.

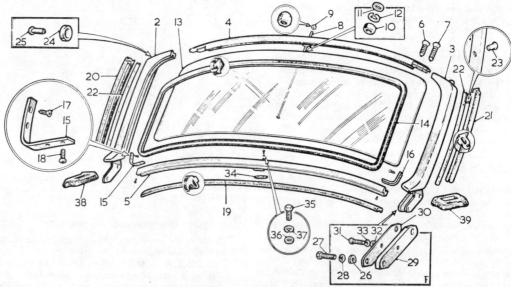

FIG 13:9 Tourer windscreen details

Key to Fig 13:9   2 Pillar—righthand   3 Pillar—lefthand   4 Rail—top   5 Rail—bottom   6 Screw—pillar to top rail 7 Screw—pillar to top rail   8 Rod—windshield centre   9 Nut—rod to top bracket   10 Nut—centre rod   11 Washer—plain 12 Washer—spring   13 Glass   14 Rubber—glazing   15 Reinforcement—bottom righthand corner   16 Reinforcement— bottom lefthand corner   17 Screw—reinforcement to pillar   18 Screw—rail to reinforcement   19 Seal—windshield to body 20 Seal—windshield pillar—righthand   21 Seal—windshield pillar—lefthand   22 Retainer—seal—pillar   23 Rivet—seat retainer to pillar   24 Fastener—dot   25 Rivet—fastener to pillar   26 Washer—foot to body   27 Screw—pillar foot to body 28 Washer—spring   29 Packing—outer   30 Packing—inner   31 Screw—packing to body   32 Washer—plain   33 Washer —spring   34 Packing—centre fixing   35 Screw—centre fixing   36 Washer—plain   37 Washer—spring   38 Grommet— seal—pillar foot righthand   39 Grommet—seal—pillar foot lefthand

Reassembly:

1 Fit the glazing rubber around the glass. Use a wax-type crayon to mark the centre of the glass at the top and bottom of the glass. This is to ensure that the top and bottom rails will be accurately aligned.

2 Refit the top and bottom rails, ensuring that their centre points are accurately aligned with the marks on the glass. Either use a long clamp to hold them in place or else loosely refit the centre rod 4.

3 Use the palm of the hand to tap the pillars back into place, working from the bottom upwards. When the pillars are in place, secure them with the screws to the top rail and reinforcing plates. Refit the lower sealing rubber 6.

4 Correctly assemble the centre rod and its nuts. **Do not overtighten the domed nut.**

Refitting:

Fibre and steel packing pieces, screwed to the side of the body, support the feet of the windscreen pillars. Normally these should not be renewed or removed but they should be checked if a new windscreen has been fitted or extensive body repairs carried out. Fit the windscreen assembly to the car and check the clearance between the foot of each pillar and the body. Adjust the fit by removing or replacing fibre packing pieces.

Refit the windscreen assembly, with the grommets fitted to the pillars and the bottom bracket packing piece in place on the body. Align the holes in the packing pieces and secure the assembly loosely in place with the special bolts and washers. Spread the bottom sealing rubber and secure the bottom bracket to the body. Tighten the windscreen pillar securing bolts. Shut the doors and check that the door ventilators align with the sealing rubber on the pillars.

13:8 GT windscreen and backlight

The windscreen and backlights on GT models, including heated backlights, are all fitted to the car by the same means.

Removal:

If the glass has broken then the weatherstrip, locking strip and finisher strips can easily be removed from the car. Make sure that all particles of glass are removed. This is most easily done using a powerful vacuum cleaner. **If the windscreen glass has broken it is absolutely essential to disconnect the demister hoses and remove any glass from the ducts or hoses.** If glass is left there, operation of the heater can blow glass into the driver's or passenger's face.

Use a blunt screwdriver to ease out the finisher strip. Prise out one end of the locking filler and withdraw it from the weatherstrip around the glass. Have an assistant outside the car to take the glass as it comes free and from inside the car press the glass firmly out, starting at a bottom corner. Remove the weatherstrip.

Carefully examine the weatherstrip and renew it if it has been cut by broken glass or shows signs of deterioration.

Check the flange in the aperture for dents or protrusions, as these can cause the new glass to break. Dress out dents using a hammer on one side and metal block on the other. Protrusions should be filed smooth to blend in with the remaining flange.

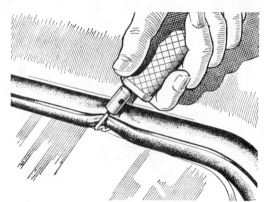

FIG 13:10 Using special tool No. **18G.468** to ease the weatherstrip lip over the glass on GT models

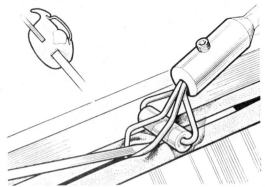

FIG 13:11 Using special tool No. **18G.468** and adaptor No. **18G.468A** to refit the locking filler strip to the weatherstrip

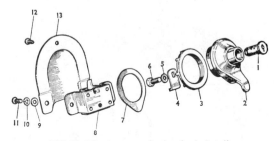

FIG 13:12 Luggage locker lock details

Key to Fig 13:12   1 Lock barrel   2 Pushbutton assembly
3 Nut   4 Operating lever   5 Washer   6 Setscrew
7 Seating washer   8 Latch lock   9 Plain washer
10 Spring washer   11 Setscrew   12 Screw (GT only)
13 Latch cover (GT only)

Refitting:

1 Refit the weatherstrip back to the aperture. Lubricate the channel into which the glass will fit with either soft soap or soap-and-water solution.

2 Place the glass into the lower channel of the weatherstrip. Have an assistant support the glass if need be. Start at a bottom corner and lift the lip of the weatherstrip over the glass, using special tool No. 18G.468 as shown in **FIG 13:10**, working all around the glass.

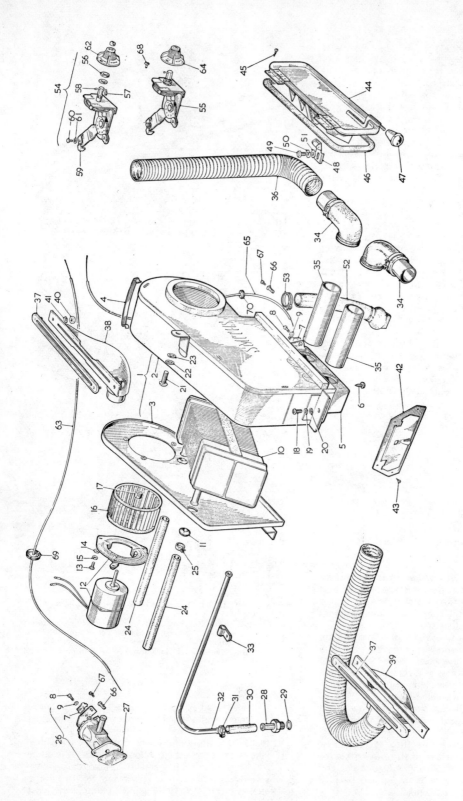

FIG 13:13 Heater details (early cars)

Key to Fig 13:13   1 Heater assembly   2 Cover   3 Cover—motor side   4 Clip   5 Outlet duct   6 Screw   7 Cable clamp   8 Bolt   9 Washer   10 Radiator   11 Grommet   12 Motor and mounting plate assembly   13 Screw   14 Washer   15 Washer   16 Runner   17 Collet nut   18 Screw   19 Washer   20 Washer   21 Screw   22 Washer   23 Washer   24 Water hose   25 Hose clip   26 Water valve assembly   27 Gasket   28 Union   29 Washer   30 Water hose—2 inch x ½ inch   31 Hose clip   32 Return pipe   33 Clip to inlet manifold   34 Demister elbow   35 Tube connector   36 Hose   37 Escutcheon   assembly—demister   38 Nozzle assembly—demister righthand   39 Nozzle assembly—demister lefthand   40 Nut   41 Washer   42 Heater outlet door   43 Screw   44 Door assembly—fresh air vent   45 Screw   46 Seal   47 Knob   48 Spring assembly—fresh air vent door   49 Screw   50 Knob   51 Washer   52 Drain and dust valve tube assembly   53 Clip   54 Clip   55 Rotary air control   56 Nut   57 Clip   58 Pin—knob   59 Cable clamp   60 Bolt   61 Washer   62 Knob—heat   63 Cable—heat control   64 Knob—air   65 Cable—air control   66 Trunnion   67 Screw—trunnion   68 Rivet   69 Grommet   70 Grommet

3 Lubricate the locking filler strip channel. Use tool No. 18G.468 with adaptor 18G.468A to refit the filler strip as shown in **FIG 13:11**. The eye of the tool opens the channel allowing the filler strip to enter and the roller then presses the weatherstrip flat. A slight side-to-side action will assist in negotiating the corners. Cut off excess filler strip to form a neat butt joint.

4 Use a blunt tool to refit the finishing strip. **No sealants should be required when refitting the glass.**

13:9 Luggage locker lid

The lid for GT models is supported by lift assisting springs while in the open position, whereas the lids on tourers are supported open by stays. Before removing the lid, support it open and carefully mark the positions of the hinges to ease refitting. Remove the support and then take out the lid to hinge bolts to free the lid.

Refit the lid in the reverse order of removal, leaving the securing bolts partially slack. Position the hinge marks, or the lid, until the lid shuts easily and is aligned with the body. Fully tighten the securing bolts.

Lock:

The details of the lock are shown in **FIG 13:12**. Do **not close the luggage locker lid while the lock is being removed or refitted.**

13:10 The bonnet

The bonnet on early cars is made of light-alloy, so care must be taken when handling it in order not to dent the material.

Maintenance:

At regular intervals lightly oil the hinge pivots, lock and safety catch.

The lock release cable is adjusted so that there is a little free movement on the control before the lock starts to open. **Do not shut the bonnet when the cable is disconnected or the cable securing trunnion screw is slack.**

The bonnet lock pin should be adjusted so that the bonnet shuts without undue pressure and yet is not loose when shut. Slacken the locknut on the locking pin and turn the locking pin up (clockwise) to tighten the bonnet, and screw the pin down if excessive pressure is required to shut the bonnet. Tighten the locknut when the adjustment is correct.

Removal:

Carefully mark the positions of the hinges on the bonnet. Support the bonnet in the open position, with the stay disconnected, and remove the two sets of bolts, nuts and washers that secure each hinge to the bonnet. Lift the bonnet clear from the car.

Refit the bonnet in the reverse order of removal, **but take care to ensure that the bonnet lock parts are accurately aligned.**

13:11 The facia and console
Removing console:

Disconnect the batteries. Remove the ashtray and four retaining screws. Turn back the carpet and pull out the

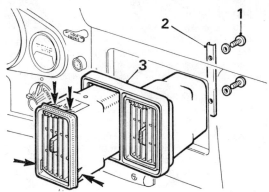

FIG 13:14 Removing face level vent, showing locating tags (arrowed)

Key to Fig 13:14   1 Screw for retaining strap   2 Strap   3 Escutcheon

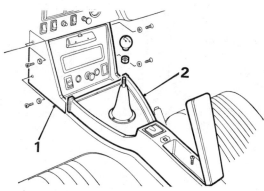

FIG 13:15 Removing console with hinged arm rest

Key to Fig 13:15   1 Console   2 Arm rest assembly

console, disconnect the wiring and remove the console assembly.

Refit the console in the reverse order of removal.

Removing the console with arm rest:

Disconnect the battery and remove the knob and locknut from the rear shift lever. See **FIG 13:15**.

Remove the four screws securing the retaining ring.

Raise the hinged arm rest, remove the retaining screw and withdraw the arm rest assembly complete with the gear shift lever gaiter and retaining ring.

Remove the four screws securing the console and partially withdraw it to gain access to the wiring behind. Disconnect the wiring and remove the console.

From car No. 410002, remove the heater control knobs, press in the retaining clips using a pin through the holes in the knobs. Remove the nuts securing the controls to the console and withdraw the controls. Remove the bulb holders. Disconnect the clock leads, remove the brackets, and withdraw the clock. Remove the warning lights, light boxes and illumination dial, and remove the console.

Refit in the reverse order.

Removing facia:

1 Disconnect the batteries. Remove the lower facia cover panels, each panel being secured by three screws.
2 Disconnect the mixture control cable from the carburetters. Remove the heater twist control knobs and free the controls from the dash by unscrewing their securing nuts.
3 Remove the tachometer. Unscrew the two knurled nuts, noting that an earth lead is secured by one nut, and pull off the bridge pieces. Partially withdraw the instruments and disconnect the wires, and then remove the instrument. Disconnect the speedometer drive cable from the back of the instrument. Unscrew the trip recorder reset retaining nut and disengage the reset from its bracket.
4 Remove the two fixing screws from the lower edge of the facia. Remove the six nuts from the facia upper edge fixing studs. Remove the two screws securing the trim piping from behind the facia.
5 Ease the facia assembly rearwards so that it clears the top fixing studs and then lift the assembly up and back to clear it from the cowls for the steering column switches. Disconnect the remainder of the wiring from the switches and instruments. Pull the mixture control cable carefully through the bulkhead and remove the facia complete with switches and instruments. If there is any doubt about the colours of the wiring cables or their correct connections then they should be labelled before disconnection.

On cars from No. 410002 proceed in a similar manner but in addition the console will have to be moved to the side for access to the facia centre fixing screws. Withdraw the face level vents. Remove the bolts securing the steering column to the facia support rail and lower the column. Remove the screw, nut, and bracket securing the glovebox to the facia support rail.

Refit the assembly in the reverse order of removal. The wiring diagram in Technical Data will be of assistance in ensuring the correct wiring connections.

13:12 The heater

The heater details are shown in **FIG 13:13**. From car No. 410002 the heater controls are situated in the centre console which will have to be moved, as necessary, as described in the previous section. Other operations are similar.

Controls:

A knob is fitted to the fresh air vent 44 to operate it. A switch is fitted to the dash for turning on the blower motor fitted to the heater. The blower should be used when the car is stationary or travelling so slowly that the air fails to circulate through the car, or when there is insufficient airflow to demist or defrost the windscreen.

Two rotary controls are fitted to the dash. The control 54 operates a cable that varies the water valve 26 to allow no, or varied quantities of, hot coolant from the engine to pass through heater radiator 10, thus controlling the temperature of the air from the heater. The other rotary control 55 varies the distribution of the air between the screen and car.

The control cable 63 is connected with the knob 62 set to OFF and the lever on the water valve 26 set to the no

flow position. The cable 65 is similarly connected with the knob 64 turned to the OFF position and the heater valve in the no flow position.

Blower motor:

This can be removed from the heater without major dismantling. Disconnect the batteries, and the blower motor wiring at the snap connectors. Remove the bolts 13 and washers 14 and 15. The motor and impeller can then be removed, attached to the motor base plate. Slacken the collet nut 17 and withdraw the impeller 16. Undo the bolts securing the motor to the base plate.

If the motor is defective it must be renewed as it is a sealed unit and cannot be repaired. Refit the motor in the reverse order of removal.

Maintenance:

In very cold weather the cooling system must be filled with an antifreeze mixture, as some water will remain in the heater if the cooling system is drained.

When flushing the cooling system, disconnect the hoses 24 and flush water through the radiator 10, using a hosepipe, until it comes out clean.

If the heater fails to produce hot air after flushing or draining there may be an air lock in the system. Slacken the connection between the hose 24 and the return pipe 32. Run the engine until water flows from the connection and the air has bled out. Tighten the connection and top up the radiator if required.

If poor operation of the heater is due to a faulty water valve 26 then the valve must be renewed as it is a sealed unit and cannot be serviced.

Removal:

1 Disconnect the batteries and the blower motor leads. Drain the cooling system.
2 Disconnect the water hoses 24 from the pipes on the radiator 10. Remove the screws securing the heater to the bulkhead, items 18 to 23.
3 Working inside the car remove the central console. Disconnect the demister ducts 36 and with one elbow 34 withdrawn remove the tube valve 52.
4 Use a pin to depress the pin 58 on the knob 64 and withdraw the knob. Take off the nut 56 and remove the air control from the dash. Free the cable 65 from the air control. Slacken the bolt on the clip 7 and withdraw the outer cable from the heater.
5 Lift the heater out of the car.
Refit the heater in the reverse order of removal.

Dismantling:

The heater assembly can be dismantled after removing the clips 4. Clean out all dirt and dust from the heater. Wash the dirt from the radiator 10 in hot water and detergent.

Reassemble the heater in the reverse order of dismantling, not forgetting to reconnect the inner cable of the control cable 65.

Face level vents:

Face level vents of the type shown in **FIG 13:14** are fitted to GHN5 and GHD5 cars after No. 258001. Later vents are similar.

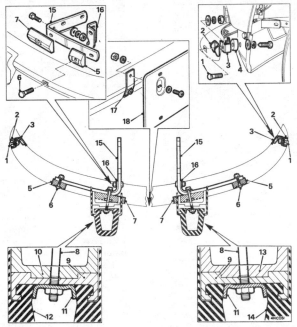

FIG 13:16   Details of late type front bumper assembly

Key to Fig 13:16   1 Small dome-head bolt   2 Small distance piece   3 Steady bracket   4 Rubber pad   5 Medium distance piece   6 Long dome-head bolt   7 Large distance piece   8 Overrider assembly securing bolt   9 Overrider mounting bracket   10 Righthand overrider support casting   11 Overrider clamping bracket   12 Righthand overrider   13 Lefthand overrider support casting   14 Lefthand overrider   15 Bumper spring   16 Lashing bracket   17 Number plate support bracket   18 Number plate

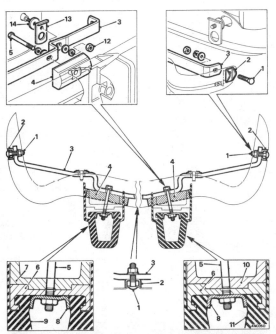

FIG 13:17   Details of late type rear bumper assembly

Key to Fig 13:17   1 Dome-head bolt   2 Small distance piece   3 Bumper spring   4 Large distance piece   5 Overrider assembly securing bolt   6 Overrider mounting bracket   7 Lefthand overrider support casting   8 Overrider clamping bracket   9 Lefthand overrider   10 Righthand overrider support casting   11 Righthand overrider   12 Bumper assembly securing nut   13 Lashing bracket   14 Large flat washer

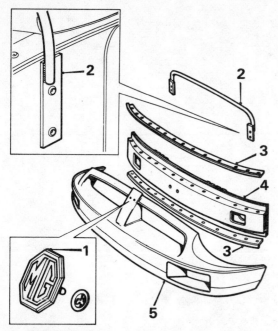

FIG 13:18   A later type front bumper assembly

Key to Fig 13:18   1 MG motif   2 Support tube
3 Clamping plate   4 Armature   5 Rubber bumper

Removal:

First remove the glovebox then disconnect the air duct hoses from the back of the vents.

Remove the two screws and the strap securing the escutcheon assembly to the facia panel and pull the complete assembly away.

In rotation ease each lower locating tag of one vent inwards and withdraw the vent slightly until the tag rests on the lip of the escutcheon.

Using a thin screwdriver blade, inserted from the back between the escutcheon and the vent, press down the two top locating tags.

Withdraw the vent from the escutcheon and repeat for the other vent.

Refitting:

Push one of the vents into the escutcheon, noting that the assemblies are marked LH and RH for left and right-hand fitting when viewed from inside the car, and ensure that the rounded corners of the vent next to the serrated wheel, register in the recess of the escutcheon with the rounded corners.

Continue to fit the assemblies in the reverse order of removal, noting that the serrated wheels of the escutcheon are at the top.

13:13 Impact absorbing bumpers

Two types of impact absorbing bumpers are fitted to later model cars in order to comply with recently introduced legislation. One type is shown in **FIGS 13:16** and **13:17**, the other in **FIG 13:18**. The procedure for removing and refitting the first type is as follows:

Front:

Remove the bolts securing each end of the bumper bar to the body, noting the rubber pad between the steady bracket and the body.

Remove the bolts securing each bumper spring to the longitudinal member and remove the complete bumper assembly.

Unscrew the nuts and dome-headed bolts, noting the small distance piece between the bracket and the bumper and the slightly longer piece between the bumper bar and the bumper spring.

The overrider assemblies are removed by unscrewing the retaining bolt, noting the large distance piece between the spring and the bar.

Remove the two bolts securing the lashing brackets to the bumper spring.

Before dismantling the overrider assemblies, mark the clamping and mounting brackets at the top to ensure correct refitting. Remove the securing screws and withdraw the clamping bracket. Slide the mounting bracket from the overrider.

Refitting is carried out in the reverse order, but make sure that the clamping bracket is correctly fitted to the overrider and note that the overriders are handed and must be fitted on the correct side of the bumper. As the fitted position of the overrider retaining bolt is angled, care must be taken not to damage the thread.

Rear:

Remove two nuts securing the bumper assembly to the mounting brackets and the three dome-headed bolts, noting the distance pieces between the bumper spring and the bumper bar.

Remove the single overrider retaining bolts, noting the large distance pieces between the bar and the spring.

Before dismantling the overrider assemblies, mark the two brackets at the top to ensure correct refitting, then remove the clamping bracket securing screws and remove the clamping bracket. Slide the mounting bracket off the overrider.

Refit by reversing the above and noting the points mentioned for refitting the front assemblies.

Second type:

Refer to **FIG 13:18**.

Disconnect the battery and then the wiring for the front parking and indicator lamps at the connectors under the bonnet. Pull the leads through the grommet and allow them to hang under the wings.

Remove the four nuts and washers securing the inner mountings of the bumper to the chassis and the four bolts securing the bumper to the outer springs.

Remove the bumper assembly, noting the two towing eyes on the outer springs. Note also that spacer plates may be fitted to the inner mountings.

Further dismantling of the bumper assembly can be carried out as necessary, noting that certain components are riveted together.

Assembly is the reverse of the removal procedure, but do not forget to fit the lamp lenses with their drain slots facing downwards.

APPENDIX

TECHNICAL DATA

HINTS ON MAINTENANCE AND OVERHAUL

GLOSSARY OF TERMS

INDEX

Inches	Decimals	Milli-metres	Inches to Millimetres		Millimetres to Inches	
			Inches	mm	mm	Inches
1/64	.015625	.3969	.001	.0254	.01	.00039
1/32	.03125	.7937	.002	.0508	.02	.00079
3/64	.046875	1.1906	.003	.0762	.03	.00118
1/16	.0625	1.5875	.004	.1016	.04	.00157
5/64	.078125	1.9844	.005	.1270	.05	.00197
3/32	.09375	2.3812	.00b	.1524	.06	.00236
7/64	.109375	2.7781	.007	.1778	.07	.00276
1/8	.125	3.1750	.008	.2032	.08	.00315
9/64	.140625	3.5719	.009	.2286	.09	.00354
5/32	.15625	3.9687	.01	.254	.1	.00394
11/64	.171875	4.3656	.02	.508	.2	.00787
3/16	.1875	4.7625	.03	.762	.3	.01181
13/64	.203125	5·1594	.04	1.016	.4	.01575
7/32	.21875	5.5562	.05	1.270	.5	.01969
15/64	.234375	5.9531	.06	1.524	.6	.02362
1/4	.25	6.3500	.07	1.778	.7	.02756
17/64	.265625	6.7469	.08	2.032	.8	.03150
9/32	.28125	7.1437	.09	2.286	.9	.03543
19/64	.296875	7.5406	.1	2.54	1	.03937
5/16	.3125	7.9375	.2	5.08	2	.07874
21/64	.328125	8.3344	.3	7.62	3	.11811
11/32	.34375	8.7312	.4	10.16	4	.15748
23/64	.359375	9.1281	.5	12.70	5	.19685
3/8	.375	9.5250	.6	15.24	6	.23622
25/64	.390625	9.9219	.7	17.78	7	.27559
13/32	.40625	10.3187	.8	20.32	8	.31496
27/64	.421875	10.7156	.9	22.86	9	.35433
7/16	.4375	11.1125	1	25.4	10	.39370
29/64	.453125	11.5094	2	50.8	11	.43307
15/32	.46875	11.9062	3	76.2	12	.47244
31/64	.484375	12.3031	4	101.6	13	.51181
1/2	.5	12.7000	5	127.0	14	.55118
33/64	.515625	13.0969	6	152.4	15	.59055
17/32	.53125	13.4937	7	177.8	16	.62992
35/64	.546875	13.8906	8	203.2	17	.66929
9/16	.5625	14.2875	9	228.6	18	.70866
37/64	.578125	14.6844	10	254.0	19	.74803
19/32	.59375	15.0812	11	279.4	20	.78740
39/64	.609375	15.4781	12	304.8	21	.82677
5/8	.625	15.8750	13	330.2	22	.86614
41/64	.640625	16.2719	14	355.6	23	.90551
21/32	.65625	16.6687	15	381.0	24	.94488
43/64	.671875	17.0656	16	406.4	25	.98425
11/16	.6875	17.4625	17	431.8	26	1.02362
45/64	.703125	17.8594	18	457.2	27	1.06299
23/32	.71875	18.2562	19	482.6	28	1.10236
47/64	.734375	18.6531	20	508.0	29	1.14173
3/4	.75	19.0500	21	533.4	30	1.18110
49/64	.765625	19.4469	22	558.8	31	1.22047
25/32	.78125	19.8437	23	584.2	32	1.25984
51/64	.796875	20.2406	24	609.6	33	1.29921
13/16	.8125	20.6375	25	635.0	34	1.33858
53/64	.828125	21.0344	26	660.4	35	1.37795
27/32	.84375	21.4312	27	685.8	36	1.41732
55/64	.859375	21.8281	28	711.2	37	1.4567
7/8	.875	22.2250	29	736.6	38	1.4961
57/64	.890625	22.6219	30	762.0	39	1.5354
29/32	.90625	23.0187	31	787.4	40	1.5748
59/64	.921875	23.4156	32	812.8	41	1.6142
15/16	.9375	23.8125	33	838.2	42	1.6535
61/64	.953125	24.2094	34	863.6	43	1.6929
31/32	.96875	24.6062	35	889.0	44	1.7323
63/64	.984375	25.0031	36	914.4	45	1.7717

UNITS	Pints to Litres	Gallons to Litres	Litres to Pints	Litres to Gallons	Miles to Kilometres	Kilometres to Miles	Lbs. per sq. In. to Kg. per sq. Cm.	Kg. per sq. Cm. to Lbs. per sq. In.
1	.57	4.55	1.76	.22	1.61	.62	.07	14.22
2	1.14	9.09	3.52	.44	3.22	1.24	.14	28.50
3	1.70	13.64	5.28	.66	4.83	1.86	.21	42.67
4	2.27	18.18	7.04	.88	6.44	2.49	.28	56.89
5	2.84	22.73	8.80	1.10	8.05	3.11	.35	71.12
6	3.41	27.28	10.56	1.32	9.66	3.73	.42	85.34
7	3.98	31.82	12.32	1.54	11.27	4.35	.49	99.56
8	4.55	36.37	14.08	1.76	12.88	4.97	.56	113.79
9		40.91	15.84	1.98	14.48	5.59	.63	128.00
10		45.46	17.60	2.20	16.09	6.21	.70	142.23
20				4.40	32.19	12.43	1.41	284.47
30				6.60	48.28	18.64	2.11	426.70
40				8.80	64.37	24.85		
50					80.47	31.07		
60					96.56	37.28		
70					112.65	43.50		
80					128.75	49.71		
90					144.84	55.92		
100					160.93	62.14		

UNITS	Lb ft to kgm	Kgm to lb ft	UNITS	Lb ft to kgm	Kgm to lb ft
1	.138	7.233	7	.967	50.631
2	.276	14.466	8	1.106	57.864
3	.414	21.699	9	1.244	65.097
4	.553	28.932	10	1.382	72.330
5	.691	36.165	20	2.765	144.660
6	.829	43.398	30	4.147	216.990

TECHNICAL DATA

Dimensions are given in inches; figures in brackets are in millimetres

ENGINE

Type	4 cylinder in-line, OHV with camshaft mounted in block, watercooled
Cubic capacity	1798 cc (109.8 cu in)

Compression ratio

High compression and emission controlled ...	8.8:1 or 9.0:1
Low compression	8.0:1
Stroke	3.5 (89)
Nominal bore	3.16 (80.26)
Firing order	1–3–4–2

Compression ratio and pressure

	Ratio	Pressure
All 18G, GA, GB, GD, GH, GG engines:		
High compression	8.8:1	160 lb/sq in (11.25 kg/sq cm)
Low compression	8:1	130 lb/sq in (9.15 kg/sq cm)
18V engine, high compression ...	9:1	170 lb/sq in (11.95 kg/sq cm)
low compression ...	8:1	170 lb/sq in (11.95 kg/sq cm)
18V engines (emission controlled) ...	9:1	170 lb/sq in (11.95 kg/sq cm)
18V engines (110 cu in, 1800 cc) from 1976 and engines equipped with catalytic converter	8:1	130 lb/sq in (9.15 kg/sq cm)

Crankshaft

Type	5 main bearing, integral balance weights
End float	.004 to .005 (.10 to .13)
Oversize thrust washers	+.003 (+.076)
Journal diameter	2.1262 to 2.127 (54.01 to 54.02)
Crankpin diameter	1.8759 to 1.8764 (47.648 to 47.661)
Shell bearing to crankshaft clearance (new) ...	.001 to .0027 (.0254 to .068)
Undersize bearings (main and big-end) ...	—.010, —.020, —.030, —.040 (—.254, —.508, —.762, —1.016)

Connecting rods

Type	Horiz. split big-end, solid small-end
Length between centres	6.5 (165.1)

Gudgeon pins

Type	Press fit in connecting rod
Diameter	.8125 to .8127 (20.63 to 20.64)
Fit in piston	Push fit at 16°C
Fit in small-end	12 lb ft minimum

Camshaft

Cam lift	.250 (6.35)
End float	.003 to .007 (.076 to .178)
Bearing to journal clearance (new)	.001 to .002 (.0254 to .0508)
Journal diameter:	
Front	1.78875 to 1.78925 (45.424 to 45.437)
Centre	1.72875 to 1.72925 (43.910 to 43.923)
Rear...	1.62275 to 1.62325 (41.218 to 41.230)
Bearing internal diameter (after fitting and line-reaming):	
Front	1.79025 to 1.79075 (45.472 to 45.485)
Centre	1.73025 to 1.73075 (43.948 to 43.961)
Rear...	1.62425 to 1.62475 (41.256 to 41.269)
Timing chain	$\frac{3}{8}$ inch (9.52 mm) pitch x 52 pitches

Tappet

Type	Barrel with flat base
Outside diameter	$\frac{13}{16}$ (20.64)
Length	2.293 to 2.303 (58.25 to 58.5)

Pistons
Skirt to cylinder clearance:
Top ...	...	...	...	...	.0021 to .0033 (.053 to .084)
Bottom ...	...	...	...	...	.0006 to .0012 (.015 to .030)
Oversize pistons	...	...	...	...	+.010, +.020, +.030, +.040 (+.254, +.508, +.762, +1.016)

Piston rings
Type: Compression—Top	...	...	...	Plain sintered alloy
Second		...	...	Tapered sintered alloy
Oil control	...	...	...	Two chrome faced rings with expander. Apex
Fitted gap: Compression	...	...	...	.012 to .022 (.305 to .6)
Oil control	...	...	...	.015 to .045 (.38 to 1.14)
Thickness: Compression—Top	...	...	.124 to .127 (3.14 to 3.22)
Second ...	...	...	.104 to .111 (2.64 to 2.81)
Oversize piston rings ...	...	...	...	+.010, +.020, +.030, +.040 (+.254, +.508, +.762, +1.016)

Valves
Head diameter:
Inlet	...	...	...	...	1.562 to 1.567 (38.67 to 38.80)
Exhaust	...	...	...	...	1.343 to 1.348 (34.11 to 34.23)
18V Inlet, early	...	...	...	1.625 to 1.630 (41.27 to 41.40)
later	...	...	...	1.562 to 1.567 (38.67 to 39.80)

Stem diameter:
Inlet...	...	...	...	...	.3422 to .3427 (8.69 to 8.70)
Exhaust	...	...	...	...	.3417 to .3422 (8.68 to 8.69)
18V ...	...	...	...	...	.3429 to .3434 (8.70 to 8.72)

Stem to guide clearance:
Inlet	...	...	...	...	.0015 to .0025 (.0381 to .0778)
Exhaust	...	...	...	...	.002 to .003 (.0508 to .0762)
18V Inlet, early	...	...	...	.0008 to .0018 (.020 to .046)
later	...	...	...	.0007 to .0019 (.020 to .048)
Exhaust	...	...	...	...	.0013 to .0024 (.03 to .06)

Valve guides
Length:
Inlet	...	...	...	...	$1\frac{7}{8}$ (47.63)
Exhaust	...	...	...	...	$2\frac{13}{64}$ (55.95)
Outside diameter	...	...	...	.5635 to .5640 (14.30 to 14.32)
Internal diameter	...	...	...	.3442 to .3447 (8.73 to 8.74)

Fitted height above head:
Inlet	...	...	...	...	.750 (19.05)
Exhaust	...	...	...	...	.625 (15.875)

Valve springs
Free length:
Inner	...	...	...	...	$1\frac{31}{32}$ (50.0)
Outer	...	...	...	...	$2\frac{9}{64}$ (54.4)
18V ...	...	...	...	...	1.92 (48.77)

Fitted length:
Inner	...	...	...	...	$1\frac{7}{16}$ (36.5)
Outer	...	...	...	...	$1\frac{9}{16}$ (39.7)
18V ...	...	...	...	...	1.44 (36.58)

Load at fitted length:
Inner	...	...	...	...	28 to 32 lb (12.7 to 14.5 kg)
Outer	...	...	...	...	72 lb (32.7 kg)
18V ...	...	...	...	...	82 lb (37.2 kg)

Valve timing
Timing marks ...	...	...	...	...	Dimples on timing sprockets

Timing check	Engine at TDC when No. 1 cylinder inlet valve is just about to open with rocker clearance set at .055 (1.4)
Inlet valve opens	16 deg. BTDC
Inlet valve closes	56 deg. ABDC
Exhaust valve opens	51 deg. BBDC
Exhaust valve closes	21 deg. ATDC

Valve rocker gear

Rocker clearance	
Running	.015 (.38) cold
Timing	.055 (1.4) cold
Shaft diameter	.624 to .625 (15.85 to 15.87)
Bush inside diameter	.6255 to .626 (15.85 to 15.9) reamed

Flywheel runout ... ... .003 (.07) maximum

Lubrication system

Oil pump	Hobourn-Eaton eccentric rotor
Oil pressure:	
Running	50 to 80 lb/sq in (3.51 to 5.6 kg/sq cm)
Idling	10 to 25 lb/sq in (.7 to 1.7 kg/sq cm)
Relief valve opens at	70 lb/sq in (4.9 kg/sq cm)
Oil filter bypass valve opens at	13 to 17 lb/sq in (.9 to 1.1 kg/sq cm)
Relief valve spring:	
Free length	3.0 (76.2)
Fitted length	$2\frac{5}{32}$ (54.7)
Fitted load	15.5 to 16.5 lbs (7.0 to 7.4 kg)

FUEL SYSTEM

Fuel pump

Type	Electrically operated SU AUF.300 or HP
Minimum flow	15 Imp gall/hr (18 US gall/hr, 68.2 litre/hr)
Suction head	18 inch (457 mm)

Carburetters (SU models):

Basic type (all models)	Twin SU HS4
Emission control	AUD 265 or AUD 326 (HS4)
Choke diameter	$1\frac{1}{2}$ (38.1)
Jet size (all models)	.090 (2.2)
Piston spring (all models)	Red
Jet needle:	
18GD, 18GG	FX (standard), No. 5 (rich), GZ (weak)
18GF	FX
18GH or 18GJ	AAE (spring-loaded)
18GK	AAL
18V 1971-72	AAU (spring-loaded)
18V 1972-74	ABD
18V 1974 on	ACD
Initial adjustment:	
Standard	12 flats down from jet level with bridge
Emission control to 1971	14 flats down from jet level with bridge
Type for 18V	Twin HIF4, AUD 434, AUD 465, AUD 493, AUD 550, AUD 616, FZX1001 or FZX1229
Bore	$1\frac{1}{2}$ (38.1)
Needle (AUD 434 and AUD616)	AAU (1972) ABD
FZX1001 and FZX1229)	ACD

Idling speed

18 GD, 18 GG	500 rev/min
18 GF, 18 GH, 18 GK, 18V 584Z, 18V 585Z, 18V 672Z, 18V 673Z	900 rev/min
18 V 581F, 18V 582F, 18V 583F, 18V 581Y, 18V 582Y, 18V 583Y	750 to 800 rev/min
18V (carburetter specification AUD 434)	750 rev/min
18V 779F, 18V 780F	850 rev/min
18V 846F, 18V 847F and all models from 1976	750 rev/min

Fast-idle speed

18 GD, 18 GG	1000 rev/min
18 GF, 18 GH, 18 GK, 18V 584Z, 18V 585Z, 18V 672Z, 18V 673Z	1300 to 1400 rev/min
Remainder except 18V 846F, 18V 847F and 1976 models	1100 to 1200 rev/min
18V 846F, 18V 847F and 1976 models	1300 rev/min

Air cleaners	Renewable element (copper paper element)
Exhaust gas analyser, except 18V 846F, 18V 847F	4.5 per cent CO maximum at idle speed
18V 846F, 18V 847F and 1976 models	3 per cent CO maximum at idle speed

Carburetter (Zenith type), specifications

Models from 1976, including cars equipped with a catalytic converter	Single Zenith 175 CD5T
Needle No. and spring colour:	
1976 onwards	45G blue
Catalytic converter models	45H blue
Choke specifications:	
Needle	K
Fast-idle cam	CT4
Fast-idle setting	.025 inch nominal
CO content (exhaust gas analyser reading)	$5\frac{1}{2} \pm 1\%$ CO maximum at normal idling speed
Idling speed	850 rev/min

IGNITION SYSTEM

Firing order	1–3–4–2
Sparking plugs	Champion N-9Y
Electrode gap:	
Models up to 1976	.024 to .026 (.62 to .66)
Models from 1976 onwards	.035 (.90)
Distributor:	
Conventional type	Lucas 25D4 or 45D4
Contact breaker gap	.014 to .016 (.35 to .40)
Rotation	Counter-clockwise
Dwell angle:	
Non-emission controlled models	57° to 63°
Emission controlled models	46° to 56°
Capacitor	.18 to .24 mfd
Distributor:	
Electronic type (contactless)	Lucas 45DE4
Pick-up air gap	.010 to .017 (.25 to .43)
Rotation	Counter-clockwise

Ignition coil:
    Models up to 1976 ... ...   Lucas HA12
    Models from 1976 (including catalytic
        converter models) ... ...   Lucas 16C6
    Primary resistance, Lucas HA12 ... ...   3.1 to 3.5 ohms (cold)
                  Lucas 16C6 ... ...   1.43 to 1.58 ohms (cold)
    Ballast resistor (with 16C6 coil) ... ...   1.3 to 1.4 ohms

Ignition timing
    Static:
        High compression ... ...   10 deg. BTDC
        Low compression ... ...   8 deg. BTDC
        Emission controlled ... ...   10 deg. BTDC
        18V engines ... ...   10 deg. BTDC
        18V engines (ECE 15) ... ...   5 deg. BTDC
        18V engines 779F and 780F ... ...   6 deg. BTDC
        18V engines 846F and 847F ... ...   7 deg. BTDC
    Stroboscopic (vacuum pipe disconnected):
        High compression ... ...   14 deg. BTDC at 600 rev/min
        Low compression ... ...   12 deg. BTDC at 600 rev/min
        Emission controlled ... ...   20 deg. BTDC at 1000 rev/min
           18GK engines ... ...   15 deg. BTDC at 1500 rev/min
           18GJ, GH, GF engines ... ...   20 deg. BTDC at 1000 rev/min
           18V engines ... ...   13 deg. BTDC at 600 rev/min
           18V engines (ECE 15) ... ...   15 deg. BTDC at 1000 rev/min
           18V engines 779F and 780F ... ...   11 deg. BTDC at 1000 rev/min
           18V engines 846F and 847F ... ...   10 deg. BTDC at 1000 rev/min
             Models from 1976 (fitted with
                Zenith carburetter) ... ...   13 deg. BTDC at 1500 rev/min
             Models fitted with catalytic converter
                and Zenith carburetter ... ...   10 deg. BTDC at 1500 rev/min

VAPOUR AND EMISSION CONTROL

Air pump
    Type ... ...   Rotary vane
    Test speed ... ...   1000 rev/min (engine)
    Test pressure ... ...   2.75 lb/sq in
    Relief valve ... ...   4.5 to 6.5 lb/sq in
    Adsorption canister:
        Type ... ...   Carbon granules with gauze filter
    Exhaust gas CO percentage ... ...   3 to 4.5%

Fuel tank ... ...   Contains capacity limiting tank and breather connected to separation tank

    Fuel line filter ... ...   Sealed renewable unit

COOLING SYSTEM

Thermostat
    Normal ... ...   82°C (180°F)
    Hot climates ... ...   74°C (165°F)
    Cold climates ... ...   88°C (190°F)
    Thermostat blanking sleeve must be fitted if thermostat is removed
Pressure cap ... ...   7 lb/sq in (from 1971 10 lb/sq in)

Fan belt
Length ... ... $35\frac{1}{2}$ (90.2) at $\frac{3}{8}$ inch width equivalent
Width ... ... $\frac{15}{32}$ (11.9)
Thickness ... ... $\frac{27}{64}$ (10.7)
Antifreeze
For safety limits see **Chapter 4, Section 4 : 7**
Specification ... ... BS.3151 to BS.3152

CLUTCH

Fluid ... ... Lockheed Disc Brake Fluid (Series 329)
Clutch
Type ... ... Borg and Beck 8 in DS.G
Diaphragm spring colour ... ... Dark blue
Facing material ... ... Wound yarn
Damper spring:
  Number of 6
  Colour ... ... Black/light green
Clutch release bearing ... ... Graphite (MY3D)

GEARBOX AND OVERDRIVE

Gearbox type ... ... 4 forward speeds with synchromesh engagement. 1 reverse speed, no synchromesh

Overdrive type ... ... Laycock LH, operating on top two speeds

Ratios
Overdrive ... ... .82:1
Overdrive overall ... ... Top 3.2:1
Third 4.43:1

Gear	Top	Third	Second	First	Reverse
Gearbox only	1.0:1	1.382:1	2.167:1	3.44:1	3.095:1
Overall	3.909:1	5.4:1	8.47:1	13.45:1	12.098:1

Top gear speed per 1000 rev/min
Standard ... ... 18 mile/hr (29 km/hr)
Overdrive ... ... 22 mile/hr (35 km/hr)
Speedometer gear ratio
Standard 10:26
Overdrive 8:21
Gear end float ... ... .005 to .008 (.13 to .20)
Countershaft gear end float ... ... .002 to .003 (.05 to .08)
Countershaft rear thrust washers ... ... .154 to .156 (3.91 to 3.96)
.157 to .158 (3.99 to 4.01)
.160 to .161 (4.06 to 4.08)
.163 to .164 (4.14 to 4.16)

Rear bearing circlip thicknesses ... ... .096 to .098 (2.43 to 2.49)
.098 to .100 (2.49 to 2.54)
.100 to .102 (2.54 to 2.59)

Synchromesh unit springs
Free length ... ... .72 (18.3)
Fitted length ... ... .385 (9.8)
Fitted load ... ... 5.5 to 6 lb (2.5 to 2.7 kg)
Synchromesh gearbox, 18V engine ... ... 18V 581F, 581Y, 584Z, 672Z, 779F and 846F type engine

Synchromesh gearbox with overdrive, 18V engine ... ... 18V 582F, 582Y, 585Z, 673Z, 780F and 847F type engine

AUTOMATIC TRANSMISSION

Torque converter ratio ... ... 2.2:1 to 1:1
Ratios (converter at 1:1):

Gear	Top	Second	First	Reverse
Gearbox	1.00:1	1.45:1	2.39:1	2.09:1
Overall	3.909:1	5.668:1	9.34:1	8.17:1

For shift speeds and operating pressures see **Chapter 7**
Automatic transmission, 18V engine ... 18V 583F—18V 583Y type engine

REAR AXLE

Type ... ... Hypoid; semi-floating
Ratio 3.909:1 (11:43)

REAR SUSPENSION

Type ... ... Semi-elliptic leaf springs
Spring
 Number of leaves ... ... 6 (including short bottom leaf)
 Interleaving 1–2, 2–3, 3–4
 Leaf width ... ... $1\frac{3}{4}$ (44.4)
 Leaf thickness ... ... 3 at $\frac{7}{32}$ (5.6), 3 at $\frac{3}{16}$ (4.8)
 Working load
  Tourer ... ... 450 ± 15 lb (181.5 ± 7 kg)
  GT ... ... 510 ± 15 lb (321.6 ± 7 kg)

FRONT SUSPENSION

Type ... ... Independent, using coil springs and unequal length wishbones

Spring	Tourer	GT
Mean coil diameter	3.238 (82.2)	3.28 (83.3)
Number of free coils ...	$7\frac{1}{2}$	7.2
Free length	$9.9 \pm .16$ (251.4 ± 1.5)	$9.1 \pm .16$ ($231 \pm .16$)
Fitted length	$7 \pm .031$ ($178 \pm .8$)	6.6 (168)
Fitted load	1030 lb (467'2 kg)	1193 ± 20 lb (541.5 ± 9.1 kg)
From car No.	293446	296196
Free length	$10.20 \pm .06$ (259.08 ± 1.5)	$9.32 \pm \frac{1}{16}$ (236.73 ± 1.6)
Static length at load: 1030 ± 20 lb (467 ± 9 kg)	7.24 (187.7)	
Static length at load: 1193 ± 20 lb (541 ± 9 kg)		6.84 (173.74)

Camber angle ... ... 1 deg. positive $^{+\frac{1}{4}\ \text{deg.}}_{-1\frac{1}{4}\ \text{deg.}}$ (unladen)

Castor angle ... ... $7^{+\frac{1}{4}\ \text{deg.}}_{-2\ \text{deg.}}$ (unladen)

Kingpin inclination (KPI) ... ... $8^{+1\ \text{deg.}}_{-\frac{3}{4}\ \text{deg.}}$ (unladen)

DAMPERS

Type ... ... Armstrong double-acting piston
Fluid ... ... Armstrong Super (Thin) Shock Absorber Fluid No. 624

 Temperate climates ... ... Mineral oil to SAE.20W specification
Arm centres
 Front 8 (203.2)
 Rear ... ... $5\frac{1}{4}$ (133)

STEERING

Type	Rack and pinion
Lubrication	Extreme pressure SAE.90 oil
Turns, lock to lock	2.93
Steering column universal joint	Hardy Spicer KO518 or GB166
Turning circle	32 ft (9.75 metre)
Toe-in	$\frac{1}{16}$ to $\frac{3}{32}$ (1.6 to 2.4)

BRAKES

Type	Front disc brakes, drum rear brakes
Adjustment	Rear brakes only
Fluid	Lockheed Disc Brake Fluid (Series 329)
Front brakes	
Type	$10\frac{3}{4}$ inch (27.3 cm) disc brake
Pad material	Don 55.FE
Rear brakes	
Type	10 inch (25.4 cm) drum brakes
Lining material	Don 24.FE
Lining dimensions	$9\frac{7}{16}$ x $1\frac{3}{4}$ x $\frac{3}{16}$ (240 x 44.4 x 4.76)
Fluid level	
Maximum	$\frac{1}{4}$ inch (6.35 mm) below bottom of filler neck
Minimum	Half-full

ELECTRICAL SYSTEM

Type	12-volt, negative earth	
Batteries		
Number	2 x 6-volt	
Type	Lucas CA9E (6-volt) (Lucas BT9E or BTZ9E to earlier cars)	
Capacity:	*CA9E*	*BT9E or BTZ9E*
10 hour rate	53 amp/hr	51 amp/hr
20 hour rate	60 amp/hr	58 amp/hr
Plates per cell	9	9
Electrolyte per cell	1 Imp pint (1.2 US pint, 570 cc)	
Alternator		
Type	Lucas 16AC or 16ACR	
Drive ratio:		
Alternator/engine speed	1.795/1	
Polarity	Negative earth only	
Maximum rotor speed	12,500 rev/min	
Rotor winding resistance	4.33 ohms ± 5 per cent at 20°C (68°F)	
Brush length		
New	.5 (12.6)	
Minimum	.2 (5) protruding when free in brushbox	
Brush spring tension	7 to 10 oz (198 to 283 gramme)	
Output	34 amps at 14 volts and 3300 rev/min engine speed	
Alternator control box		
16AC alternator	Lucas 4TR (bulkhead mounted)	
16ACR alternator	Lucas 8TR or 11TR (integral in alternator)	

Starter motor

Type	Lucas M418G pre-engaged
Brush spring tension	36 oz (1.02 kg)
Minimum brush length	$\frac{5}{16}$ (8)
Light running current	70 amp at 5800 to 6500 rev/min
Lock torque	17 lb ft (2.35 kg m) at 465 amps
Torque at 1000 rev/min	7 lb ft (.97 kg m) at 260 amps

Solenoid ... ... Integral with motor

Closing coil resistance...	.13 to .15 ohm
Holding coil resistance	.63 to .73 ohm

Starter motor

Type	Lucas 2M100 pre-engaged
Brush spring tension	36 oz (1.02 kg)
Minimum brush length	$\frac{3}{8}$ inch (9·5 mm)
Minimum commutator thickness ...	0.140 inch (3.5 mm)
Lock torque	14.4 lb ft (2.02 kg m) with 463 amps
Torque at 1000 rpm	7.3 lb ft (1.02 kg m) with 300 amps
Light running current	40 amp at 6000 rpm (approx.)
Maximum armature end-float	0.010 inch (0.25 mm)
Solenoid: Closing (series) winding resistance ...	0.25 to 0.27 ohm
Hold-on (shunt) winding resistance	0.76 to 0.80 ohm

Windscreen wiper motor

Type	Lucas 14W (two-speed)
Light running speed:	
Normal	46 to 52 rev/min
High-speed	60 to 70 rev/min
Light running current:	
Normal	1.5 amp
High-speed	2.0 amp
Minimum brush length:	
Earth brush	$\frac{3}{16}$ inch (4.8 mm)
Normal brush	$\frac{3}{16}$ (4.8)
High-speed brush	.280 (7.1)
Brush spring pressure	5 to 7 oz (140 to 200 gramme), (brush bottom aligned with brushbox slot end)

CAPACITIES

	Imperial	US	Litres
Cooling system	9½ pints	11.4 pints	5.4
GHN5/GHD5 cars, from No. 410002	11½ pints	13.8 pints	6.6
with heater	12 pints	14.4 pints	6.8
Engine sump	7½ pints	9 pints	4.26
Fuel tank:			
Standard	12 galls	14 galls	54
USA models	—	12 galls	45.4
Gearbox	5¼ pints	6 pints	3
Gearbox and overdrive	6 pints	7 pints	3.4
Automatic gearbox	10½ pints	12.7 pints	6
Oil cooler	¾ pint	.9 pint	.42
Rear axle	1½ pints	2 pints	.85
Steering rack	⅓ pint	.39 pint	.19

TORQUE WRENCH SETTINGS

Unless otherwise stated these are given in lb ft, and the figures in bracket are in kg m.

Engine

Big-end bolts ...	35 to 40 (4.8 to 5.5)
Big-end nuts (12-sided)	33 (4.5)
Crankshaft pulley nut	70 (9.6)
Clutch attachment	25 to 30 (3.4 to 4.1)
Cylinder head ...	45 to 50 (6.2 to 6.9)
Flywheel attachment	40 (5.5)
Manifold attachments ...	15 (2.1)
Oil filter centre bolt	15 (2.1)
Oil pump attachment ...	14 (1.9)
Rear plate:	
$\frac{5}{16}$ bolts	30 (4.1)
$\frac{3}{8}$ bolts	30 (4.1)
Rocker cover	4 (.56)
Rocker pedestal	25 (3.4)
Sump ...	6 (.8)
Timing cover:	
$\frac{1}{4}$ bolts	6 (.8)
$\frac{5}{16}$ bolts	14 (1.9)
Water outlet elbow	8 (1.1)
Water pump attachment	17 (2.4)

Automatic gearbox

Converter to drive plate	25 to 30 (3.46 to 4.15)
Transmission case to converter	8 to 13 (1.1 to 1.8)
Extension housing to transmission	8 to 13 (1.1 to 1.8)
Oil pan attachments ...	8 to 13 (1.1 to 1.8)
Pressure adaptor plug ...	4 to 5 (.55 to .69)
Drain plug	8 to 10 (1.1 to 1.38)
Governor to counterweight	4 to 5 (.55 to .69)
Governor coverplate	20 to 48 lb in (.23 to .552)
Front servo adjusting screw locknut	15 to 20 (2.07 to 2.77)
Rear servo adjusting screw locknut	25 to 30 (3.46 to 4.15)
Starter inhibitor switch locknuts	4 to 6 (.55 to .83)
Filler tube sleeve to case	20 to 30 (2.07 to 4.15)
Filler tube to sleeve	17 to 18 (2.35 to 2.49)
Stone guard screws	17 to 19 lb in (.196 to .219)
Driving flange nut	55 to 60 (7.6 to 8.3)
Centre support bolts	10 to 18 (1.38 to 2.49)

Rear axle and suspension

Axle shaft nut	150 (20.6) and aligned to next splitpin hole
Pinion nut	135 to 145 (18.6 to 20.0)
Damper bolts ...	55 to 60 (7.6 to 8.3)
Road wheel nuts	60 to 65 (8.3 to 9)

Front suspension

Subframe to frame	44 to 46 (6.08 to 6.36)
Damper bolts ...	43 to 45 (5.9 to 6.2)
Hub retaining nut	40 to 70 (5.5 to 9.7)
Road wheel nuts	60 to 65 (8.3 to 9)

Steering

Steering arm bolts	60 to 65 (8.3 to 9)
Steering column clamp bolts	12 to 17 (1.6 to 2.35)
Steering lever ball joint	34 to 35 (4.7 to 4.8)
Steering tie rod locknut	33.3 to 37.5 (4.6 to 5.2)
Steering universal joint bolt	20 to 22 (2.8 to 3.0)

Steering wheel:

$\frac{9}{16}$ UNF ... ... 27 to 29 (3.73 to 4.01)

$\frac{11}{16}$ UNF ... ... 41 to 43 (5.66 to 5.94)

Brakes

Brake pressure failure switch (Nylon) ... ... 15 lb in (.173)

Brake pressure failure switch end plug ... 200 lb in (2.3)

Caliper mounting ... ... 40 to 45 (5.5 to 6.2)

Disc to hub ... ... 40 to 45 (5.5 to 6.2)

Hydraulic pipeline union

$\frac{3}{8}$ UNF ... ... 5 to 7 (.69 to .96)

$\frac{7}{16}$ UNF ... ... 7 to 10 (.96 to 1.38)

Tandem master cylinder port adaptors ... 33 (4.56)

Tandem master cylinder reservoir bolts ... 5 (.69)

Electrical

Alternator shaft nut ... ... 25 to 30 (3.46 to 4.15)

Wiper motor yoke bolts ... ... 20 lb in (.23)

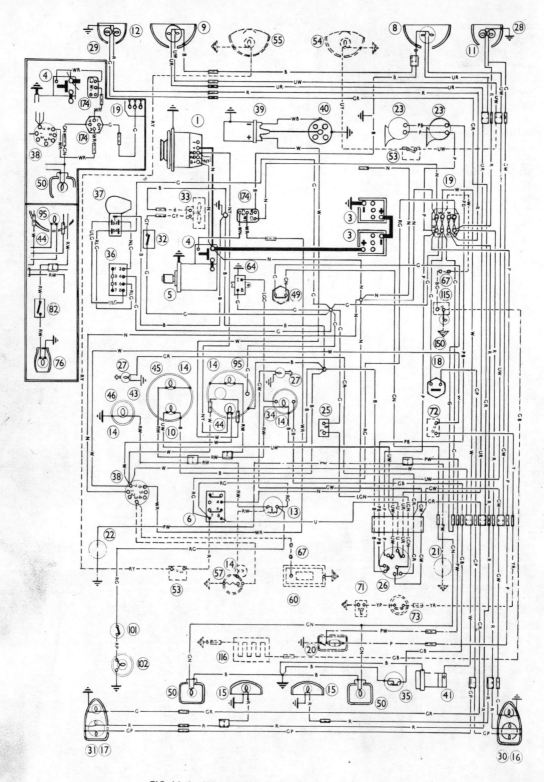

FIG 14:1   Wiring diagram for MGB 1969-70 models

Keys to Figs 14:1, 14:2, 14:3, 14:4, 14:5 and 14:6 1 Alternator or dynamo 2 Control box 3 Batteries (6-volt) 4 Starter sole-noid 5 Starter motor 6 Lighting switch 7 Headlamp dipswitch 8 Righthand headlamp 9 Lefthand headlamp 10 High-beam warning lamp 11 Righthand parking lamp 12 Lefthand parking lamp 13 Panel lamp switch or rheostat switch 14 Panel lamps 15 Number plate illumination lamp 16 Righthand stop and tail lamp 17 Lefthand stop and tail lamp 18 Stop lamp switch 19 Fuse unit 20 Interior courtesy lamp or map light (early cars) 21 Righthand door switch 22 Lefthand door switch 23 Horns 24 Horn-push 25 Flasher unit 26 Direction indicator switch or Direction indicator/headlamp flasher or Combined direction indicator/headlamp flasher/headlamp high-low beam/horn-push switch 27 Direction indicator warning lamps 28 Righthand front flasher lamp 29 Lefthand front flasher lamp 30 Righthand rear flasher lamp 31 Lefthand rear flasher lamp 32 Heater booster motor switch 33 Heater booster motor, or fresh-air motor 34 Fuel gauge 35 Fuel gauge tank unit 36 Windshield wiper switch 37 Windshield wiper motor 38 Ignition/starter switch 39 Ignition coil 40 Distributor 41 Fuel pump 43 Oil pressure gauge 44 Ignition warning lamp 45 Speedometer 46 Coolant temperature gauge 47 Coolant temperature transmitter 49 Reverse lamp switch 50 Reverse lamp 53 Fog and driving lamp switch 54 Driving lamp 55 Fog lamp 57 Cigar-lighter illuminated 59 Map light switch (early cars) 60 Radio 64 Bi-metal instrument voltage stabilizer 65 Luggage compartment lamp 66 Luggage compartment lamp switch 67 Line fuse 68 Overdrive relay unit 71 Overdrive solenoid 72 Overdrive manual control switch 73 Overdrive gear switch 74 Overdrive throttle switch 76 Automatic gearbox gear selector illumination lamp 77 Windscreen washer pump 82 Switch illumination lamp 95 Tachometer 101 Courtesy or map light switch 102 Courtesy or map light 115 Heated back-light switch (GT only) 116 Heated back-light (GT only) 118 Combined windshield washer and wiper switch 131 Combined reverse lamp switch and automatic transmission safety switch 147 Oil pressure transmitter 150 Heated back-light warning lamp (GT only) 152 Hazard warning lamp 153 Hazard warning switch 154 Hazard warning flasher unit 159 Brake pressure warning lamp and lamp test push 160 Brake pressure failure switch 168 Ignition key audible warning buzzer 169 Ignition key audible warning door switch 170 Righthand front side-marker lamp 171 Lefthand front side-marker lamp 172 Righthand rear side-marker lamp 173 Lefthand rear side-marker lamp 174 Starter solenoid relay 198 Drivers seat belt buckle switch 199 Passengers seat belt buckle switch 200 Passengers seat switch 201 Gearbox switch seat belt warning 202 Warning light—fasten belts 203 Line diode

Key to Figs 14:7, 14:8 and 14:9 1 Alternator 3 Batteries (6-volt) or battery (12-volt) 4 Starter solenoid 5 Starter motor 6 Lighting switch 7 Headlamp dip switch 8 Headlamp dip beam 9 Headlamp main beam 10 Headlamp main beam warning lamp 11 Righthand parking lamp 12 Lefthand parking lamp 13 Panel lamp rheostat switch 14 Panel illumination lamp 15 Number plate illumination lamps 16 Stop lamp 17 Righthand tail lamp 18 Stop lamp switch 19 Fuse unit (4-way) 20 Interior courtesy lamp 21 Interior lamp door switch 22 Lefthand tail lamp 23 Horn 24 Horn push 25 Flasher unit 26 Direction indicator switch 27 Direction indicator warning lamp 28 Righthand front direction indicator lamp 29 Lefthand front direction indicator lamp 30 Righthand rear direction indicator lamp 31 Lefthand rear direction indicator lamp 32 Heater motor switch 33 Heater motor 34 Fuel gauge 35 Fuel gauge tank unit 37 Windscreen wiper motor 38 Ignition/starter switch 39 Ignition coil 40 Distributor 41 Fuel pump 43 Oil pressure gauge 44 Ignition warning lamp 45 Headlamp flasher switch 46 Coolant temperature gauge 47 Coolant temperature transmitter 49 Reverse lamp switch 50 Reverse lamp 53 Fog lamp switch* 54 Fog lamp* 55 Driving lamp* 57 Cigar lighter—illuminated* 58 Driving lamp switch* 60 Radio* 64 Instrument voltage stabiliser 65 Luggage compartment lamp switch 66 Luggage compartment lamp 67 Line fuse 71 Overdrive solenoid* 72 Overdrive manual control switch* 73 Overdrive gear switch* 76 Automatic gearbox gear selector illumination lamp (early cars) 77 Windscreen washer pump 82 Switch illumination lamp 95 Tachometer 115 Heated back-light switch* (GT only) 116 Heated back-light* (GT only) 118 Combined windscreen washer and wiper switch 150 Heated back-light warning lamp* (GT only) 152 Hazard warning lamp 153 Hazard warning switch 154 Hazard warning flasher unit 159 Brake pressure warning lamp and lamp test-push 160 Brake pressure failure switch 168 Audible warning buzzer 169 Ignition key audible warning door switch 170 Righthand front side-marker lamp 171 Lefthand front side-marker lamp 172 Righthand rear side-marker lamp 173 Lefthand rear side-marker lamp 174 Starter solenoid relay 196 Running-on control valve 197 Running-on control valve oil pressure switch 198 Driver's seat belt buckle switch 199 Passenger's seat belt buckle switch 200 Passenger seat switch 201 Seat belt warning gearbox switch 202 'Fasten belts' warning light 203 Line diode 208 Cigar lighter illumination 211 Heater control illumination lamp 240 Heated back-light relay 244 Driver's seat switch 245 Sequential seat belt control unit

* Optional fitment circuits shown dotted

CABLE COLOUR CODE

Key to Cable Colour Code: **N** Brown **U** Blue **R** Red **P** Purple **G** Green **LG** Light green **W** White **Y** Yellow **B** Black **K** Pink **O** Orange **S** Slate
When a cable has two colour code letters the first denotes the main colour and the second denotes the tracer colour

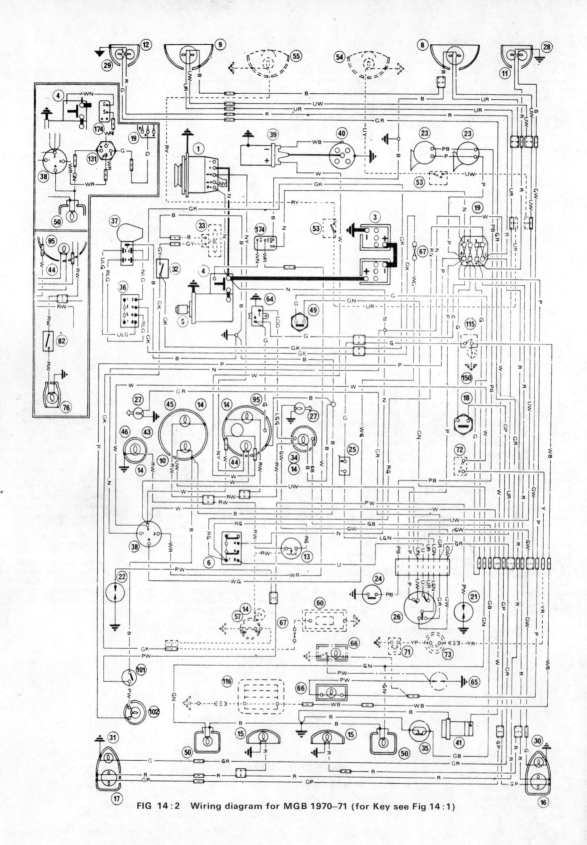

FIG 14:2 Wiring diagram for MGB 1970–71 (for Key see Fig 14:1)

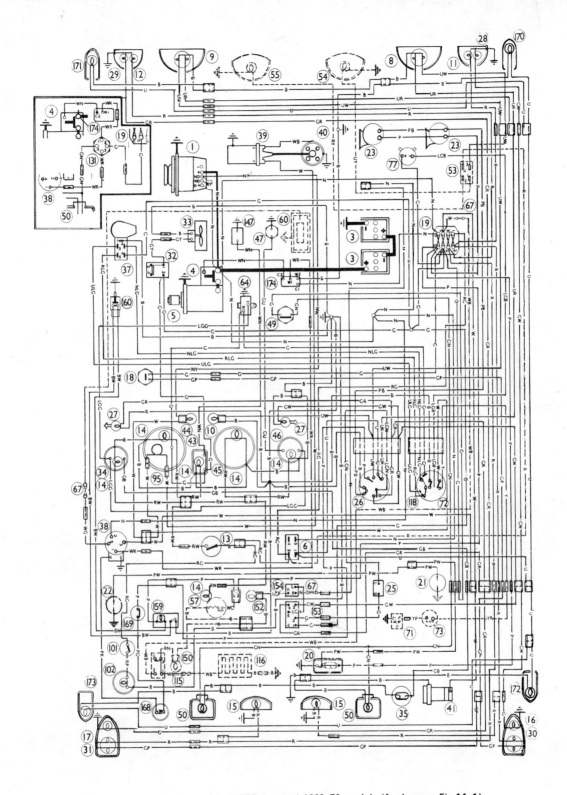

FIG 14:3   Wiring diagram for MGB (export) 1969–70 models (for key see Fig 14:1)

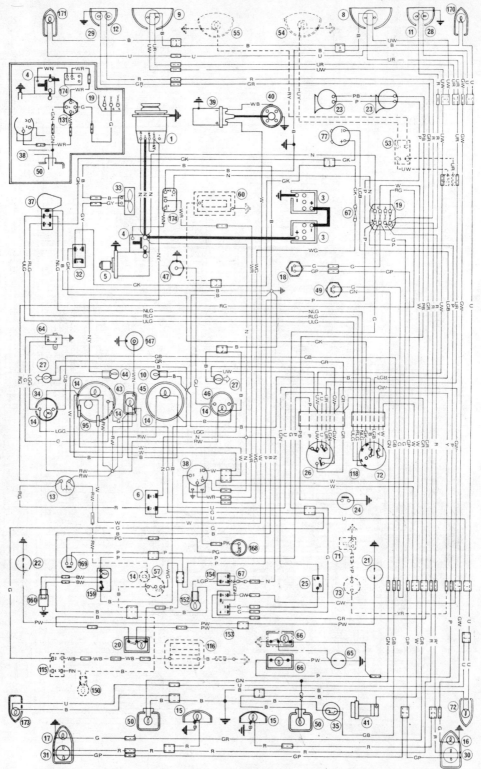

FIG 14:4   Wiring diagram for MGB (export) 1970–71 models (for key see Fig 14:1)

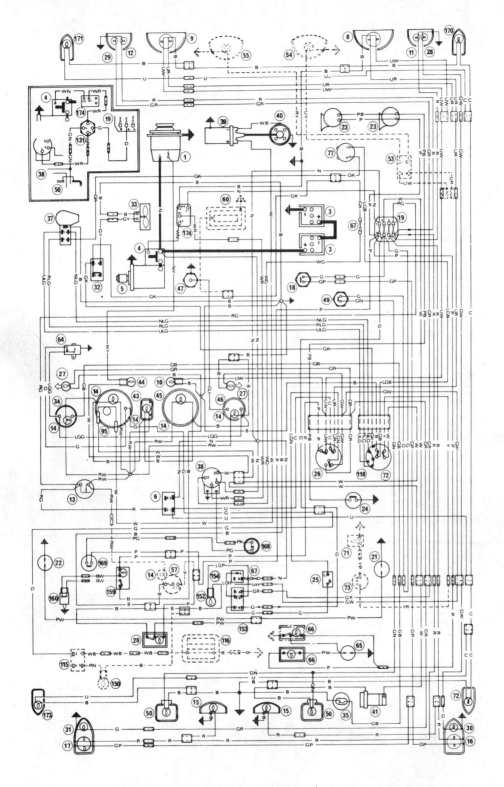

FIG 14:5   Wiring diagram for MGB (export) 1971-72 models (for key see FIG 14:1)

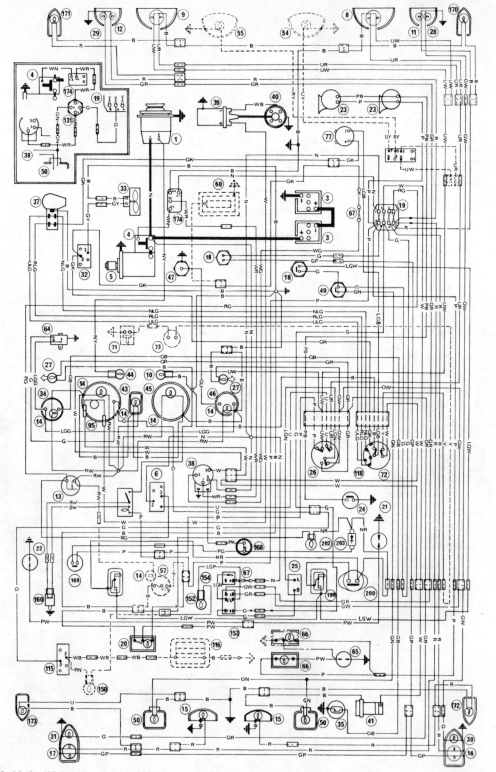

FIG 14:6 Wiring diagram for MGB (export) 1971-72 models with seat belt warning (for key see FIG 14:1)

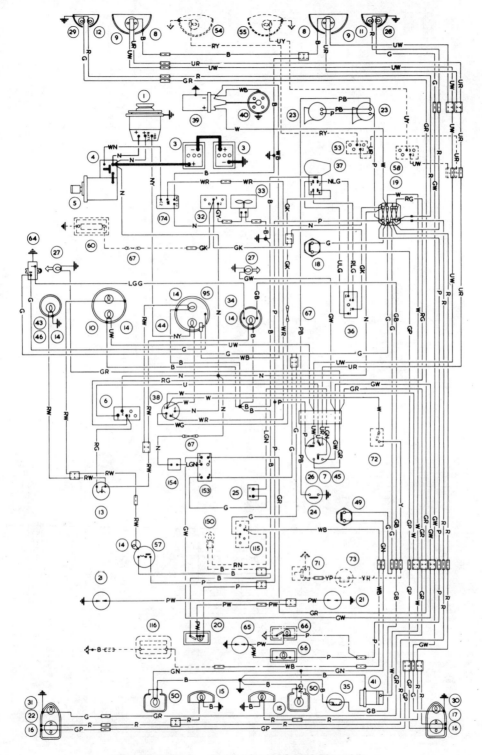

FIG 14:7   Wiring diagram for MGB 1973-74 models

Key opposite FIG 14:1

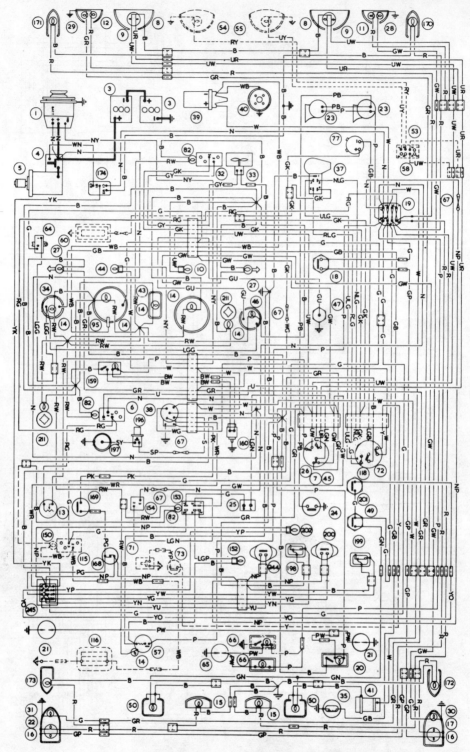

FIG 14:8   Wiring diagram for MGB (export) 1973-74 models

Key opposite FIG 14:1

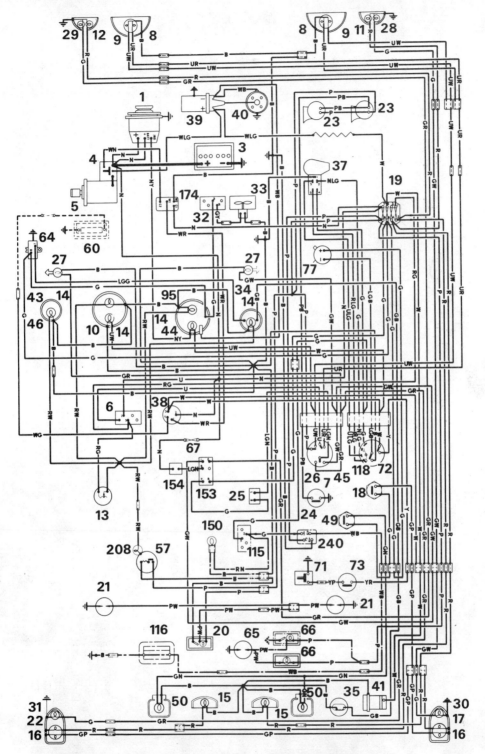

FIG 14:9 Wiring diagram for MGB 1975-76 models

Key opposite FIG 14:1

MGB 70

NOTES

HINTS ON MAINTENANCE AND OVERHAUL

There are few things more rewarding than the restoration of a vehicle's original peak of efficiency and smooth performance.

The following notes are intended to help the owner to reach that state of perfection. Providing that he possesses the basic manual skills he should have no difficulty in performing most of the operations detailed in this manual. It must be stressed, however, that where recommended in the manual, highly-skilled operations ought to be entrusted to experts, who have the necessary equipment, to carry out the work satisfactorily.

Quality of workmanship:

The hazardous driving conditions on the roads to-day demand that vehicles should be as nearly perfect, mechanically, as possible. It is therefore most important that amateur work be carried out with care, bearing in mind the often inadequate working conditions, and also the inferior tools which may have to be used. It is easy to counsel perfection in all things, and we recognise that it may be setting an impossibly high standard. We do, however, suggest that every care should be taken to ensure that a vehicle is as safe to take on the road as it is humanly possible to make it.

Safe working conditions:

Even though a vehicle may be stationary, it is still potentially dangerous if certain sensible precautions are not taken when working on it while it is supported on jacks or blocks. It is indeed preferable not to use jacks alone, but to supplement them with carefully placed blocks, so that there will be plenty of support if the car rolls off the jacks during a strenuous manoeuvre. Axle stands are an excellent way of providing a rigid base which is not readily disturbed. Piles of bricks are a dangerous substitute. Be careful not to get under heavy loads on lifting tackle, the load could fall. It is preferable not to work alone when lifting an engine, or when working underneath a vehicle which is supported well off the ground. To be trapped, particularly under the vehicle, may have unpleasant results if help is not quickly forthcoming. Make some provision, however humble, to deal with fires. Always disconnect a battery if there is a likelihood of electrical shorts. These may start a fire if there is leaking fuel about. This applies particularly to leads which can carry a heavy current, like those in the starter circuit. While on the subject of electricity, we must also stress the danger of using equipment which is run off the mains and which has no earth or has faulty wiring or connections. So many workshops have damp floors, and electrical shocks are of such a nature that it is sometimes impossible to let go of a live lead or piece of equipment due to the muscular spasms which take place.

Work demanding special care:

This involves the servicing of braking, steering and suspension systems. On the road, failure of the braking system may be disastrous. Make quite sure that there can be no possibility of failure through the bursting of rusty brake pipes or rotten hoses, nor to a sudden loss of pressure due to defective seals or valves.

Problems:

The chief problems which may face an operator are:
1 External dirt.
2 Difficulty in undoing tight fixings.
3 Dismantling unfamiliar mechanisms.
4 Deciding in what respect parts are defective.
5 Confusion about the correct order for reassembly.
6 Adjusting running clearance.
7 Road testing.
8 Final tuning.

Practical suggestions to solve the problems:

1 Preliminary cleaning of large parts—engines, transmissions, steering, suspensions, etc,—should be carried out before removal from the car. Where road dirt and mud alone are present, wash clean with a high-pressure water jet, brushing to remove stubborn adhesions, and allow to drain and dry. Where oil or grease is also present, wash down with a proprietary compound (Gunk, Teepol etc,) applying with a stiff brush—an old paint brush is suitable—into all crevices. Cover the distributor and ignition coils with a polythene bag and then apply a strong water jet to clear the loosened deposits. Allow to drain and dry. The assemblies will then be sufficiently clean to remove and transfer to the bench for the next stage.

On the bench, further cleaning can be carried out, first wiping the parts as free as possible from grease with old newspaper. Avoid using rag or cotton waste which can leave clogging fibres behind. Any remaining grease can be removed with a brush dipped in paraffin. If necessary, traces of paraffin can be removed by carbon tetrachloride. Avoid using paraffin or petrol in large quantities for cleaning in enclosed areas, such as garages, on account of the high fire risk.

When all exteriors have been cleaned, and not before, dismantling can be commenced. This ensures that dirt will not enter into interiors and orifices revealed by dismantling. In the next phases, where components have to be cleaned, use carbon tetrachloride in preference to petrol and keep the containers covered except when in use. After the components have been cleaned, plug small holes with tapered hard wood plugs cut to size and blank off larger orifices with grease-proof paper and masking tape. Do not use soft wood plugs or matchsticks as they may break.

2 It is not advisable to hammer on the end of a screw thread, but if it must be done, first screw on a nut to protect the thread, and use a lead hammer. This applies particularly to the removal of tapered cotters. Nuts and bolts seem to 'grow' together, especially in exhaust systems. If penetrating oil does not work, try the judicious application of heat, but be careful of starting a fire. Asbestos sheet or cloth is useful to isolate heat.

Tight bushes or pieces of tail-pipe rusted into a silencer can be removed by splitting them with an open-ended hacksaw. Tight screws can sometimes be started by a tap from a hammer on the end of a suitable screwdriver. Many tight fittings will yield to the judicious use of a hammer, but it must be a soft-faced hammer if damage is to be avoided, use a heavy block on the opposite side to absorb shock. Any parts of the steering system which have been damaged should be renewed, as attempts to repair them may lead to cracking and subsequent failure, and steering ball joints should be disconnected using a recommended tool to prevent damage.

3 It often happens that an owner is baffled when trying to dismantle an unfamiliar piece of equipment. So many modern devices are pressed together or assembled by spinning-over flanges, that they must be sawn apart. The intention is that the whole assembly must be renewed. However, parts which appear to be in one piece to the naked eye, may reveal close-fitting joint lines when inspected with a magnifying glass, and, this may provide the necessary clue to dismantling. Lefthanded screw threads are used where rotational forces would tend to unscrew a righthanded screw thread.

Be very careful when dismantling mechanisms which may come apart suddenly. Work in an enclosed space where the parts will be contained, and drape a piece of cloth over the device if springs are likely to fly in all directions. Mark everything which might be reassembled in the wrong position, scratched symbols may be used on unstressed parts, or a sequence of tiny dots from a centre punch can be useful. Stressed parts should never be scratched or centre-popped as this may lead to cracking under working conditions. Store parts which look alike in the correct order for reassembly. Never rely upon memory to assist in the assembly of complicated mechanisms, especially when they will be dismantled for a long time, but make notes, and drawings to supplement the diagrams in the manual, and put labels on detached wires. Rust stains may indicate unlubricated wear. This can sometimes be seen round the outside edge of a bearing cup in a universal joint. Look for bright rubbing marks on parts which normally should not make heavy contact. These might prove that something is bent or running out of truth. For example, there might be bright marks on one side of a piston, at the top near the ring grooves, and others at the bottom of the skirt on the other side. This could well be the clue to a bent connecting rod. Suspected cracks can be proved by heating the component in a light oil to approximately 100°C, removing, drying off, and dusting with french chalk, if a crack is present the oil retained in the crack will stain the french chalk.

4 In determining wear, and the degree, against the permissible limits set in the manual, accurate measurement can only be achieved by the use of a micrometer. In many cases, the wear is given to the fourth place of decimals; that is in ten-thousandths of an inch. This can be read by the vernier scale on the barrel of a good micrometer. Bore diameters are more difficult to determine. If, however, the matching shaft is accurately measured, the degree of play in the bore can be felt as a guide to its suitability. In other cases, the shank of a twist drill of known diameter is a handy check.

Many methods have been devised for determining the clearance between bearing surfaces. To-day the best and simplest is by the use of Plastigage, obtainable from most garages. A thin plastic thread is laid between the two surfaces and the bearing is tightened, flattening the thread. On removal, the width of the thread is compared with a scale supplied with the thread and the clearance is read off directly. Sometimes joint faces leak persistently, even after gasket renewal. The fault will then be traceable to distortion, dirt or burrs. Studs which are screwed into soft metal frequently raise burrs at the point of entry. A quick cure for this is to chamfer the edge of the hole in the part which fits over the stud.

5 **Always check a replacement part with the original one before it is fitted.**

If parts are not marked, and the order for reassembly is not known, a little detective work will help. Look for marks which are due to wear to see if they can be mated. Joint faces may not be identical due to manufacturing errors, and parts which overlap may be stained, giving a clue to the correct position. Most fixings leave identifying marks especially if they were painted over on assembly. It is then easier to decide whether a nut, for instance, has a plain, a spring, or a shakeproof washer under it. All running surfaces become 'bedded' together after long spells of work and tiny imperfections on one part will be found to have left corresponding marks on the other. This is particularly true of shafts and bearings and even a score on a cylinder wall will show on the piston.

6 Checking end float or rocker clearances by feeler gauge may not always give accurate results because of wear. For instance, the rocker tip which bears on a valve stem may be deeply pitted, in which case the feeler will simply be bridging a depression. Thrust washers may also wear depressions in opposing faces to make accurate measurement difficult. End float is then easier to check by using a dial gauge. It is common practice to adjust end play in bearing assemblies, like front hubs with taper rollers, by doing up the axle nut until the hub becomes stiff to turn and then backing it off a little. Do not use this method with ballbearing hubs as the assembly is often preloaded by tightening the axle nut to its fullest extent. If the splitpin hole will not line up, file the base of the nut a little.

Steering assemblies often wear in the straight-ahead position. If any part is adjusted, make sure that it remains free when moved from lock to lock. Do not be surprised if an assembly like a steering gearbox, which is known to be carefully adjusted outside the car, becomes stiff when it is bolted in place. This will be due to distortion of the case by the pull of the mounting bolts, particularly if the mounting points are not all touching together. This problem may be met in other equipment and is cured by careful attention to the alignment of mounting points.

When a spanner is stamped with a size and A/F it means that the dimension is the width between the jaws and has no connection with ANF, which is the designation for the American National Fine thread. Coarse threads like Whitworth are rarely used on cars to-day except for studs which screw into soft aluminium or cast iron. For this reason it might be found that the top end of a cylinder head stud has a fine thread and the lower end a coarse thread to screw into the cylinder block. If the car has mainly UNF threads then it is likely that any coarse threads will be UNC, which are not the same as Whitworth. Small sizes have the same number of threads in Whitworth and UNC, but in the $\frac{1}{2}$ inch size for example, there are twelve threads to the inch in the former and thirteen in the latter.

7   After a major overhaul, particularly if a great deal of work has been done on the braking, steering and suspension systems, it is advisable to approach the problem of testing with care. If the braking system has been overhauled, apply heavy pressure to the brake pedal and get a second operator to check every possible source of leakage. The brakes may work extremely well, but a leak could cause complete failure after a few miles.

Do not fit the hub caps until every wheel nut has been checked for tightness, and make sure the tyre pressures are correct. Check the levels of coolant, lubricants and hydraulic fluids. Being satisfied that all is well, take the car on the road and test the brakes at once. Check the steering and the action of the handbrake. Do all this at moderate speeds on quiet roads, and make sure there is no other vehicle behind you when you try a rapid stop.

Finally, remember that many parts settle down after a time, so check for tightness of all fixings after the car has been on the road for a hundred miles or so.

8   It is useless to tune an engine which has not reached its normal running temperature. In the same way, the tune of an engine which is stiff after a rebore will be different when the engine is again running free. Remember too, that rocker clearances on pushrod operated valve gear will change when the cylinder head nuts are tightened after an initial period of running with a new head gasket.

Trouble may not always be due to what seems the obvious cause. Ignition, carburation and mechanical condition are interdependent and spitting back through the carburetter, which might be attributed to a weak mixture, can be caused by a sticking inlet valve.

For one final hint on tuning, never adjust more than one thing at a time or it will be impossible to tell which adjustment produced the desired result.

NOTES

GLOSSARY OF TERMS

Allen key   Cranked wrench of hexagonal section for use with socket head screws.

Alternator   Electrical generator producing alternating current. Rectified to direct current for battery charging.

Ambient temperature   Surrounding atmospheric temperature.

Annulus   Used in engineering to indicate the outer ring gear of an epicyclic gear train.

Armature   The shaft carrying the windings, which rotates in the magnetic field of a generator or starter motor. That part of a solenoid or relay which is activated by the magnetic field.

Axial   In line with, or pertaining to, an axis.

Backlash   Play in meshing gears.

Balance lever   A bar where force applied at the centre is equally divided between connections at the ends.

Banjo axle   Axle casing with large diameter housing for the crownwheel and differential.

Bendix pinion   A self-engaging and self-disengaging drive on a starter motor shaft.

Bevel pinion   A conical shaped gearwheel, designed to mesh with a similar gear with an axis usually at 90 deg. to its own.

bhp   Brake horse power, measured on a dynamometer.

bmep   Brake mean effective pressure. Average pressure on a piston during the working stroke.

Brake cylinder   Cylinder with hydraulically operated piston(s) acting on brake shoes or pad(s).

Brake regulator   Control valve fitted in hydraulic braking system which limits brake pressure to rear brakes during heavy braking to prevent rear wheel locking.

Camber   Angle at which a wheel is tilted from the vertical.

Capacitor   Modern term for an electrical condenser. Part of distributor assembly, connected across contact breaker points, acts as an interference suppressor.

Castellated   Top face of a nut, slotted across the flats, to take a locking splitpin.

Castor   Angle at which the kingpin or swivel pin is tilted when viewed from the side.

cc   Cubic centimetres. Engine capacity is arrived at by multiplying the area of the bore in sq cm by the stroke in cm by the number of cylinders.

Clevis   U-shaped forked connector used with a clevis pin, usually at handbrake connections.

Collet   A type of collar, usually split and located in a groove in a shaft, and held in place by a retainer. The arrangement used to retain the spring(s) on a valve stem in most cases.

Commutator   Rotating segmented current distributor between armature windings and brushes in generator or motor.

Compression ratio   The ratio, or quantitative relation, of the total volume (piston at bottom of stroke) to the unswept volume (piston at top of stroke) in an engine cylinder.

Condenser   See capacitor.

Core plug   Plug for blanking off a manufacturing hole in a casting.

Crownwheel   Large bevel gear in rear axle, driven by a bevel pinion attached to the propeller shaft. Sometimes called a 'ring gear'.

'C'-spanner   Like a 'C' with a handle. For use on screwed collars without flats, but with slots or holes.

Damper   Modern term for shock-absorber, used in vehicle suspension systems to damp out spring oscillations.

Depression   The lowering of atmospheric pressure as in the inlet manifold and carburetter.

Dowel   Close tolerance pin, peg, tube, or bolt, which accurately locates mating parts.

Drag link   Rod connecting steering box drop arm (pitman arm) to nearest front wheel steering arm in certain types of steering systems.

Dry liner   Thinwall tube pressed into cylinder bore

Dry sump   Lubrication system where all oil is scavenged from the sump, and returned to a separate tank.

Dynamo   See Generator.

Electrode   Terminal, part of an electrical component, such as the points or 'Electrodes' of a sparking plug.

Electrolyte   In lead-acid car batteries a solution of sulphuric acid and distilled water.

End float   The axial movement between associated parts, end play.

EP   Extreme pressure. In lubricants, special grades for heavily loaded bearing surfaces, such as gear teeth in a gearbox, or crownwheel and pinion in a rear axle.

Fade	Of brakes. Reduced efficiency due to overheating.
Field coils	Windings on the polepieces of motors and generators.
Fillets	Narrow finishing strips usually applied to interior bodywork.
First motion shaft	Input shaft from clutch to gearbox.
Fullflow filter	Filters in which all the oil is pumped to the engine. If the element becomes clogged, a bypass valve operates to pass unfiltered oil to the engine.
FWD	Front wheel drive.
Gear pump	Two meshing gears in a close fitting casing. Oil is carried from the inlet round the outside of both gears in the spaces between the gear teeth and casing to the outlet, the meshing gear teeth prevent oil passing back to the inlet, and the oil is forced through the outlet port.
Generator	Modern term for 'Dynamo'. When rotated produces electrical current.
Grommet	A ring of protective or sealing material. Can be used to protect pipes or leads passing through bulkheads.
Grubscrew	Fully threaded headless screw with screwdriver slot. Used for locking, or alignment purposes.
Gudgeon pin	Shaft which connects a piston to its connecting rod. Sometimes called 'wrist pin', or 'piston pin'.
Halfshaft	One of a pair transmitting drive from the differential.
Helical	In spiral form. The teeth of helical gears are cut at a spiral angle to the side faces of the gearwheel.
Hot spot	Hot area that assists vapourisation of fuel on its way to cylinders. Often provided by close contact between inlet and exhaust manifolds.
HT	High Tension. Applied to electrical current produced by the ignition coil for the sparking plugs.
Hydrometer	A device for checking specific gravity of liquids. Used to check specific gravity of electrolyte.
Hypoid bevel gears	A form of bevel gear used in the rear axle drive gears. The bevel pinion meshes below the centre line of the crownwheel, giving a lower propeller shaft line.
Idler	A device for passing on movement. A free running gear between driving and driven gears. A lever transmitting track rod movement to a side rod in steering gear.
Impeller	A centrifugal pumping element. Used in water pumps to stimulate flow.

Journals	Those parts of a shaft that are in contact with the bearings.
Kingpin	The main vertical pin which carries the front wheel spindle, and permits steering movement. May be called 'steering pin' or 'swivel pin'.
Layshaft	The shaft which carries the laygear in the gearbox. The laygear is driven by the first motion shaft and drives the third motion shaft according to the gear selected. Sometimes called the 'countershaft' or 'second motion shaft.'
lb ft	A measure of twist or torque. A pull of 10 lb at a radius of 1 ft is a torque of 10 lb ft.
lb/sq in	Pounds per square inch.
Little-end	The small, or piston end of a connecting rod. Sometimes called the 'small-end'.
LT	Low Tension. The current output from the battery.
Mandrel	Accurately manufactured bar or rod used for test or centring purposes.
Manifold	A pipe, duct, or chamber, with several branches.
Needle rollers	Bearing rollers with a length many times their diameter.
Oil bath	Reservoir which lubricates parts by immersion. In air filters, a separate oil supply for wetting a wire mesh element to hold the dust.
Oil wetted	In air filters, a wire mesh element lightly oiled to trap and hold airborne dust.
Overlap	Period during which inlet and exhaust valves are open together.
Panhard rod	Bar connected between fixed point on chassis and another on axle to control sideways movement.
Pawl	Pivoted catch which engages in the teeth of a ratchet to permit movement in one direction only.
Peg spanner	Tool with pegs, or pins, to engage in holes or slots in the part to be turned.
Pendant pedals	Pedals with levers that are pivoted at the top end.
Phillips screwdriver	A cross-point screwdriver for use with the cross-slotted heads of Phillips screws.
Pinion	A small gear, usually in relation to another gear.
Piston-type damper	Shock absorber in which damping is controlled by a piston working in a closed oil-filled cylinder.
Preloading	Preset static pressure on ball or roller bearings not due to working loads.
Radial	Radiating from a centre, like the spokes of a wheel.

Radius rod	Pivoted arm confining movement of a part to an arc of fixed radius.	**TDC**	Top Dead Centre. The highest point reached by a piston in a cylinder, with the crank and connecting rod in line.
Ratchet	Toothed wheel or rack which can move in one direction only, movement in the other being prevented by a pawl.	**Thermostat**	Automatic device for regulating temperature. Used in vehicle coolant systems to open a valve which restricts circulation at low temperature.
Ring gear	A gear tooth ring attached to outer periphery of flywheel. Starter pinion engages with it during starting.	**Third motion shaft**	Output shaft of gearbox.
Runout	Amount by which rotating part is out of true.	**Threequarter floating axle**	Outer end of rear axle halfshaft flanged and bolted to wheel hub, which runs on bearing mounted on outside of axle casing. Vehicle weight is not carried by the axle shaft.
Semi-floating axle	Outer end of rear axle halfshaft is carried on bearing inside axle casing. Wheel hub is secured to end of shaft.		
		Thrust bearing or washer	Used to reduce friction in rotating parts subject to axial loads.
Servo	A hydraulic or pneumatic system for assisting, or, augmenting a physical effort. See 'Vacuum Servo'.	**Torque**	Turning or twisting effort. See 'lb ft'.
		Track rod	The bar(s) across the vehicle which connect the steering arms and maintain the front wheels in their correct alignment.
Setscrew	One which is threaded for the full length of the shank.		
Shackle	A coupling link, used in the form of two parallel pins connected by side plates to secure the end of the master suspension spring and absorb the effects of deflection.	**UJ**	Universal joint. A coupling between shafts which permits angular movement.
		UNF	Unified National Fine screw thread.
Shell bearing	Thinwalled steel shell lined with anti-friction metal. Usually semi-circular and used in pairs for main and big-end bearings.	**Vacuum servo**	Device used in brake system, using difference between atmospheric pressure and inlet manifold depression to operate a piston which acts to augment brake pressure as required. See 'Servo'.
Shock absorber	See 'Damper'.		
Silentbloc	Rubber bush bonded to inner and outer metal sleeves.		
		Venturi	A restriction or 'choke' in a tube, as in a carburetter, used to increase velocity to obtain a reduction in pressure.
Socket-head screw	Screw with hexagonal socket for an Allen key.		
Solenoid	A coil of wire creating a magnetic field when electric current passes through it. Used with a soft iron core to operate contacts or a mechanical device.	**Vernier**	A sliding scale for obtaining fractional readings of the graduations of an adjacent scale.
		Welch plug	A domed thin metal disc which is partially flattened to lock in a recess. Used to plug core holes in castings.
Spur gear	A gear with teeth cut axially across the periphery.		
Stub axle	Short axle fixed at one end only.	**Wet liner**	Removable cylinder barrel, sealed against coolant leakage, where the coolant is in direct contact with the outer surface.
Tachometer	An instrument for accurate measurement of rotating speed. Usually indicates in revolutions per minute.		
		Wet sump	A reservoir attached to the crankcase to hold the lubricating oil.

NOTES

INDEX

NOTES

NOTES

NOTES